MY PHILOSOPHY

by BENEDETTO CROCE

GIAMBATTISTA VICO

HISTORICAL MATERIALISM
AND THE ECONOMICS OF KARL MARX

THE POETRY OF DANTE

HISTORY OF EUROPE
IN THE NINETEENTH CENTURY

HISTORY
AS THE STORY OF LIBERTY

POLITICS AND MORALS

BENEDETTO CROCE

MY PHILOSOPHY

AND OTHER ESSAYS ON THE
MORAL AND POLITICAL PROBLEMS
OF OUR TIME

Selected by R. Klibansky

Translated by E. F. Carritt

London

GEORGE ALLEN & UNWIN LTD

FIRST PUBLISHED IN 1949
SECOND IMPRESSION 1951

PRINTED IN GREAT BRITAIN BY
JAS. TRUSCOTT AND SON LTD.

TRANSLATOR'S NOTE

The selection of these essays was not my own. Many of their
metaphysical presuppositions and conclusions I am unable to accept.
But my admiration for their author as a writer on aesthetics and
politics and also as a man induced me to adventure their translation.
Translations are notoriously frail ; for, as the French proverb has
it, when they are handsome, they are not faithful and when faithful
not handsome. I have contented myself with plainness.

E. F. CARRITT

CONTENTS

CONTENTS

Problems of Ethics and Aesthetics

Philosophy of History

Various Thoughts

DISCOURSES ON
PHILOSOPHY

❧ I ❧

MY PHILOSOPHY

I HAVE ALWAYS DECLINED the request to expound my philosophy shortly in a popular way, partly because philosophy, like any other work of man, can only be really understood by those who are of the trade, and partly because this possessive 'my' has a bad sound. Any craftsman who takes up the job which a fellow-worker or predecessor has dropped, and carries it on towards perfection does not call it 'his' but 'our' work. But I have now reached the age when, as Giovanni Prati wrote, there rises in the heart 'the sadness of the days that are no more.' It was his fortune to know sadness but not, as we do, to despair in the encircling gloom of slaughter and destruction of all that we held dear or sacred. I have reached the age when a man's life seems a past that he can survey at a single glance, and when he himself takes his place in 'history', or to put it more plainly, he looks at himself as if he were dead. That is why I am now willing to comply briefly, so far as is modest and reasonable, with the request.

Consistently with my simile of a craft as always a matter of collaboration, we must get rid of the pretence or illusion that a philosopher's work or 'system' is a self-completed revelation of the so-called 'mystery of reality'. A definitive pronouncement of total truth would mean the burial of thought and all its doubts, and, with them, of man himself, who would not know what to do with his thought if he did not exercise it in order to live a human life. Man thinks and will always think and always doubt, though he could not think if he did not already live in the truth, in the light of God. In his continual progress man stumbles from time to time upon obstacles which have a certain common nature; he meets with clouds and darkness and perplexity which he must clear away if he is to advance in thought and in its corresponding action. A man is a philosopher in the strict or eminent sense if he removes one more of these stumbling-blocks, great or small, if he dispels one of these clouds, or lightens one darkness, so that by the result of his work the activities of civilisation and morality, slowly perhaps but certainly, enjoy increase.

Hence we see the folly of supposing that philosophies are like either clever, 'brainy' inventions or dreams, which may be believed and arouse fanatical enthusiasm, but fade away, one after the other, as each philosopher contradicts and supersedes the last. Such transitoriness is only found in the frivolous ignorance of vulgar and careless readers; the fact is quite different. The truths definitely attained by philosophers are not mutually destructive but are accumulated and integrated, and govern the life and thought even of the plain man who may be quite unaware of it. When, pray, was destroyed the truth which Socrates gave to men by emphasising, as against the rhetorical and dilettante scepticism of the sophist, the force of logical conception, inference and definition? When was destroyed the truth of Descartes which, by reminding man that he was thinking, gave him the only proof of his own reality? When the truth of Vico, who related thought with action and asserted that men can know their history because they themselves made it? And when that of Kant, who forever destroyed sensationalism and abstract intellectualism by his discovery of the synthesis *a priori* and by his new idea of judgment, which showed that categories would be empty without intuitions, and intuitions without categories blind? And who has ever destroyed or eradicated the truth of Hegel, that the principle of contradiction 'A is A, and not-A is not-A' must be profoundly modified, since reality is not static but living, not fixed but changing, and therefore demands the new principle that 'A is both A and not-A,' so that rationalist logic gives place to the dialectic?

Some part of my philosophical work is conditioned by the demand so powerfully and persuasively expressed by Hegel. For while I have not found it possible to substitute for the history that has taken place, from which I must start, another history that has not taken place, as he requires, yet my work, like that of every thinker, great or little, could only be done in connection and correlation with what preceded it. Hegel was the last great speculative genius who has appeared in the history of philosophy, a genius of the class of Plato and Aristotle, of Descartes, Vico and Kant. After him there have only been minor talents, not to speak of mere followers who do not count. But about Hegel I felt with distress, what I saw clearly, that— quoting Catullus when in love with Lesbia—I could live neither with him nor without him. Certainly I could not do without him, though I was well aware of the bitter revolt against his philosophy during the nineteenth century, which accused him of system-mongering, of violence to the facts, of sophistic trickery and in general of visionary raving, or, worse, of charlatanism. For all that, nobody was able to refute effectively his criticism of the traditional logic, and all attempts to do so by Trendelenburg and others remained unconvincing and petty, the controversy ending with the proclamation of a victory which was purely imaginary. What is more, the substantial truth of his dialectic had been absorbed into the blood of a whole generation, in whose minds the principle of historical thinking, which he had put forward, flourished. Even the natural sciences adopted a historical method of their own in the theory of evolution, of which the new positivism claimed to be the philosophy. Political thought also abandoned the eighteenth century faith in intellectualism, rationalism, enlightenment and jacobin radicalism, so that the new revolutionary movement, which was adumbrated as socialism or communism, aspired to scientific status by adopting and adapting to its own ends the historical method of Hegel; and in its theoretical expression in Russia today it still wears the Hegelian garment.

On the other hand the orthodox Hegelians, some of whom in Italy were worthy of all honour, treated the works of Hegel as gospel, and made of his philosophy a religion complete with exegesis, dogma and ancillary superstitions, so that his school became a congregation of the faithful. It was no longer possible to expect from them the necessary criticism and correction of the master's formulas, or even any incentive to such criticism, since Hegelianism, as they represented it, now crystallised into a hard and fast dogma, had lost the stimulus of the genuine Hegel, who had been his own constant critic and, to the day of his death, a prey to internal conflicts. Against this Hegel of theirs I rebelled; I rebelled because of my love for history which I saw either neglected by them or treated as *a priori* dialectic, not as the dialectic which ought to arise from the recorded facts and a sympathetic interpretation of the documents; I rebelled because of my love of poetry also, which I saw reduced, in the style of Baumgarten, to a confused perception and an immature philosophy which fused concepts and conceptual contrasts into imagery. Finally, I rebelled because I found it impossible to find any meaning for the dialectical transitions, asserted by this Hegel, from the 'Idea' to Nature and Nature to Spirit or for the return from Spirit to a restoration of the 'Idea'; in fact I found meaningless almost all the triads which at every step he constructed and overcame by sophistic solutions which gave his system a specious plausibility and coherence.

And yet one had to settle one's account with Hegel or not advance at all; nor did I find in myself the sublime courage of Campanella, in whose mouth the poem of Alessandro Poerio puts the proud defiance of Aristotle: 'Nor, seated on the throne of the centuries, could I tremble to challenge the Stagirite—You are my opponent!' Consequently, my opposition was cautious and even timid, accompanied by an uneasy feeling that there might be in Hegel some great truth hidden beneath his artificial formulas. I thought one could not have finished with the truth or with the formulas by contemptuously throwing all away in a bundle, without first finding out what the sticks in the bundle were and why they had been fastened together. At last, when my time had come, I saw before me the real logic of the philosophy Hegel had created, the Dialectic, taking shape out of the tangle. At the same time all the shackles fell away which had hampered and constricted this great thinker, and which owed their strength to the theological, academic and political traditions of his time and country and to his own ambition to herald a new and final philosophy that should say the last word on universal history. So soon as I had thus understood the all-too-human failings of his divine genius I was emboldened patiently to disentangle the knot which bound Hegel the philosopher to Hegel the man of human passions and designs, not yet or no longer a philosopher; which bound the discoverer of the dialectic to the builder of a closed system, the bold and deep thinker to the credulous weaver of dialectical triads. This conclusion took shape in my well-known book: *What is Living and what is Dead in Hegel's Philosophy*.[1]

It is not worth while enumerating the criticisms which were at once made on this book by the surviving Hegelians or by their dwindling disciples and imitators. I was accused of deficiency in speculative method because I distinguished within a philosophic system what was living and what was dead, what true and what false, whereas, as they said, echoing the words of Hegel like parrots, a system is the realization of a given principle, which may and should be criticised as a single whole on some different and better principle, but must not be divided up and criticised in its separate parts. But the very thing I was deliberately denying was the indivisible unity of philosophic systems. Apart from prejudice, I clearly saw behind the apparent unity a series or complex of particular problems, some successfully solved and others not, systematised up to a point, but only in pro-visional systems, which always must be and always are open to reconsideration in the light of later experience and later inevitable problems arising by historical necessity. I could not see in each system the realisation of a new and limited principle exhausting itself therein, since in my view the one and only principle of philo-sophy is the eternal and universal nature of thought itself. So, too, I could not accept their demands that the categories or forms of spiritual activity should be deduced or developed one from another in an orderly progression by demonstrating their logical self-contradictions. Such a wearisome 'ballet of bloodless categories,'[2] finding a final rest in one supreme ultimate category is precisely the 'panlogism' or pure rationalism which weakened Hegel's vitality and effectiveness and against which I rebelled. For my part, I closed my account with Hegel, profiting, without scruple, by his great

[1] Bari, 1907. English translation: London, 1915.

[2] The phrase is from F. H. Bradley: *Principles of Logic*. The Italian is *susseguirsi e inseguirsi di contradizioni logiche* (translator's note).

discoveries as the wherewithal to treat by different methods and different ideas those problems on which he had forced arbitrary and fanciful solutions.

Thus in æsthetics and the philosophy of language, in moral philosophy and the philosophies of economics and law, as well as elsewhere, I proposed and defended conclusions quite different from Hegel's. In logic also I saw clearly that the relations of the natural and historical sciences to philosophy compelled me to throw overboard the two imaginary sciences which he invented and elaborated, the *Philosophy of Nature* and the *Philosophy of History*, and to reinterpret his *Phenomenology of Spirit*, reshaping it as a '*Phenomenology of Error*' (and also of the search for truth). His treatment of the history of philosophy gave a new dignity to the subject, but I had to deny his historical order of categories in the development, while preserving his identification of philosophy with its history. And so it was with all his works. The main point is that the more I reflected on his dialectic, of which I recognised the substantial truth, the more I saw that it had been itself vitiated by theological and academic salvage from the traditional metaphysic, and by the habits of abstract logic, which accounted for his arbitrary and cursory treatment of particular problems, in spite of the flashes of genius, which his mind struck in every direction, and of his experience and penetration in human affairs. He had a manly, severe and at the same time wide view of morality; yet, constrained by his triadic scheme and his own German temperament, with too little political sense and too much reverence for authority, he subordinated it to the state and particularly to the Prussian state, which, to his mind, had achieved the perfect constitution. He had, what is rare among philosophers, a knowledge and a love for poetry, music and the arts of form; yet he corrupted their innocent nature, rationalising them by introducing conceptual, cultural and social values instead of the purely æsthetic. He had emphasised at least as strongly as any other thinker of his time the difference and the contrast between the method of the understanding in sciences and that of the reason in philosophy; yet he fused the two in a single process where one was propædeutic and the other completion. He had a conspicuously realistic temper, yet often forgot the clear evidence of fact; his philosophy was emphatically one of immanence, yet opened the door to transcendence. The systematic machinery which he had set in motion caught him and dragged him in its wheels, crushing the seeds of all his best thoughts.

How did he understand the kind of opposition which provides the 'moments' or stages for his dialectic? What is the origin of the 'contradiction' which for Hegel was not an insuperable exclusion, like that of good and evil for Parsees and Manicheans, but always leads to a reconciliation? As I investigated the origin of the contraries and analysed the thought that lay behind them, I could not resist the conclusion that their opposition arises only within the nature of their own substratum; it is kindled precisely by the evolution from one form of that substrate to another, from one spiritual activity to another, the two being only distinguishable within a unity. Hegel, on the other hand, used the formula of mere contrariety, to which he obstinately adhered and which he carried so far as to make it generative of all reality. In this way he falsified the dialectical complex of spirit, one in its various activities, since he denied the reality of them all, interpreting them slightingly as so many unsuccessful attempts at the truth of philosophy, which would be attained only in the mystic realisation of the Idea. This was an initial error which had the gravest consequences, since as I have said, it infects and vitiates his whole system. And in spite of all, this force of contrariety, which had been miraculously dreamt of by the ancient Heraclitus, Heraclitus the Obscure, and which was now called up and re-enlisted and marshalled by Hegel as a necessary instrument for the advance of modern thought, remains, with all his imperfections and eccentricities of expression, his immortal title to be called the regenerator of philosophy.

And so, since modern thought cannot do without this force of contrariety nor the synthesis which at once retains and overcomes the opposing elements, it is to be found throughout in the new philosophic home which I have made for myself and arranged and fitted up, a home new in its foundations and plans and passages and in the use of its rooms, since all are pretty different from those which Hegel had bequeathed. The relation which I there establish between mind or spirit and nature is no longer a dualistic one where the two terms are related by the mediation of God or the Idea, but a unity in which spirit, for its own purposes, fashions the idea of nature or the external world; and thus any intrusion of transcendence is absolutely excluded. The threefold classification, which goes back to the Stoics and was used for centuries by the Schoolmen, and which Hegel found surviving in the philosophy of Wolff, distinguished a 'rational' philosophy, a 'real' philosophy and a 'metaphysic' which united them, corresponding severally to the 'philosophy of spirit,' the 'philosophy of nature' and 'metaphysical logic.' My affirmation of the absolutely spiritual nature of reality annuls this distinction and leaves only the philosophy of spirit, which resolves the other two into itself. Hegel's categories or forms of the spirit were purely logical and therefore logically inadequate. The last of them, that was to comprise all the rest, cannot be defended in its unrelatedness to the others which it had superseded and resolved into itself. All of them, the last included, have now given place to the eternal alternation of the eternal values or categories or activities of spirit; each of them in its operation presupposes the others, since all are necessary to the whole, and no one can claim a primacy that belongs only to the whole cycle or to the spirit itself. Many criticisms and censures and even rather flat satires have been made on my 'four' categories, as if truth, beauty, morality or goodness and utility were private inventions of mine rather than spiritual activities and ideals to which men constantly give these names—names that are not without meaning. And I have been insistently urged to unify these categories in the Hegelian way, that is to say, to annihilate them or give them up, which I steadily refused to do. In this philosophy of mine, then, poetry is poetry and not philosophy; action and morality are what they are, not poetry or philosophy; and philosophy is itself, neither poetry nor action nor morality, yet it concerns itself with all these as they concern themselves with it. Even morality, which from a certain point of view might be called the unifying capacity of the spirit, can only realise this capacity by interacting with the others at their own level, moderating and governing them indeed, but as a *primus inter pares*, respecting their autonomy, and not as a tyrant.

Nor does historical knowledge any longer, as used to be thought, stand opposed and inferior to philosophy, since history is philosophy in the concrete. If we may elaborate and amend the Kantian definition of judgment, history is the only judgment properly so called, and includes in itself philosophy, which is only living philosophy in history and as history. That is why, since I had to find a name for my edifice, to the term 'idealism,' which has become vague and equivocal, I preferred 'absolute history.'[1]

I must protest against the identification of this philosophy, some of whose features I have indicated, with Hegelianism, and against its baptism as 'Italian neo-Hegelianism.' I protest for the simple reason that we cannot believe in 'schools' of philosophy, in revivals, returns, renewals or patchwork of any sort. We must hold fast to the truth that thinking, if it is really thinking, is always the thinking of the mind or, better, of the historical moment, in which it is done; that it is always original and not reducible or derivative; that only on these conditions can it be universal or necessary; and that to treat thought in any other way[2] is to misunderstand its veridical character and to materialise it unphilosophically as an event conditioned and determined by the past. I hope it is not necessary to state that in these remarks I am not indulging the *laudum immensa cupido* which sometimes exhibits itself as the gross personal vanity of refusing to acknowledge the influence of a master. What can be more delightful or more restful than a loyal confidence in the person and the teaching of a master? Can anyone have failed to experience this delightful security, especially in his youth, or to long that it might last for ever, as one longs always for some faithful heart, the one heart faithful above all others, on which to rest one's own, in perfect confidence? I too have experienced this happiness; I remember with what longing and excitement I awaited, with what a thrill of joy I found the men or the books that could clear my confusion and dispel my doubts; by them I judged myself, with them I identified myself, in them I lost myself; they were my masters. But if an unchanging and untroubled bond is the rare gift that fortune gives to her favourites

[1] *Storicismo assoluto.*

[2] On the prefix 'neo' in philosophy see my *Discorsi di varia filosofia*, I, 107-15, Bari, 1945.

in love and in pure friendship, we must not expect it in our relations with the masters of our intellectual life, just because they help us to think for ourselves and to deal for ourselves with the new situations in which we are or shall be placed. So sometimes, though they may not know it or wish to know it, they make us different from themselves and even enemies or opponents. This is what has happened to me with the philosophy of Hegel. I salute him and shall always honour him as a master among the greatest I have had. But I should have been an unworthy disciple if I had failed, whenever I thought necessary and in whatever extent and degree, to develop or correct or harmonise or replace his doctrines and even to rebuild the whole structure. I had to criticise his idea of a final system from the idea, which I wish had been his, of a provisional dynamic system constantly developing and of provisional and dynamic systematisation.

As to the future fate of this philosophy of 'mine' (as I may call it for clearness in this last statement), like all others it will be superseded (as I have often superseded it in my lifetime and shall so long as I live and think) by the *unda quæ supervenit undam*, by the growth and widening of the human spirit. And yet the truths which I have been able to discover and to establish remain and will remain. Great men or little men, we can neither hope nor look for more than that.

Sorrento, 4th January, 1945

🍃 2 🍃

THE MORAL PROBLEM
OF OUR TIME

HISTORICAL MOVEMENTS start at the top and penetrate down-wards; the opposite is impossible. That is a proposition of which we ought to need no demonstration or reminder. Yet not only do we need both reminder and elucidation of it, but it is apt today to arouse murmurs of protest and to earn for its authors the facile condemnation of hide-bound Tory or reactionary, as if reason were not always a 'reaction' against unreason, and common sense against common nonsense. In this proper sense all thoughtful men are reactionaries, though they are by nature revolutionaries, the only true and constant revolutionaries, the shakers of the world. But according to the current myth it is the 'masses' who alone, it is supposed, can change the course of history and leave their mark upon it by their mysterious omnipotence. Theirs is the secret monopoly of irresistible power and wisdom, whose oracular whispers we must piously hear or solicit and obediently fulfil. Mazzini spoke a nobler, as well as a humaner language when he called them 'the People.' It was the people, in his view, who should alone have achieved liberation from the foreigner, the downfall of native tyrants, national unity, the proclamation of the republic, and the federation of nations. Brave, sound of heart, contemptuous of the royal armies and stronger, more single-minded than mercenaries could ever be, it should have conquered by daring to kindle its own fiery cross from the Alps to Sicily. Yet when we look below the surface, behind the imagery to the reality, when we watch the actual course of history, we discover that this 'People' is nothing but the great soul of Mazzini. His sublimely obstinate ideal was realized by men distinguished in thought, knowledge and moral enthusiasm, by bands of volunteers, few of whom came from the artisan or peasant classes, by the royal armies, by wise diplomacy. These were the forces which created an Italy free and independent, republican in spirit and in action, if not in form, which honoured Mazzini as its forerunner and educator, the first author of the mighty work.

But soon Mazzini's 'People' was replaced by another collective entity, born of socialism or communism, which the apostle of Italy would not accept, since he detected its hated materialist basis against which he was never weary of protesting. But here, too, when we attend to realities, this collective being, the 'proletariate,' as it was called, is not to be discovered among those who founded and guided communist or socialist policy, nor in those who constructed its theory and principles, nor in those who formed its associations, parties, sects and institutions. These were all philosophers, men of learning, writers, technicians, industrialists or politicians, nearly all members of the upper classes. Saint-Simon, besides being the designer of considerable engineering works, was a count; Enfantin and Considérant had studied at the *Ecole Polytechnique*; Owen was a factory owner. Apart from the Utopians, who go back to Plato, More and Campanella, among socialists who claimed to be scientific was Marx, who got his doctorate in philosophy with a thesis on Epicurus, and constructed a new theory of history with corresponding logic and ethics, as well as a new doctrine of economic value and production. Lassale likewise wrote a dissertation on Heraclitus and a criticism of acquired rights, besides tragedies and other literary works. Engels had engaged in industry and commerce, and was a prolific writer of wide culture, mainly inspired by Hegel. William Liebknecht was a university student, teacher and journalist; I still remember him as an old man who wanted to see Italy before he died and was introduced to me by Turati to guide him through Naples, and who, one day in the Museum, before the groups of the Tyrannicides, burst out with the famous Greek eulogy of Callistratus. More recently, Antonio Labriola, my teacher in marxism, was a university professor and a philosopher trained in the Herbartian school, but a convert to Hegelianism. Georges Sorel was a civil engineer, and student of history and political economy. Lenin, among his thirty odd volumes, published a criticism of Empiriocriticism; Trotsky was a still more accomplished writer. So it was with all of them; only as a curiosity was any notice taken of some naive sociological compilation from the pen of a worker or some little tract on logic like the one Marx delighted to honour in one of the prefaces to Capital, but to which no student of logic had ever paid the least attention. Indeed, if the simple proletariate had ever dreamed of criticising its masters it might have paid them in their own coin and condemned them all as 'bourgeois.'

In all this there is of course no intention to underrate the seriousness, importance and weight of these social movements, but only to establish the fact that historical influences always came from above. If the 'masses' and their needs were not always with us there would be no historical development, just as if we had no passions or feelings, loves and sorrows, we should not have the arts and poetry for which they provide the material. But art and poetry as we know them would not exist without the genius which creates this form, the form of beauty; and consequently their history is the history of artistic genius and not of the feelings and passions of mankind. Even we critics and historians of literature have had to abandon our pretty pet the myth of popular poetry, the wild native wood-note of the people, which was supposed from time to time to liquefy the trite and desiccated poetry of art and to issue in new forms and new works of genius. Deeper and more accurate research has revealed, always present at the birth of every poet and every epoch of poetry, the traditions of advanced culture and the genius of individuals. Thus Homer appeared as the leader of an organised school of bards, and, Shakespeare as a pupil of the Italian and Elizabethan renaissance, well versed in the refinements of Italian art; even the medieval epic was influenced by Latin models, and the Provencal and Romance-Latin lyric by Latin church poetry and the liturgical chant.[1]

[1]See my introduction to my *Poesia popolare e poesia d'arte*, and the recent book of Guido Errante on the *Lirica romanza delle origini* (New York, 1943).

All this is very natural and obvious, but it is easy to explain (since everything is explicable) how it was lost sight of. Yet it is brought before our eyes again by any philosophical analysis, by every reading of history, both of which make clear the primacy of genius in thought, art and action; as it is also by the well-known saying that political changes are always preceded by changes in thought and culture.

It must be admitted that, though the myth of the People or the Masses denied all credit for man's highest and noblest productions to the so-called great men whom the world-spirit from time to time calls upon, and transferred it to collective entities, yet it did not debase or degrade the intrinsic quality of these productions. This was left to one of those charlatan philosophies which characterised the extremist wing of the Hegelian school between 1840 and 1848. This sect could neither advance beyond Hegel by freeing him from the mill-stone of scholastic intellectualism, nor preserve the profound and fruitful truths which he had discovered and emphasised. The work of debasement was due to Marx, a man of prophetic and subversive genius, who could call up apocalyptic visions and invent fiery slogans, but was little gifted for criticism, philosophy or science, and whose theoretical work was the laborious effort of his early years, soon dropped, and left unfinished in his later life. His Historical Materialism, which was strictly neither materialism nor history, was an intolerant denial of human values or, what comes to the same thing, their nullification by subordinating them all to his one ruling interest, economic welfare and the social revolution. The age of 'enlightenment,' the eighteenth century, had delighted to rationalise religion as an invention of priestcraft, but in the language of Marx religion, thought, poetry, morality, every mental activity outside economic action became deception, camouflage, a mere super-structure on the one reality of the economic war. Homer had sung, Plato philosophised, Jesus and Paul had transformed the moral consciousness, quite unaware that they were only minor and indirect tools in a class-warfare to which their work was reducible without remainder. No doubt there are many would-be poems, many would-be religious doctrines, many moral professions, which are really inspired by economic ends, and many economic activities which cloak themselves in such forms. But these very words imply that the cloak is not the reality, for propagandist art and science are not art or science and partisan morality is what we call hypocrisy. It is hard to know if we should ascribe to sheer grossness or sheer thoughtlessness the ability to identify such obvious tricks of political and economic propaganda with truth, beauty, morality and religion. Yet this monstrous identification was made by Marx and his faithful Engels in a book which they wrote together in 1845-46 on *German Ideology*, and which gave a definitive direction to this mental development. To give a single example : in this book Kant's ethics of the 'good will,' which gave the death-blow to all hedonistic morals, was summarily dismissed by explaining it as the projected image of the frustration felt at that time by the German bourgeoisie, who, not being able to compete in industry and commerce with the French or English, consoled themselves with the 'Good Will' ![1] The path so light-heartedly entered on was cheerfully followed again and again in Germany, Italy and other European countries during the latter part of the last century, when historical materialism was the fashion and even regarded as a revelation of the *arcana imperii*, the hidden secret of politics. But it was a monstrous game of which people soon tired, and in the end historians returned to the wise old criteria of research and reasoning, distinguishing truth from falsehood, beauty from ugliness and right from wrong. This annihilating analysis of values has lasted in Russia ever since the victorious revolution made the Marxist theory an article of faith. Even there some seeds of doubt may be noticed from time to time springing up. For example, during some years Shakespeare's plays were interpreted in terms of class-economics, till the idea occurred that their subject was not the economic class, as was the orthodox and popular view, but human beings called Hamlet or Macbeth.[2] A more despicable form taken by this denial of spiritual values is seen in so-called Nazism or Fascism,

[1] *Conversazioni critiche*, V, 226-29, where is also recorded the explanation there given by Marx of the German war of independence against Napoleon, as dictated by the need for sugar and coffee, which were cut off by the continental blockade. These early editions of Marxist doctrine throw no little light on its true meaning and value.

[2] See my *Pagine sparse*, iii, 79-80.

in which they are treated as dependent upon race or upon the political aims of the faction which has seized power; on which no more words need be wasted.

It is not surprising that this chimerical economic determination, the insidious enemy of intellect, should have obscured and dethroned the governing moral idea of liberty, which in the early nineteenth century was set up as the ideal and religion of the modern world. And in fact it was boasted by Marx and his disciples, and has often been repeated even to our own day, that the veil had at last been torn from the naked and shameful fact and that this cried-up liberty was merely a by-product of capitalist economy, whose motive was the profit to be derived from *laisser-faire*, free competition, and the labour fund of the proletariate, a form of exploitation which replaced those of slavery and serfdom. In this way it was argued that the theory and history of political liberty must stand and fall with capitalism.[1]

Is there then any substance or truth in this theory of historical interpretation? There is certainly error, which being the negation of truth, must have its true grounds in misunderstood facts that are the causes of its false views, illicit inferences and ambiguities of idea and argument. I will call attention to two of these grounds.

The first may be called the fallacy of contiguity in time. The same important widening and developments of thought, knowledge and culture which united to arouse a new consciousness of liberty and of the liberal ideal, were also, on another side, thanks to the advances in science and technique, contributory causes of what was later called the industrial revolution. This involved an increasing use and productivity of machinery and mechanised methods and new relations between the social classes, in which the industrious middle class now gained the upper hand. How great and surprising, how impetuous and rapid was the rise in the production of wealth under capitalism, and how the face of the world was thereby changed, was specially celebrated in the pages, half epic, half lyrical, of the *Communist Manifesto* published by Marx and Engels in 1848. The coincidence of

[1]Among the most recent exponents of this view is H. J. Laski, *The Rise of European Liberalism, An Essay in Interpretation* (London, 1936). And see my *Conversazioni critiche*, V, 287-90.

new enthusiasm in the moral-political and in the economic field was neatly expressed in the early part of the nineteenth century by the saying that the universal slogan of the day was: 'We want liberal institutions and steam ships.' Minds not given to close criticism of ideas and their origin, but easily swayed by what impressed their imagination, readily confused and identified these two movements, which, though naturally parallel, were quite distinct in their own natures. Moreover, it was not then remembered that the cradle of modern liberty had not been the world of business, but the world of the religious wars, the assertion of natural rights, the demand for the liberty of the nonconformist churches, the spread of toleration, the world where philosophy and science were bursting the bonds which impeded their rapid progress. It was easy to fall into the optimistic illusion that by a single activity and a single principle man had opened for himself a certain and straight road to the better life, in which he would have at once spiritual and material redemption.

The other grain of truth excusing the materialist fallacy of identifying liberty and capitalism was dependent on the first and of minor importance. The coincidence of progress in liberty and in industrialisation, being illicitly converted into an identity, was used in defence of economic interests which were thus idealised and borrowed the sanctity of moral claims. This kind of special pleading is so common a fallacy in similar cases that it would have been surprising if it had not occurred here.

But the profound difference between liberty and capitalism and between their several theories was soon recognised by the wiser liberals. The most striking example of this was Sismondi, whose *Histoire des Républiques Italiennes au Moyen Age* was inspired by liberal ideas and who, with Constant, was the first to expound and preach the idea of modern liberty as different from that of the ancients. He must always be remembered with gratitude by Italians for his help in our national revolution. He was a pupil of Adam Smith and in his treatise on political economy, written in 1803, had accepted without reservation both the complete exclusion of state intervention in the production of wealth and the orthodox creed of free competition. His conversion on this point took place in 1818 and was solemnised in his *Nouveaux Essais* published the next year. He himself gave as its cause his experience of the grinding down of the working class under the dominant industrialism, and the poverty of the peasants, whose former prosperity had been destroyed by the agrarian changes. More probably his change of view was brought about or at least stimulated by the polemics, schemes, and experiments of Robert Owen, to which his attention had been directed.[1] Consequently, he set out to insist that the state must acknowledge the responsibilities of the moral consciousness and intervene with remedial schemes in economic life ; and, whether his actual proposals were practical and sound or not, they at least showed that the ideas of moral freedom and of economic free competition, so far from being identical, might easily conflict, and that the former, as the supreme court of appeal, is always competent to over-ride the latter in order to resolve the antagonisms of human life.

It would not be uninstructive to trace in detail the series of objections, corrections and reservations, now no longer to be suppressed, which arose in the liberal conscience against the heavy burden that abstract economic theories were trying to lay upon it. These first took shape in writers like Carlyle and Ruskin, and in admissions forced step-by-step from systematic economists that there were limits to economic laws which must be modified by non-economic conceptions. This was followed by political activities such as the great English enquiry into the conditions of factory workers, and laws for their regulation, which in England followed close upon the triumph of free trade. Then in due course there followed the increase of social legislation during the latter half of the nineteenth century, with progressive relaxation of repression by the recognition of the workers' rights of combination, the right to strike and so on. Even Marxist socialism, which claimed once and for all to cut at the roots of these evils and conflicts by the purely economic method of communist equality, turned out both utopian and ineffective, as was implied, at the end of the nineteenth century in the so-called 'crisis of marxism.' This had to give place to the programme of

The most accurate research into the historical causes of Sismondi's conversion is in a recent memoir by W. Rappard of the University of Geneva, the *Revue d'Alger*, a.I., 1944, parts I, II.

'reformism,' a succession of measures opportune to the exigencies of time and place, and such as the course of history permitted and required. This involved a revision of the marxist theory of history, which like its Hegelian model, though by a different route, had issued in a stagnation or complete negation of the historical process from which it had professed to start. But the development here referred to is an important part of nineteenth century history, a knowledge of which must here be presupposed.

In abstract terms the development consisted in distinguishing between political or moral liberation and economic liberalism, with a subordination or absorption of the second by the first, a distinction which perhaps the Italian language alone can indicate by different words, *Liberalismo* (liberation) and *Liberismo* (*Laisser-faire*). Economic science itself underlined the distinction by adopting the less pretentious name of 'pure economics' instead of 'political economy,' the one given it at its birth. The terms in which pure economics work are abstractions far removed from the actual and occasional solutions of social and historical problems, and therefore equally removed from both *laisser-faire* and state-controlled economy. Though rejected and abused by the marxists as another trick for the defence of capitalism, pure economics in fact effected the purification of other systems from capitalist presuppositions since its theories dealt with economics in abstraction, with *homo œconomicus*, the individual in no social medium. The distinction still lacked a philosophical basis till this was worked out by the Philosophy of Spirit,[1] which recognised two grades of practical activity, the one egoistic or economic, the other universal or moral, both necessary, of which the second continually subdues and refashions the first. Since this solution of the problem we no longer think, as the phrase used to go, of 'moralising economics,' on the contrary we demand that it should assert its own nature yet more strictly, not as immoral but as non-moral, for that way is its function and its truth. At the same time we demand that the moral conscience should intervene to bring it under its supremacy, for human life is subject to this sole authority, which alone is competent to give the ultimate decision in moral conflicts by

[1] The title of Croce's philosophical system. (Translator's note.)

prescribing the action which may reconcile them. There is no question of a final choice between the advantages of a free market, in which supply and demand depend upon individual whims or wants, and the advantage of planning, controlling and disciplinary action in the interest of social necessities; nor between the tendencies towards private property with private enterprise and those towards common property with state-controlled enterprise. No final choice is open between motives both absolutely essential to human life. The sole practical problem is how to act in every situation appropriately, that is to say morally, so as to realise the greatest amount of human liberty and spontaneity that circumstances allow. Every other formula of justice, which demands to be implemented by exclusive adherence in all circumstances to one or other of the rival economic doctrines, is utopian, and it cannot be our duty to do what is impossible. Morality consists only in effecting something and the ineffectiveness of utopian schemes is tested by the touchstone of historical conditions. This is as true of the individualist utopia of Bastiat as of the communistic utopia of Marx, which, as all who know his thought now recognise, has certainly not been realised in Russia on either the economic or political side. There is no justice under the sun except the justice which is done in individual cases, with the proverbial regard for time, place and the circumstances by which cases are altered. Every verdict of justice is unique, so that when applied to another case it is unjust, and what spells liberty in one case is oppression and slavery in another. The description of a world of universal and indefeasible justice does not even make a good fairy story; for the imagination cannot even fancy what is self-contradictory, and the romances which have tried to describe such a world are stupid and tedious. It is a platitude, but one which people get it into their heads to deny, that it takes all sorts to make a world; that is to say, it is a world of oppositions and conflicts, whose purpose is not the prosperity of the individual but the self-development of the world, the creation of ever higher and more complex forms of life, the divine drama of existence. This is no paradox or metaphysical cutting of the knot; it is the fact which we experience every moment, the reality which some call tragic and some sublime.

The only doctrine which adequately represents this law of reality is the moral and religious doctrine of freedom, freedom which cannot be dependent on our physical and economic needs or compromise with them, but is their natural ruler, intent, as occasion may demand, either to satisfy them and procure happiness by a good life or to renounce them all by a good death. When people repeat, as so often today, that man cannot be free unless he is prosperous, or in some determinate (though mathematically indeterminable) degree prosperous, they forget once more the simple fact, attested by history and experience, that good men sacrifice their happiness and life itself in reverence to duty and to human dignity. To forget this is the unpardonable sin of preferring a finite value to an infinite.

As a result of this separation from economic *laisser-faire* the ideal of liberalism has seemed to be left like a disembodied spirit, since, divorced from its former partner, it has not been united to any other economic system. But to discard embarrassing accretions is not to lose in stature, but rather an opportunity for growth. It is rather gain than loss when poetry disencumbers itself of some specially presented subject and takes the world as its theme, with liberty to fasten on this or that aspect as the spirit of poetical imagination moves it. Still, the taunts and laments at the decay of liberty began when the parliaments of Europe no longer saw the two traditional parties of conservatives and progressives confronting one another in debate, but in their place, numerous economic sects arising to discuss and compromise on public business. More lately these chidings and lamentations have increased and finally issued bulletins of the serious illness and at last of the death of liberty, accounts not always received with becoming regret, not always elegiac but sometimes bacchic and triumphant. At present these certificates of death or of extreme senile decay appear almost daily in books and newspapers, supported however or accompanied by statements which rather contradict them. I open a newspaper and read there: 'In England liberalism as a party is absolutely dead; even as an attitude of mind it has been replaced by socialism of the Fabian type, which is its antithesis.' Yet the writer adds, 'The English are by temperament liberals,'[1] which

[1]In the socialist journal *Avanti* (Rome, 19th September, 1944), in an article headed 'England's Secrets' by an author with long experience of English life. The same paper (13th January, 1945) says: 'English democracy is something imponderable, not to be identified with a party; it has its roots in the character of British men and women and is on a plane transcending parties'.

is a direct contradiction. Here in fact is the recognition of the effective dominance which liberalism still has in that country; it is also an omen encouraging other countries to achieve this steady and sure estate, and to safeguard it on the same terms, as a matter of temperament, something which has passed into their blood and marrow and become second nature. The Fabianism here spoken of is simply the practical and progressive acceptance of economic reforms, which previously had only appeared in socialist programmes; and this acceptance is evidence that the old liberal alliance with *laisser-faire* has been broken off. I am reading an instructive book entitled *The Deflation of American Ideals*[1]; and how has this deflation been effected? By the abandonment of the thoughtless optimism of the nineteenth century, especially between 1840 and 1870; by the reaffirmation of the moral and religious character of liberalism as against the economic shackles which it had forged and the criticism it had thereby incurred; by the new-won conviction that men would not become free merely by the overthrow of capitalism, but they must control the great corporations and concentrations of power and direct them to social purposes. So such 'deflation' might more properly be called 'reform.' As to the obituary notices of liberty, they require for confirmation something more than the abuse and horse-laughter showered on its empty tomb in Italy and elsewhere by a lewd and drunken mob. This is a question of ideals and principles, and what was needed was to prove that liberalism has been replaced by some other logically consistent principle and ideal, a proof which has not yet been even stated in any clear and reasonable form. In Russia, if liberalism has not matured under the new order, we must remember that it had not under the old; at present it has been set aside and all attention directed to the economic revolution and the technical organisation of resources, in which great results have been achieved. And even here, if we look to the future, it is liberty which we must anticipate, the liberty that now is lacking but which will be achieved in due time. Men are exhausted and appalled by the startling extent and horror of the slaughter and destruction which

[1]Sub-title: *An Ethical Guide for New Dealers*, by Edgar Kemler, Littaker Fellow, Harvard University. (Washington, 1941.)

surround them, and by the loss of the spiritual traditions and experiences, the civilised ideas, the moral habits and refined feelings which were their heritage. With disillusioned minds, forgetful of a past that has sunk below the horizon, they yearn and pray for some miraculous new birth, but the renewal, long heralded and announced, neither dawns in their minds nor stirs with promise in their hearts. Certainly their longing cannot be satisfied by schemes daily elaborated for dreary political mechanisms of repression, or by new holy alliances; whatever other uses these have, they are not of a nature to stimulate moral life. On the other hand the need cannot be met by the deliberate political refurbishing of old creeds which only in the vigour of youth and manhood had the fiery warrior spirit of self-sacrifice, inspiring great thoughts and actions and teaching men how to die. Why then do we see so little of this 'rebirth' of which we hear so much? Why is it still unborn? Simply because it is looked for in the future; but its name is liberty which exists today, yesterday and forever. Liberty is the steadfast pole-star which guides voyagers in life's stormy sea; it is the only guide to new worlds, new thoughts, new outlooks, a new order and a new life. The world, which cannot perish and which has the will to live, must always return to the paths of liberty; however men may deny and blaspheme it, be they few or many, they cannot change the law of the world.

Still liberalism, as already remarked, has outgrown, along with other errors of inexperience and resulting superficiality, the optimistic illusion of a progress without impediment and without reaction, and has constantly developed its historical sense of the 'dialectic,' the ebb and flow of human affairs. It does not blind itself to the fact that today the realisation and expansion of liberty is checked by an obstacle whose strength or whose dead weight it seems unable to overcome; but it is not dismayed or downcast. This opposition is commonly, though rather metaphorically, ascribed to the current materialism; but, strictly speaking, materialism, being a metaphysical theory, is as unrelated to moral or other action as that of Thales or any pre-Socratics; for it was Socrates who brought philosophy down from heaven to investigate the mind of man and formulate its laws. It is well known that the most fanatical material-

33

C

ists in theory, when it comes to action, often turn out in fact to be philanthropic humanitarians, liberals or democrats. Sometimes also this opposing force is ascribed to communism. But whatever the materialist pronouncements of Marx (and they were fairly incoherent) and whatever the doctrines of such tendency popular in Russia, communism in itself, being a purely economic reform of the social fabric, is not materialist, not even in the special sense in which historical materialism put it forward as the denial of all human values other than utilitarian. Moreover whatever materialist tendencies we may find to blame in communism are to be found no less in some of the governments which professed to oppose it with deification of the superman or dictator. Perhaps the aptest name for this opposing force, and one that naturally suggests itself, is, 'atavism,' or 'the atavistic conception of life.' Pure atavism is something in its nature blind and irrational, and delights to boast itself so; it obeys and recognises no laws but only the frantic impulse to action, without stopping to note what the action is or why it should be done. When the force which opposes us has been thus defined by the name atavism, we see it as no longer confined to one particular time or place; it escapes the contemporary frame in which we first see it, and is recognised as the latest form of the movement, or rather the pretentious disintegration, called irrationalism, whose first chronic symptoms appeared in the late eighteenth and early nineteenth century under the name of romanticism.

Romanticism, in fact, in any definable sense, leaving aside the colloquial and literary uses of the word, is sheer irrationalism. It is a particular form of irrationalism owing its birth and features to a conflict in minds which have lost and yet will not abandon the transcendental religion handed down to them. Such a mind is ready, though it does not know it, for the revelation of immanence, in which is preserved all that had permanent value in Christianity; and from this painful dilemma it ventures the most fantastic schemes of escape. Its original and just attack on the abstract intellectualism of the 'enlightenment,' on the eighteenth century mathematical 'reason' whose only function was 'reasoning', was exaggerated, in its enthusiasm, into a rebellion against all reason, even reason in a

34

more profound sense which might have corrected the other. The proof of this is that when the first sentimental rebellion was developed into a philosophical criticism, eminently by the work of Hegel, and the new idea of a dialectical reason replaced the old one, the revolt continued in multitudinous forms as one of romantic and capricious feeling and of unbridled fancy. Thus it was that in philosophy Hegel, and in poetry Goethe, declared themselves strongly opposed to romanticism and defined it as a disease, which indeed it was. This is not the place to analyse romanticism more closely or to repeat the history of its development.[1] The early romantics in all their melancholy, abandonment and despair, still showed bright sparks of magnanimity. Among their successors the morbid element grew, complications set in and issued in all sorts of perversions. At last we saw, and still have before our eyes the union of romanticism with party and war, war waged on the plea not of the spiritual cult of the nation but on the brutish superstition of race, with monstrous bloodshed accompanied by taunts and torture and with the deliberate destruction of all that human genius and human toil have created in centuries. Every spark of idealism, every feeling of common humanity is mocked and extinguished. This state of mind[2] has innumerable repercussions of all kinds in every sphere of life, echoes in which the ear can distinguish more or less clearly the same note; in politics, in philosophy, in literature, in painting, in sculpture; among nationalists and communists, revolutionaries and reactionaries; it is as if all had drunk of the same poisoned well. We are tempted to say this is the spirit of the age[3] demanding expression for itself in the words of men's lips and the work of their hands. But the extent of this turbulent manifestation does not rise to the sublime, nor stir our feelings of awe; for decay and diseases are also widely enough spread, but not for that admired or loved or envied. Those who in the face of such things and in the midst of them *sibi constant*,

[1] For this I refer to what I said in my *Storia di Europa rel secolo decimonono*.

[2] I analysed an instance of this frame of mind in my *Misticismo politico tedesco*, in *Pagine politiche*, Bari, Laterza, 1945, pp. 9-16. Since writing this I have seen the proofs of *Il nazismo e la civiltà d'Europa* by C. Antoni for the review of *La nuova Europa*, 28th January, 1945, which similarly traces nazism to romanticism.

[3] See my note *Filosofia moderna e filosofia dei tempi* in the volume *Il carattere della filosofia moderna* (Bari, 1941), pp. 261-66.

who hold fast to the ancient and eternal laws of thought and action, who do not sacrifice reason for irrationality, these men may be sad and anxious, but, as Aristotle said of Anaxagoras, they feel and know that they are sober among drunkards.

But faced by this hostile power, men despair of speedy victory and at the slowness of their advance and the tardy signs of the victory that must be theirs. They hold fast the belief that, though much in the world is hostile to truth, goodness and beauty, yet nothing in it happens in vain. And so there rise to their lips the words of Dante, that the just eyes of God are turned elsewhere or that in his unsearchable providence he is fashioning a good invisible to our eyes. In the meantime they lean more closely on the one source of strength which never fails the man who trusts it, on the consciousness of a call and a duty, the unfailing source of spiritual refreshment and renewal, to save him from despair of life.

And this duty is always a thing of reason, not of unreason; it dwells in hearts that burn with the fire of the human ideal, of civilisation, of liberty, of untiring work. We must keep ourselves rational and live rationally because we are Christians, and be deeply Christian because we are rational, as I have explained elsewhere;[1] for Christianity and reason, however it may seem at the moment, can never be outdone or outmoded. Are the faithful then few, as is asserted by those who would sow discouragement? Perhaps even today they are more than is thought; witness the number of the leaders and the literal crowds of followers in the different countries of Europe and America, and their obstinate resistance, and the encouraging signs of reawakening and revival. But whether they be few or many, it may be they have secret allies, unknown to them, even among their present enemies, who on their side are discontented, uneasy and divided among themselves. For reason alone really unites men, and apart from reason there is only the treacherous convergence of fancies, caprices and passing interests. These arguments give comfort and courage to stand firm and to use every effort in the defence of that cause for which alone it is good to live and good to die.   *Sorrento*, 15*th December*, 1944

[1] *Why we cannot help calling ourselves Christians*, translated in the present volume.

❧ 3 ❧

WHY WE CANNOT HELP CALLING
OURSELVES CHRISTIANS

THE CLAIM to the name of Christian is seldom free from some suspicion of pious unction and hypocrisy, since it is a name often adopted from complacency and as a cloak for something very different from the Christian spirit. The citation of evidence for this would be easy, but must be forgone, since it would give occasion for criticism and debate irrelevant to the purpose of this essay. Here, my object is simply to demonstrate by an appeal to history that we cannot avoid acknowledging and confessing that we are Christians, and that the name merely registers a fact.

The rise of Christianity was the greatest revolution that the human race has ever accomplished. It is not surprising that something so great, so wide and so deep, so far-reaching in its effects, so unforeseen and so irresistible in its development, should have been thought, and might still be thought, a miracle, a revelation from on high, a direct intervention of God in human affairs, giving them new laws and setting them on an entirely new path.

No other revolutions will bear comparison with this; even the great discoveries which mark epochs in human history beside it seem incidental and limited. There are no exceptions: not the revolution of the Greeks in poetry, art, philosophy and civil liberty, nor that of the Romans in law, not to speak of writing, mathematics, medicine and the other, more ancient, discoveries which we owe to Egypt and the East. And though the revolutions and discoveries which have followed in modern times were not so incidental and limited as their ancient predecessors, but touched the whole man in his very soul, they can only be conceived as dependent on the Christian revolution and derivative from its original and lasting stimulus.

The reason for this is that the Christian revolution worked upon the very centre of the soul, upon the moral consciousness, and by emphasizing the inner essence of that consciousness, almost seemed to confer on it a new power, a new spiritual quality, which had hitherto been lacking in humanity. Pre-Christian men, heroes and men of genius, did marvellous deeds, created magnificent art, and handed down to us rich treasures of style, of thought and experience ; but in all of them we find wanting that authentic touch of brotherhood in one communion which Christianity alone has given to human life.

Yet this was no miracle invading the course of history and installing itself there as an alien and transcendent power. Nor was it that other kind of metaphysical miracle which some philosophers, and chief among them Hegel, have invented when they set themselves to conceive history as a long process in which the spirit acquired one-by-one its constituent elements or categories—scientific knowledge, the state, liberty, each at its fixed time, and, with Christianity, inward morality. For the spirit is always the full realisation of itself, and its history is the history of its own creations, continuous and infinite, in which it manifests its eternal nature. Neither the Greeks nor the Romans nor the Orientals brought forth into the world those universal ideas of which they are emphatically called creators. Only in virtue of already possessing these could they attain to the lofty acts and achievements unexampled, by which they set their seal on the fateful crises of human history. And so too the Christian revolution was a historical process, with its place in the general historical process as the most fateful of all its crises. Experiments, precursors, foreshadowings of Christianity have been recorded, as for every human deed, for a poem or a political act ; but the light which they have been thought to transmit to it they really received by reflection from what was afterwards brought about. No deed is ever brought to birth by the aggregation or combination of other deeds, but always and only by an act of original creation; it never pre-exists in its antecedents.

At the appearance of Christianity, the moral consciousness awoke to new moods of joy and labour, at once eager and confident, with the sense of sin which always besets us, but also with the power that always resists and conquers it; humble yet proud, and finding its exaltation in its humility and its joy in the service of the Lord. And this consciousness kept itself pure and undefiled, intolerant of every pleasure which distracted it or put it in conflict with itself, ever suspicious of the tinsel praise or blame of society. It drew its laws solely from the inner voice, not from external commands or precepts, all of which are useless for the problems to be solved at every moment, for the attainment of the moral end, and all of which forced men back, one way or another, to the sensual sty of utility. Its passion was love: love of all men without distinction of race or class, bond or free; love of all creatures, of the world which is the work of God, and of God who is the God of love, who is not far from men but came down to them, and in whom we live and move and have our being.

From such an experience, which was at once feeling, action and thought, arose a new vision and a new interpretation of reality, a reality no longer sought in the world of objects divorced from an experiencing subject and substituted for it, but in that which is the eternal creator of all things and the sole principle of explanation. And thus prevailed the conception of the spirit, so that God himself was no longer conceived as an abstract identity with no distinguishable qualities[1] and therefore impassive and inert, but was at once identity and difference, because living and the source of all life, one in three.

This new moral attitude and this new conception were partly disguised in myths—the kingdom of heaven, the resurrection of the dead, baptismal regeneration, the expiation and redemption which atone the sins of those elected to the kingdom, predestination, grace and so on. They passed painfully from grosser myths to others that were finer and more transparent; they were not always consistently thought out, but entangled themselves in contradictions which left

[1] *Indifferenziata.*

men uncertain and perplexed, but none the less they were in substance as we have summarized them, and as every man feels them
echo in his heart when he calls himself a Christian. A new action, a
new conception, a new poetical inspiration is not, and must not be
thought of, as it is presented in abstraction and by the reproductive
fancy, as if it were something physically self-contained and isolated,
but rather as a force insinuating itself among other forces, sometimes
entangled by them, sometimes losing its way, sometimes advancing
slowly and with difficulty, or finally yielding to other forces which
it cannot altogether conquer and absorb; but in the hour of defeat
finding renewal and a militant resurrection. To understand such a
creation in its true and fundamental character we must separate it
from these irrelevancies, pass over all these incidents, and view it, not
in its puzzles and contradictions, its entanglements and its haltings,
its mistakes and wanderings, but in its primal impulse and in its
dominating tendency. So in a work of poetry what counts is the
poetry in it and not the prosaic matter which is mixed with it or
accompanies it, the *maculæ* which are to be found even in Homer or
in Dante. It may be objected, with feelings of mistrust, and in phrases
of magisterial criticism, that in this way we are 'idealising' facts and
doctrines and not regarding them in their concrete reality; but such
'idealisation', which need not be blind to accidents and adulterations,
and certainly need not deny them, is, as we have said, nothing but the
'understanding' which understands them. If we take the opposite
way, we shall treat on the same level the reasoning and the myths,
the consistencies and the inconsistencies, the certainties and the
uncertainties of a thinker, and we shall necessarily conclude that his
system is no system but a mass of contradictions, vitiated by fallacies
and rotten from beginning to end. And this is the favourite habit of
many critics and historians, who seem delighted to discover in the
deeds and thoughts and creations of the past their own moral incapacity and mental confusion.[1]

[1] I must be allowed to remark that contemporary Italian literature has, in the volumes
of Omodeo on Christian origins, a work which to a rare degree combines not only a keen
historical sense for fine shades of development with vigorous philosophical thought,
but also the apprehension of events in their individuality with an equal apprehension
of the links which bind them to their past and to their future.

It was no less necessary that the evolution of truth, which Christianity had so vastly intensified and accelerated, should be halted for a time, and that the Christian revolution should have a breathing space, which in history may last for centuries, and should make itself at home. And the voice of censure and lamentation has been raised, and is still heard, over this fall of religious enthusiasm from the high levels on which it had moved, and over the petrifaction of religious thought into practical politics, a solidification which is death. But such polemic against the institution of the Church or the Churches is as unreasonable as one against Universities and other places of learning, where science, which is unceasing criticism and self-criticism, is changed to something fixed in examinations and text-books, and is learned by rote, either for practical purposes or, in better disposed minds, as something to keep by one in the attempt or accomplishment of new scientific advances. We cannot eliminate from the life of the spirit this phase in which the intellectual process of inquiry terminates in the acquisition of doctrine and there is begun that process of action to which doctrine leads. This termination may, from one point of view, seem to be the death of truth, as in a certain sense it is, since real truth consists simply in its own self-creation. But from another point of view, that of the preservation of truth for a new life and for a recommencement of the process, it is less a death than a hidden and protected seed which will germinate and throw out new shoots. In this way the Catholic Christian Church did not always hesitate to formulate the unthinkable merely because her thoughts had not yet been thought out; and she fashioned her dogmas, her rites, her sacramental system, her hierarchy, her discipline, her temporal power, her finance and economy, her law and law-courts with the appropriate legal casuistry. She designed and carried out compromises and bargains with appetites which she could neither govern or extinguish, nor leave free and unbridled. And this activity was beneficial in overcoming both pagan state-craft and other newer enemies arising from her own nursery in the East which she had long outgrown. These latter were specially dangerous because they bore in their faces many features of her own, as did the Gnostics and the Manicheans. Beneficial, too, was her foresight in rebuilding upon spiritual foundations the falling or fallen Roman Empire, and in embracing and preserving the tradition shared by Rome with all ancient civilisation. In this way the Church enjoyed that long and glorious reign known as the Middle Ages, the distinction and name of which appear to have arisen by chance, but were in fact suggested by a correct intuition of the truth. And in that period she not only completed the conversion and latinisation and civilising of the Germans and other barbarians, checked the infiltration of revived heresies, dualistic, pessimistic, ascetic, pantheistic, nihilistic; not only inspired the defence of European civilisation threatened by Islam, but upheld the moral and religious demands which surpass and dominate those of sheer politics. In virtue of all this, the Church fairly claimed the right of sovereignty over the whole world, however serious were often the actual malversations or corruptions of this right.

No more valid are the other charges commonly brought against the Catholic Christian Church for the corruption which was allowed to enter and often to spread pretty widely; for every institution carries within itself the danger of corruption, or parts which monopolise the life of the whole, or selfish or political motives which displace morality; and in fact every institution suffers such accidents and perpetually struggles to overcome them and to recover its healthy constitution. Just the same thing happened, if in less scandalous and more underhand ways, to the churches which rose up against the catholic mother, with accusations of corruption, under the name of evangelical and protestant confessions. The Catholic Christian Church, as has been remarked, even in the Middle Ages, more than once availed herself of the Christian spirits which were spontaneously kindled within or without her borders, and by using them for her own purposes, was rejuvenated and reformed. Later, partly through the corruption of the popes, the clergy and the friars, partly through the general change of the political situation which had robbed her of her medieval sovereignty and blunted her spiritual weapons, but finally through the criticism of the new scientific and philosophical thought which rendered scholasticism antiquated, the church seemed on the verge of ruin. Yet once more she prudently reformed herself and, saving all which political wisdom could save, continued her work with the greatest triumphs in the lately-discovered countries of the New World. An institution does not perish through accidental and superficial errors, but only when it no longer satisfies any need, or so far as the quantity and quality of the needs which it satisfies are lowered. What may be the present situation of the Catholic Church in these respects is not the business of the present discussion to enquire.

We must now take up our argument at the point where we interposed the above comments on the essential truth of Christianity and on its relation to the Church or churches. We have recognised the necessity that the growth and progress of Christian thought should for a time be halted. This is, in fact, what happens, if we may compare great things with small ones, whenever the writer of a book resists the temptation of *infinitum perfectionis* and hands it over to the printer and the public. The next step was that the progress had to be resumed and revised and carried to greater heights. What we have once thought is not thought once for all and done with; a deed is no barren deed, stricken with sterility, but always pregnant, always, to borrow a phrase from Leibniz, *gros de l'avenir*. Jesus, Paul, the author of the fourth gospel, and all who during the first age of Christianity in various ways co-operated with them, were men of profound practical genius. So fiery and ceaseless was the travail of their life and thought that they seemed to require their teaching to be received not only as a fount of water springing up to everlasting life or as a vine whose branches bring forth fruit, but as a ceaseless activity, living and adaptive, to dominate the course of history and to satisfy new needs and demands, which they themselves did not feel or dream of, which would be conceived later in the womb of reality. Such continuity, at once a change and growth, can never be achieved without a clearer definition, correction and modification of the original conceptions, or the addition of new ones and the completion of new systems. It can never, therefore, be a mere repetition nor the absurdity of a line-by-line commentary; that is to say it is no mechanical task, as, on the whole, with the exception of some brilliant efforts, was the work of the Middle Ages, but a gift of native aptitude and genius. Consequently, we must hold that those men most effectively carried on the religious work of Christianity who, starting from its conceptions, but permeating them with the criticism and research of later ages, produced substantial advances both in thought and life. And, in spite of some superficial anti-christianity, these were in fact the humanists of the renaissance, who understood the value of poetry and art and of politics and the secular life, and revindicated for them a place in the perfect humanity as against medieval supernaturalism and asceticism. And with them in some respects were the great reformers who widened the Pauline doctrines to a universal significance by freeing them from the topical references and the hopes and the expectations of his time. So too were the austere founders of physico-mathematical science, by their stimulus to the discovery of new materials for human civilisation ; and the preachers of natural religion and natural rights and of tolerance, forerunners of later liberal ideas ; and the triumphant reasoners of the age of enlightenment who reformed social and political life, discarding what remained of medieval feudalism and clerical privilege, putting to flight the dense clouds of superstition and prejudice, and creating a new and burning enthusiasm for what is good and true by a rebirth of the Christian and humanitarian spirit. Behind them came the practical revolutionaries who spread their achievement from France all over Europe. Last of all came the philosophers, Vico, Kant, Fichte and Hegel, who directly or indirectly succeeded in giving critical and speculative range to the idea of the Spirit which Christianity had substituted for ancient realism. It was they who conceived the idea of reality as a development. Their united influence overcame first encyclopædist rationalism by the idea of evolution, next the jacobin cult of abstract liberty by liberal institutions, and lastly abstract jacobin cosmopolitanism by respecting and promoting independence and liberty for the peculiar cultures of the various peoples or, as they were called, nationalities. These philosophers, and all like them, were disowned by the Church of Rome, anxious, as she had to be, to protect her institutions and the settlement of her dogmas by the council of Trent. Finally, she condemned them, together with the whole modern world in a papal syllabus, without however being able to oppose the lay science, culture and civilisation by a science, civilisation and culture of her own. She was, and still is, bound to deny as a blasphemy the rightful claim of these men to be called Christians, yet they were workers in the Lord's vineyard, who by their toil, their sacrifices and their blood have made fruitful the truth first founded by Jesus; a truth developed indeed by the early Christian thinkers, but only as every thought must be developed, which can never be at first more than a sketch, always to be completed by new touches and new lines. Nor can she on any account consent to the idea that there are Christians outside all the churches no less real than those within, and all the more intensely Christian because free. But we who write neither to please nor to displease the churchmen, and who in our respect for truth understand the logic of their intellectual and moral position and the laws of their behaviour, are bound to ratify that meaning of the name 'Christian' which history shows to be legitimate and necessary.

A very significant proof of this historical interpretation is the fact that the continual and violent anti-ecclesiastical polemic which runs through the centuries of the modern era has always paused in silent reverence before the record of the person of Jesus, feeling that to attack him would be to attack themselves, the grounds of their own ideal, their own hearts' blood. Now and again, some poet, using the right of poets to enact in symbol and metaphor every ideal and counter-ideal as their passions move them, has seen in Jesus, Jesus who loved happiness and willed it, an enemy of joy and an apostle of sadness, and, like Goethe and the Italian Carducci, has ended with a palinode. Moods of nostalgia for the serene paganism of antiquity were also the fruit of poetical and imaginative moods, contradicted, often enough, by the very opposite moods and imaginations in those, who for a time, had entertained them.[1] The careless fun and mockery which has innocently enough been turned in streams on every glorious character and deed of history, has never seemed innocent or permissible against the figure of Jesus, nor has

[1]Something that these admirers of neo-paganism overlooked may be expressed in the words which J. Burckhardt puts into the mouth of the Vatican Hermes: 'We had everything; the splendour of the heavenly gods, beauty, eternal youth, endless mirth; but we were not happy, because we were not good'. (cf. M. Arnold, *Pagan and Medieval Religious Sentiment* in *Essays in Criticism*, first series. Translator's note.)

that figure ever accommodated itself to representation on the stage, except in the naïve mystery plays of the middle ages and their popular survivals to which even the Church has shown itself indulgent and indeed favourable. Another proof of the same truth may be found in the Christian colouring of the affectations and slogans which have often been adopted by those political and social movements of the modern world, which were most definitely anti-ecclesiastical. Thus the eighteenth century rationalist followers of Voltaire could talk of 'The Celestial City' which they had constructed, of 'The Garden of Eden,' which they placed in ancient Rome or in some happy arcadia, and of 'Nature', which for them took the place of the Bible and the Church, or the like.[1] The revolutions of modern times invoke their 'evangelists', send out their 'apostles' and glorify their 'martyrs'.

The truth is that, though we are children of the whole of history and its blood flows in our veins, yet ancient ethics and religion were taken up and dissolved in the Christian idea of conscience and moral inspiration, and in the new idea of God in whom we live and move and have our being, who cannot be Zeus or Jehovah nor even, in spite of the worship offered to him in our days, the Germanic Wotan; and it is precisely for this reason that in our moral life and our thought we feel ourselves literally children of Christianity. No man can tell whether another religious revelation, equal or superior to what Hegel called 'Absolute religion,' will come to pass for the human race in some future of which today we can see no dawn. But this we know, that in our own times our thought inevitably works on the lines laid down by Christianity. We are for ever struggling to mediate between the bitter opposites, continually recurring, of conscience and external law, morals and expediency, immanence and transcendence, liberty and authority, the heavenly and the earthly which go to make up man. It is from the successful reconciliation of some individual form of such oppositions that there arises in us the joy of inward peace; from the consciousness that we can never reconcile them completely nor exhaust their full meaning arises the manly pride in an unending

[1] See Carl L. Becker, *The Heavenly City of the Eighteenth Century Philosophers*. (Newhaven.)

warfare and an unending labour, the need for which will never be wanting to us or to our children's children; for it is the warfare and the toil of life. To keep alight or to rekindle and to feed the fire of Christian sentiment is a constantly recurring need, alternating between hopes and fears, more pressing and more tormenting today than ever. The Christian God is still our God, and the philosophies to which we owe allegiance call him Spirit, which is always beyond us and yet always our very selves. If we no longer worship him as a mystery, it is because we know that he will always be a mystery in the eyes of the abstract, intellectualist logic undeservedly credited and honoured as 'human logic', but that he is transparent truth to the eye of that concrete logic which may well be called 'divine', if the word be used in the Christian sense of that to which man always raises himself, and which, for ever uniting him with God, makes him truly man.

PHILOSOPHY OF
POLITICS

D

4

UNPOLITICAL MAN

MANKIND NEVER WEARIES of advising and reminding its poets, philosophers and historians to keep clear of the tendencious passions of politics. The universal truth of pure humanity can indeed only be reached in their works by rising above private aims and passions such as are eminently those classed under the name of 'politics'. It is impossible to concentrate upon the eternal truth which is above all private interests, and at the same time to look on some one of these interests with favour and to promote it. Or at least this can only be done by a more or less skilful hypocrisy, which may sometimes serve the politician's aim, but brings a blush of shame to the man who reverences the chastity of truth and beauty, and who feels that the mere suggestion is an insult to his moral character and a threat to the very roots of his higher life. The poet or philosopher or historian who stoops to such deception and trickery is, to that extent, not what he professes himself but a mere politician or rather the tool of politicians. He cannot but have a bad conscience, for his act is in contradiction with the assumed character of a free intelligence, with the function he has undertaken, and with the tacit contract between himself and society not to fail in this peculiar duty. The only exception is the more or less innocent simplicity (an exception we must allow, since 'the kinds of fool are infinite') which does not clearly know what it is doing. As a rule, behind all such unprofessional behaviour we find the motive of self-interest, a fear of loss or a hope of gain. When we meet with such sham artistic or scientific products, we can always be sure that we are justified in asking their authors: 'What did you get for it? What was the price?' The philosopher or the historian or the poet gets nothing for it; his work is priceless. He shoots his golden arrow against the sun and is glad to watch its flight; if he wants anything more, it is only that others should share his pleasure and emulate him with such arrows of their own.

Another piece of urgent advice given by society to the artists and philosophers is to abstain, even in their practical life, from political activity, or at least from any ambition to play a conspicuous or leading part. There is a difference amounting almost to opposition, both between the habits and capacities to be cultivated and also between the experiences to be sought by the two professions. Artists and philosophers relate ideas or shape visions; politicians work on men's passions and interests, to unite or to embroil them; the very virtue of the one class is the defect of the other. The man of thought or contemplation, if dragged into the arena of political conflict, can do little good and some evil; the little good cannot make up to society for its loss in distracting him from the work for which he was born and bred. This second piece of advice cannot have the peremptory unconditional character of the first, since philosophers and artists are not abstract thought or imagination but men; their activity is primarily directed to these pursuits but is not thereby exhausted. Moreover, the state and society itself treat them as members and citizens call on them for services in peace and war. Thereby they are stimulated in some degree to share in political discussion and conflict and to join a political party, if only as auxiliaries assigned the work for which they are suited. Their work is 'cloister-work', as Ariosto called it (who, by the way, had to be governor of Garfagnana), that is to say, not the dirty work of sham poetry and sham philosophy, but legitimate, straightforward political propaganda.

Are then the first unconditional prohibition of adulterating pure art and science and the second conditional precept to keep political activities within very narrow limits intended to make artists and philosophers indifferent to politics—unpolitical men? Could artists and philosophers for their part accept the latter precept and obey it?

In order to obey it they would have to tear out from the organic texture of their interests the whole life of political activity. But the concrete man unites in his soul interests for every activity of life, and his blood is warmed by them all. The philosopher and the historian trace out the relation and the dialectical connections of these activities; the poet lives them over again and portrays their living semblance. If one were to be cut out, if one were banished from the mind, the effect of the mutilation would be that all the others would pale before the sight and wither in the heart. The love for another human being, the affection for family and children, are of necessity an interest in the moral and political society that surrounds us, in which we ourselves and those whom we love draw our breath. If in the height of passion we vainly try to evade one of these activities, and (to keep to our example) to shun politics, that is really the effort not of disinterestedness but of self-interest, which surrenders to what it would escape. In the same way, the mistaken attempt of the philosopher to deny one of these activities turns out a reaffirmation of it; the poet who sighs to escape from politics is really obsessed by them; the shepherd of Erminia[1] in his solitary lodging among trees and streams is always mindful of the court intrigues. A man could only suppress his political interest by at the same time suppressing all his others; he would not be unpolitical only but apathetic, and total apathy is death, the death of thought and imagination, of philosophy and poetry, which have no subject matter but the life of the passions. These alone move our imagination, prompt us to define our ideas and to verify our history and, less directly, to invent the formulas of science and the symbolism of mathematics. And the passions are always grievous: 'alas, it was in grief that Italian song had birth,' wrote Leopardi; and the grief which inspires thought no less than poetry is not the crude degrading pain of egotism, but care and sorrow for human society. It is true that the intellectual activities of imagination and understanding subdue passion by using it as their material, but in subduing it they do not exterminate it, rather they tame and domesticate it. So far from losing interest in it, they are enough interested to make it their own. In fact, the proper purpose of the maxims with which we started is to produce not an unpolitical man but, if we may so speak more exactly, a 'sympolitical' one, who is concerned in politics as in every human activity. He is concerned not

[1]Tasso; *Gerusalemme Liberata*, Canto VII. (Translator's note.)

to produce bad propagandist poetry, philosophy or history, still less to undertake political activities outside his province, but simply to transmute his passionate concern into pure poetry, philosophy or history ; and this he could not do if he had not this passionate concern, if his mind were indifferent, that is to say empty.

The proof of this interpretation of our maxims is to be found in the contempt with which society itself regards writers who are really unpolitical, calling them versifiers, mere literary men, dreary æsthetes, dull commentators, pedantic philosophisers of bloodless categories, with many other compliments. It is to be found too in the 'decadence' ascribed to periods in which such writers were the rule, as in the Italian counter-reformation and sixteenth century, when political or 'sympolitical' writers were the exception.

This discussion may be summed up in a way which seems apt to our own times. When, as so often, you hear a writer of genuine thought or a poet of genuine feeling declare, 'I am absolutely un-political', say to him, 'You don't know yourself well enough'. But when you hear the same remark from a poet without feeling and therefore without real imagination, or from a philosopher or historian without intimate feeling for human nature and therefore without understanding of it, some dry manipulator of forms and formulas, then you can say, 'You know yourself pretty well !'

1931

5

THE STATE AS FRIEND
AND AS ENEMY

THE STATE HAS SUFFERED, even in the sphere of theory, the extremes of love and hatred, of eulogy and vilification. Even its ideal nature has been diversely interpreted and treated as a manifestation now of good, now of evil, the highest good or the greatest evil. It has been loved and worshipped by the 'statolatrists' who under various names and disguises have figured in the history of ideas and of political alignments. It has been hated and reviled by anarchists, who likewise have their various disguises and names. Various, in fact, are the motives leading to either attitude, some noble and some mean. The 'anarchists' have sometimes been moved by a thirst for the freer development of human powers or even by a vision of the purest and most abstract moral ideal, or, like the anchorites, by the horror of social brutalities; but sometimes by a morbid intolerance of duty and discipline. The 'statolatrists' at some times have been moved by an austere reverence for the moral law and at others have truckled to the powers that be or tried to propitiate them and use them for their own purposes. But whatever the psychological motives discernible in each case according to the historical situation and the temperaments and characters of individuals, they all lead to the same error, in which men are led astray by false imaginations of good and evil. The theoretical formula for this kind of error is 'the fallacious denial or misinterpretation of some necessary stage or element in life and reality'.

This is certainly not the place to go over again the whole dialectical process by which the conception of the practical spirit is reached; it is enough for our present purpose to recall the conclusion : that the two stages or elements of expediency or might and of morality or right are equally indispensable ; that these severally correspond to the coercive state and to the free ethical will ; that they do not stand in a relation of opposition but of mutual implication. If the element of utility and force disappeared, so too would that of morality which is based upon it and can only work through it. And conversely, if the element of utility and force should usurp the prerogative of its superior, the moral consciousness, the human drama would lose all meaning, life and purpose ; an insignificant, blind vibration to vanish again in the void. The necessity of both these elements is recognised, though in an imperfect and inconsistent way, by certain doctrines which allow the state to be a condition or an instrument of morality, but one that can and must be superseded in its functions. On their view the perfectly moral life would be one which, having completely realised itself, is emancipated from any bondage or any relation to the state and dismisses it as something no longer required. In other language, the necessity of the state is here at once asserted and denied, since it is reduced from a timeless and unconditional necessity to one that is only contingent and temporary.

I will confine myself, by way of example, to two historical forms of this doctrine, very different in origin yet substantially identical. One is the traditional teaching of the church that the earthly city of state-organisation is necessary for sinful man but no longer for the citizen of the kingdom of heaven. The other is the Marxist doctrine which sees the human race, throughout its history, struggling in an economic class-war, oppressed by a governing class and its instrument the state. In this struggle humanity goes through a series of stages to the conclusion of the class-war and the consequent abolition of the state with the transition from the reign of necessity to the reign of liberty. This parallel suggests some not unprofitable reflections on the degree to which the historical materialism of Marx was influenced by Judaic and other unhistorical ideas of a millenium. This degradation of the state to a merely educative function is to be found also with an altered accent in writers of a very different tendency, such as

Fichte. According to him the state was to develop a superior generation which, when it had been perfected, would kick away the ladder
by which it had climbed. Here we cannot help noticing a very
inadequate grasp of the essentially polemical and critical nature of
the moral consciousness, which, in such abstract perfection and self-
sufficiency, far from being perfected, would be stifled.

These favourable and unfavourable attitudes are mainly of theoretical interest as more or less successful efforts of thought to define
and value the state and its relations. But devotion and hostility, more
directly practical and moral, are inspired by states in the concrete, by
this or that particular state. I say 'moral', because I do not intend, nor
would it be profitable, to consider the attitude of individuals to the
state arising from accidental situations or a conflict of interests. In
such cases the devotion would be mere complicity in profit, and the
hostility a rivalry for favours, easily bribed to complicity. If then our
principle has been established that the state is indispensable to the
moral life, both as the basis for its development and as the appropriate
material for its activity, what would be a genuine devotion to the
state and to its political life? It could only be a love for the field in
which the moral man must work, and with him the thinker and the
artist, a field where alone the delight of labour can be tasted. We love
the state as we love our home, our family, the country round us, our
friends, and companions. All these are the conditions and the objects
both of our congenial activities and of our duties. These loves are not
without their anxieties and their sorrows or they would not be loves,
which are always bitter-sweet.

In this aspect devotion to the state is collaboration with it, putting
the best part of ourselves into its political life—our affections, the
truths which make our effective creed, and our ideals. Such a participation is what is called liberty; for liberty is not opposition to the
state or an offence against its majesty, but the life of the state itself,
unless we think that the blood circulating in our veins and constantly
renewing itself is a lawless disturbance of the sovereign calm of our
physiological organism. There is no conceivable liberty within a
state except political liberty or, as we have said, collaboration in its
life. It is in vain that theorists have laboured to delimit the state and

individual liberty, to define how far the state should control and how far respect individual freedom of action. Vainly have they tried to prescribe and reserve the sphere of liberty as being that of the family or of religion or of science or art or of all together. None of these are effectively free except so far as they can influence the life of the state ; confined to their special interests, however much honoured and indulged, they lack the sap which should nourish them, and feed upon themselves and wither. So when Italy entered on her *risorgimento*, the demand, already made by Vico, was heard on all sides that her philosophers should not be 'monks' but 'politicians', and her poets neither courtiers nor academicians but citizens. Her ideal of the 'honest man' was no longer one who honestly attends to his own business and keeps clear of politics but, instead, one who is wide awake to the connection of his private life with the public, of his family with the state, who watches his children not with an eye to segregating them from the surrounding society, but with one that sees them as at once its members and its subjects, sharing its strength and weakness and responsibilities, its glories and its shame.

History reveals this love of a state in action, a state which need not always have just the constitutional form which we admire and take for granted today ; still less need it be transfigured into the 'ideal state' unknown to history, but imagined either in the naïve belief that it once existed in the past and has been corrupted or with the hope of one day realising it upon earth. This ideal state is equally unknown to sound theory, which only recognises states that really exist or have existed. But whenever a man has been able to work within a state and to realise there his moral ideal, he has loved it and been devoted to it, and for it has gladly sacrificed his life ; a state which perhaps, in the various stages of civilisation was theocratic or feudal, absolute or democratic, multi-national or national. On the other hand, whenever the relation of collaboration was broken by too serious obstacles and the state excluded the individual, pursuing ends which were indifferent or repugnant to him, then his 'consent' was lacking. By consent I mean moral approval, not the interested truckling which is never lacking to any government, even the most tyrannical. When this moral consent is lacking, love turns to hatred, new names and adjectives replace the old; the revered monarch becomes the loath-some tyrant, the priest is detested as a greedy churchman, the sovereign of a multi-national state becomes the 'foreign oppressor', and so on. Hence arise revolutions to restore consent and love for a new form of state.

In revolutions the break in the relation of consent and love is, if we may so express ourselves, the fault of the state, which has become headstrong and incapable of representing the natural impulses or the moral demands of its members. In 'reaction' the break comes from opposite causes, through the incapacity of natural impulses to rise to the demands of morality and so to find a channel for themselves in institutions where they can benefit the state. When this danger threatens, the danger of 'a relapse into anarchy' as it is called, the primary and fundamental human need for social order reacts against it and reacts in a one-sided way in the form of self-interest and violence.

All reaction is preceded by an absolute or relative weakness of men's moral nature. Sometimes this consists in a conventionally comfortable and superficial way of life which chills men's ideal enthusiasms, and in a decadence and corruption of the 'governing or 'political' classes, who become, as it is said, 'drones'; sometimes in the emergence of new ideals lacking able and experienced promoters and defenders, and consequently politically premature. Those who suffer by the reaction are generally led by their sufferings to interpret the harshness of the state, which is no longer representative, as treachery and hostility, nor are their feelings and consequent illusions unnatural. But those among them whose moral consciousness has not been weakened, or has quickly regained its strength, are more ready to blame themselves or, what comes to the same thing, their party, as responsible. In the resulting reaction they do not see harshness and sinister motives, or not these only, but mainly an objective necessity. They recognise that every part of our spiritual life, like the health of our organism, is from time to time upset by diseases, and that history develops through crises, which are aspects of the development itself, through pains and sufferings which are in fact remedies. There are drugs and remedies which a philosopher has described as 'incapable

of assimilation', but which yet are calculated to stimulate the recu-
perative powers by provoking reaction and rebellion. Wise men do
not despair even when liberty, achieved by the incredible efforts of
past generations and apparently unshakably established, seems to
vanish from the world or from the world they live in. They know
that nothing is built for ever, nor any gain permanent, for nothing of
this sort is materialised beyond the fate of human mortality, not even
the light of truth. Every truth may be denied and obscured and stifled.
And just as the individual must every day and every hour renew his
self-mastery, so human societies must constantly regain their equilibrium. Our thought rejects as fatuous the idea of a static life without
change, and even our feelings rebel against the imagination of an
inertia which could bring nothing but boredom and yawning. So
men of good will will not lose heart, but bracing themselves or
repressing their pain at the rupture of cordial co-operation with the
state, they set about the work of reform. And, to begin with, they
will reform themselves; and, by purging themselves of all that was
weak and selfish, they will begin to bind up the breach and so serve
the state and manifest their love for it, if not as it is, as it will be. To
understand the necessity of what has happened does not imply, as
mean minds find it convenient to think, coming to terms with it by
silencing the voice of conscience and minding their own business. On
the contrary, it implies obedience to conscience, which bids us to
work and, as the first condition of work, to abandon comfortable and
flattering fictions and grasp reality as a whole. Reality includes our
opponents but also ourselves with our will and feelings and with
those ideal aims that go beyond ourselves and our individual
existence.

Since reaction restores a social order, which had broken down and
revindicates the state's fundamental and permanent function, its
character and value is sheerly political. Its direct purpose is accomplished in the repression of violence and anarchy and in the restoration
of state authority. Another purpose it cannot directly pursue but only
negatively facilitate, by enforcing privation or what the doctors call
'diet'. This purpose is to call a truce and give time for moral forces
to awaken to their responsibilities and so make possible a renewal of

ethical and moral unity, of consent, of mutual advantage and of love. This is the direct and proper purpose, not of politics, but of the social forces themselves, one which they pursue by positive means; and when they are weak and sluggish, to that extent they retard its attainment and necessitate the phenomena of reaction. For regeneration is a task alien to the very nature of reaction because opposite and complementary to the one it is performing. It cannot by one and the same action break the bond between government and consent and also preserve it or bind it up again. If ever reaction is tempered by such a double policy, that is a sign that its necessity is gradually passing away and its work completed.

Yet the need for restoring this bond of mutual benefit and affection is so deep and strong, and the forces of reaction themselves feel it so urgently that they most often apply themselves to the two contradictory and impossible tasks. They are ambitious of deserving honour and glory, of conciliating moral approval; and consequently they surround themselves with culture and enlist under their patronage the plastic and poetic arts. This is not mere political expediency or deliberate design of propaganda, but has a certain degree of sincerity, for the reactionaries are after all men, not personifications of reaction, and as men they cannot help feeling the need I have described and trying to satisfy it. So the counter-reformation or catholic reaction, in the latter half of the sixteenth and much of the following century, produced a culture, a learning, a school of history, a literature and an art in its own service. So, too, the absolute monarchies, restored after the French revolution and the Napoleonic wars, were anxious to have their reactionary political theorists and historians, and set to work architects and painters. So, too, in our own day the totalitarian Russian state descends into the philosophical arena and equips itself with the dialectic of Hegelian Marxism and a materialist metaphysic, opens schools of poetry, boasts its new proletarian art and claims to initiate a glorious rebirth of thought and civilisation. Similarly in Germany, with wonderful and indeed breathless speed, there now rises on the horizon and spreads over the intellectual heaven the new culture of the boasted Third Reich, the theory of the pure Aryan race, of Germanic Christianity, philosophy and science, and finally of

German mathematics. Volumes of verse and prose are piled up which would indeed prove the intellectual enthusiasm and achievement of this nationalism if quantity were the same as quality and printed paper were digested thought.

But the weak point of a culture fostered or rather fabricated by reaction is precisely this, that quantity does not beget quality and that appearance is not reality. *Durum et durum non faciunt murum*, you must have mortar as well as bricks to build a wall, and here the mortar stands for genius which is not made to order or merely because it would be useful. Nor yet is it bred by intoxicated fanaticism, which can be had to order, but which is not pure, spontaneous genius, and, when stock is taken, turns out to have been barren. History and criticism pass over with contempt or silence the fanatical and servile works which aped history and philosophy and poetry in the counter-reformation and the revival of absolutism. And so they pass or will pass over the philosophic crudities of the Bolsheviks and their frigid, inhuman art, and over the present silly theories of German professors and pastors, who are not ashamed to assert that the first duty of a man of science or religion is to Germany and only then to truth or conscience, or who have discovered that Christianity was born of a 'Nordic inspiration'. The real culture of reactionary periods is to be sought and found in the opponents of reaction: during the Italian counter-reformation in Bruno, Campanella and Galileo; during the restoration of absolutism in those who opposed it or stood aside or, to some extent, in those who gave it their political obedience but not their hearts or their whole hearts. The Napoleonic period, too, only attained literary eminence in opposition writers like Chateaubriand and Madame de Staël. Napoleon, for all his military and political genius, revealed the poverty of his feelings for poetry when, to prove his admiration for Corneille, he said that if he had lived in his time, he would have made him a duke.

Yet the ethical and cultural ambition of reaction has great importance and in its way some value. It has value so far as, in its rough handling of the tender things of the mind, it stimulates and strengthens by reaction the pious affection and religious reverence which true worshippers feel for them, and the determination to protect them by every devotion and sacrifice. It has value too because, however rough its handling, and however diminished and mutilated the culture it imposes, it induces others to enter the intellectual world. And that world has a logic of its own which sooner or later opens the way to a discernment of true and false culture, of beauty and ugliness, of sincerity and affectation, of solidity and hollowness. Above all, it has value because it proclaims and reminds us of something that reaction can never give us in spite of our thirst for it; and thereby it portends that the reactionary process must sooner or later come to an end. In the last analysis reaction consists in the proclamation of a state of siege, except that in a state of siege the military, though they take over the policing of the city and publish edicts forbidding assembly and enforcing a curfew and the delivery of arms, do not meddle with philosophy and poetry or even with morality and religion. They know that a state of siege is temporary and do not claim that it should regulate every detail of human life. Reactionaries either do not know this truth or will not confess it or cannot bring themselves to act in conformity with it; yet by the violence they do to nature they are forced to reveal to others and to themselves that their state of siege can only be transitory.

How long this temporary stage may last, whether months or years or half a century, is the question asked, alike by gentle and simple, of the philosopher who defines political ideas and traces their dialectical development. But the philosopher has logical not chronological foresight, or, to speak more accurately, he has no foresight but only insight into the 'relations of ideas.' Historical prophecy is not in the field of the sciences, which only deal with facts, that is to say with the past living in the present and the present rooted in the past; it expatiates in the fields of sentiment and imagination. The making or hearing of such prophecies is popular because it is an easier field to work in than the other, indeed better fitted for a playing-field or a playground. It is easier too than the field of practical work which demands personal decision and responsibility in taking and upholding a position in life's struggle, not with prophetic vision but only with character and conscience.

1933

❧ 6 ❧

AN ESSAY IN COMMUNIST
PHILOSOPHY

I HAVE BEEN courteously presented with a copy of a little work[1] which I received with the welcome that a literary curiosity deserves, since it was translated and printed in Naples, a city where the sun shines on the statues of Thomas Aquinas, Giordano Bruno and Vico. These names might surely at least have suggested something less naïve than the confused heap of horrid philosophical fallacies which fill its pages.

What is 'dialectical materialism'? Is it, like all philosophical theories, something of universal validity? No, it is the theory of a party; the 'general theory of the Marx-Lenin party'. And what is its nature? It is dialectical in method and materialist in its conception of physical phenomena; as if materialism did not mean mechanism and determinism, the direct contrary of dialectic!

What did Marx do to the Hegelian dialectic? He professed to accept only the 'rational kernel' and to reject the 'idealist husk'. In fact he did the opposite; he missed the invaluable and epoch-making revolution in logic and the logical basis of historical thinking, but preserved the relics of an antiquated metaphysic, only substituting for Hegel's God, which was called the 'Idea', his own, which he called 'Matter', though both come to the same thing, something which works behind the scenes of history.

'Metaphysics considers nature as a chance collection of objects or phenomena in isolated independence of one another, not as a single

[1]Stalin, *Materialismo dialettico e materialismo storico*, edited by the Italian Communist Party, Naples, 1944.

connected whole'. On the contrary, a metaphysic, however insecurely based, is usually distinguished by its deduction of all natural facts from its single presupposed principle.

'Our consciousness and thought, however independent or self-determined they may seem, are simply the product of a material, bodily organ, the brain, which is a reflection of matter existing independently of consciousness'. But what is this 'reflection'? Is it a mirror held up to nature? Is there not something childish in taking so naïve a metaphor literally? 'Matter is not created by spirit, spirit is itself the supreme creation of matter.' A creation so 'supreme' that it ventures to deny its creator, demonstrating that matter is its creation, an abstraction which it has constructed for its own scientific purposes!

'Lenin condemned the *Empirio-criticism* of Ernest Mach as a "fideism" or "phenomenalism" which is a symptom or defence of bourgeois society'. But the theory of Mach and others of his persuasion is merely an examination into the logic of the physical or natural sciences as distinct from the logic of philosophy and history. It must be studied and, if necessary, criticised and refuted, by strict logic, and not in some supposed political or social interest.

'The science of history, if it is really to be a science, must no longer reduce the history of social development to the actions of kings and commanders'. No longer? It seems to me that for more than two centuries, to say the least (and strictly one should go back as far as Christianity) historians have revolted against a history of kings and battles and have set in its place a history of civilisation, of the constant acquisitions and development of humanity. 'History ought rather to be, above all, the history of those who have produced the material goods, the history of the peoples and the working masses'. Are we or are we not, in our history of the peoples, to include among the working masses, or more simply among the workers for humanity, Homer, Sophocles, Plato, Aristotle, Pheidias, Michelangelo, Dante and Kant, not to speak of Jesus and Paul? Or might we include Paul as a carpet and mat-maker, a trade he is said to have followed, and Spinoza as a lens-polisher, which is how he earned his living?

But enough! The game is a pretty one but too easy to last long. In

E

a note prefixed to the pamphlet we are told that this essay of Stalin is 'the simplest and yet most profound which has yet been written on the theory of Marx and Lenin'. Yet, in fact, Marx never in his life gave any theoretical justification for the paradoxes which, as a youth, in the convulsions of the left wing of a moribund hegelian school, he had invented. He confined himself thereafter to dogmatic repetition. These paradoxes, which were popularised in a grosser form by his superficial imitator Engels and more grossly still by Lenin, who lacked all philosophic training, these paradoxes, chewed over again by Stalin without any mental digestion, are philosophical extravagances and words without meaning. This is not to deny that Marx and even his faithful and industrious Engels, as well as Lenin and Stalin, are men of great importance who have counted and still count for much in the social and political history of our times. It is the more grievous to have to treat them, especially the last three, as on the level of clowns in some popular farce. But what is one to do? Garibaldi is still Garibaldi though he wrote vile verses and stories which find no mention in any history of literature.

Again, in the prefatory note, we read : 'This essay is a formidable ideological weapon for refuting bourgeois theories, and as intelligent and effective propaganda for the doctrine of Marx and Engels'. Effective it may be, though I should not say intelligent. It may be effective as a text-book of prejudices and superstitions, a legend of prodigies and miracles, a catechism of obscure and damnatory dogmas, which repeated more or less by rote may impress or stun the ignorant and simple-minded. How much it will profit civilisation and human progress, moral culture and good faith in social relations, I leave to the judgment of those who have thought about such matters.

No man who is alive to the immense possibilities of history, of the human mind and society, is blind to the profound social changes which the future may bring about. But he may still ask why the most noble and generous ideas and the most serious and realistic purposes should not be reasonably argued with a scrupulously critical mind and with respect for the scientific tradition of centuries. That is why in my beginning I mentioned those men of genius who, in the course of history, have done honour to Naples, to Italy and to the world. And since we have champions of communism among our neighbours, I cannot refrain from expressing the hope that they will free themselves from these superstitions and sectarian formulas, which are not philosophy or science but pseudo-philosophy and pseudo-science. These formulas came from the marxist party of Western Europe, and when, during the 'crisis of marxism', they had there been riddled by criticism, they emigrated to Russia. There the lower intellectual level of culture at that time saved them from any critical revision and only rendered them more hasty, fantastic and fanatical. I therefore hope that our friends will undertake the study necessary for the assimilation of our intellectual heritage, and that, abandoning the mechanical repetition of formulas, they may become the reformers, renewers and regenerators of a communism bringing true moral and intellectual progress for mankind—if such an ideal is ever to become real in human society or in any part of it.[1]

La Liberta, Naples, March, 1944.

[1]Under the title '*The Arms of Criticism*' and '*Armed Criticism*', the following note was published in the journal *La Libertà* of Naples (year I, No. 5, 6th April, 1944) as an answer to a somewhat unreasonable reply from the communist organ in Naples to the above critical remarks, which were perfectly calm and objective and intended to be quite friendly.

SORRENTO, *2nd April*, 1944.

DEAR FRIENDS,

The note in which *La Libertà* has thought proper to reply to you, solely in the interests of truth, and to be precise, of exactitude in quotation, was written by the editorial staff while I was absent from Naples and unaware of what was happening. This does not prevent me from approving of it in every syllable. If I had myself had to reply, this is what I should have said; to your threat that the 'critical arms' which I had adopted must be met by 'armed criticism', that is, by physical force, I should have answered with an old story which it brought to my mind. An officer was dancing in a ball-room when a man near him whispered, 'How badly he dances.' The gallant gentleman overheard and, having finished his dance, planted himself fiercely before the honest bourgeois and exclaimed: 'Sir, I would have you know that if I dance badly I fight well'. What do you suppose was the reply of the good man, who was not to be frightened out of his logic? Simply this: 'Then I advise you always to fight and never to dance'. And so I advise you to use violence or threaten it if it pleases you, but to leave dialectic, idealism, materialism and philosophy alone. Perhaps such a reply seems undignified in a philosopher; but we are in Naples, a city in which it is at least allowed to laugh, I will not say at communists, but with communists, of whom I know a good many and whom, outside their ferocious press campaigns, I have found charming and sensible people.

Yours, etc.

7

NOTE ON THE HISTORY OF COMMUNISM AS PRACTICAL POLITICS

ABOUT FIFTY YEARS AGO a History of Socialism and Communism was begun in Germany by a group of the most influential socialist and marxist writers under the direction of Bernstein and Kautsky. It was carried on by the co-operation of specialists in the manner of the national and universal histories composed by learned 'bourgeois'. When the first volume appeared[1] I was winning my spurs as a writer and objected in an essay that this 'history' lacked development and therefore was rather 'a kind of anthology of all proletarian rebellions and of all the social theories which founded themselves more or less on common ownership'.[2] Had I gone deeper I must have asserted in so many words that communism was essentially incapable of being made the subject of a history.

The subject of history must be something positive not negative: but the essence of communism, its fundamental and governing idea, the chief article of its creed, is no positive policy or institution but a mere beating of the air which expresses itself most crudely in its ideal of life as a peace without differences or rivalries, where indeed the ideals and feelings of all the citizens are the same, and their needs all the same and all satisfied. Such a condition would completely remove the necessity and even the possibility of mutual conflict, defeat and victory, and consequently the need for state regulation. Every error of theory has of course some practical ground or stimulus,

[1]*Geschichte des Sozialismus in Einzel-Darstellungen* (Stuttgart, Dietz, 1895).
[2]*Materialismo storico ed economia marxistica* (VI ed., Bari, 1941), pp. 185-6.

and here this is obviously to be found in the pain and grief of conflict, which men strive to evade by wishful dreaming of a life without struggle, which would be a death in life.

For these reasons communism is essentially not only a utopia but a Utopia which may be called absolute, unchangeable, unattainable in any age, even if it is placed in the most distant and final future. Historical utopias which have seemed successful have been either more or less religious sects, which founded little colonies, or the Jesuit missions in Paraguay, or cenobites and similar offshoots of the churches. All of them pretty soon became corrupt and dissolved themselves or decayed, and, apart from this, they never stood on their own feet but were parts of some non-communist society, of which they were either parasites or devices for performing some special function. It is impossible to construct such utopias even in fancy except by reducing men to robots without nerves or blood or imagination or thought or will. Certainly this is so unless the communism is paradoxically confined, as in some naïve ancient ideals or patterns of cities, to aristocratic governors like Plato's, or has a slave class, like Thomas More's, subjected to it so that it becomes as Vico would have said (who talked of 'aristocratic liberty') an 'aristocratic communism'.

The liberal conception of life and history has not for its antithesis the thesis of communism, as an enemy with whom it contends on equal terms. That would be to exalt the communist conception to a philosophic rank which in fact it does not deserve, and at the same time to degrade liberalism by anticipating and expecting some unspeakable, undiscoverable third stage in which both should be synthesised. The relation of the liberal conception to the communistic is like that between a man of experience and one of none who is carried away by his fancy and wallows in misunderstandings and ambiguities. The liberal conception recognises that life is a continual movement and therefore consists in perpetual conflicts and conciliations which perpetually give rise to new conflicts. It is a continual movement towards equality and peace and a continual rebirth of inequality and turmoil, the ruin of peace and well-being. It is impossible to make either of these 'moments' the end of life, for the end of life is simply life in its fullness, the sacred mystery of existence which we must worship and not presumptuously profane by destructive tinkering with the very mainspring of action and of life itself. But the liberal conception also recognises that man can, and in fact does, 'sublate' this conflict to continually higher levels; this is the faith which inspires the activity, the perpetual progress and enrichment and refinement of human life. The wise cannot pass over with indifference or mockery the errors of the ignorant; they take note of them and understand their causes in the hardships and pains and desires of humanity and try to remove these causes. So the liberal mind ponders the assertions and the claims of communism, and though it cannot help seeing the obvious contradictions in its panacea, and though it criticises the fallacies which are always arising in new forms, yet at the same time it tries to satisfy the particular practical claims of communism wherever the means exist, or more gradually as the means can be provided. It satisfies them, but only so far as they rightly follow from the well-considered nature and results of mental and moral liberty. A liberal constitution gives men all that it should: freedom of speech and of the press, of association, of propaganda, of elections, representation, voting, majority rights. Men can use these means, if they know how, to enquire into political and economic affairs, to convince others and so recruit adherents to their policies; but they must not expect to be allowed the violent seizure of power in order to satisfy their demands. Not that the liberal mind absolutely condemns all so-called revolutions, all breaks with legality and interruptions of the regular course of human society; for history, in which the liberal mind is nourished, has taught it that there are necessary and beneficent revolutions, surgical operations, as one might say, to assist timely births obstructed by accidental obstacles. But surgical operations are never without danger, and, if the birth supposed to be timely is in fact premature, the result may be fatal, or, in plain words, premature revolutions may give rise to anarchy and reaction and barbarism. Consequently the liberal mind only admits of tumultuous revolution in extreme cases, which for its part it does its utmost to avoid by substituting, wherever possible, evolution for revolution, and negotiation and gradual compromise for civil war.

The nineteenth century, in which liberty was best realised and most self-conscious, received in the poem of Faust—no divine comedy but the human comedy of the new age—the symbol of this advance. Faust seeks a moment so completely beautiful that he can bid time to stand still; but he cannot find it, and when at last he thinks he has succeeded and the words escape his lips, he has found, instead of a moment in which he can take his ease for ever, an ideal surpassing all moments of material enjoyment, the ideal of unwearying free activity,[1] and for this reason his soul does not fall into the hands of Mephistopheles. This is a secular conception implying a theory of immanence, whereas the communist conception, by its essential materialism, implies a sort of transcendence on the part of the material principle. By its materialist creed indeed, communism comes into conflict with the christian churches, and especially with the Catholic Church, yet it has a certain contact with the latter in the mortification it imposes on the pride of thought and action. Another point of contact is the tendency of communism to consider as on a very low level, among children and men devoted entirely and therefore mistakenly to the pursuit of livelihood,[2] races which the Catholic Church can receive as being thus spiritually exonerated, and can bring under its sway by indicating to them, as a compensation for their wretched life on earth, a heavenly beatitude.

At any rate, the contrast between the liberal spirit and communism, with its impetuous simplifications and fiery outbursts of revenge, hatred and destruction, is a sharp one. It is a contrast which must be clearly understood if we are not to be taken in by illusions of easy mutual understandings and agreements which are certainly desirable, but will be pretty slow and difficult. Such understandings will require that one of the parties should raise itself by the lessons of experience

[1] In well-known lines which cannot be too often reconsidered:
> Das ist der Weisheit letzter Schluss:
> Nur der verdient sich Freiheit wie das Leben,
> Der täglich sie erobern muss.
> Und so verbringt, umrungen von Gefahr,
> Hier Kindheit, Mann und Greis sein tüchtig Jahr.
> Solch' ein Gewimmel möcht' ich sehn,
> Auf freiem Grund mit freiem Volke stehen,
> Zum Augenblick dürft' ich sagen:
> Verweile doch, du bist so schon !

[2] *bisogni del benessere.*

and by reflection to a higher stage of mental culture, from which, when it looks back on its previous ideas and policies it will see them illuminated and transfigured, no longer as indefinite and utopian, but as definite and historical. Today, even when communists or socialists profess and believe themselves converted to liberalism, their culture, their feelings, their spiritual needs, their historical knowledge and understanding are altogether too different and too inferior. At the bottom of their hearts they still cherish the ideal of a static society, in which, as they euphemistically say, 'social justice' will be realised, with 'freedom' as a by-product. 'Free' is for them an *epitheton ornans*, or rather freedom is something to which they do lip-service, but of which their idea is entirely superficial as of something almost passive. Evidence of this has been seen recently in a book by Henri de Man, much read in Italy a few years ago, in which he announced his outgrowth from Marxism and conversion to a liberal or liberal-socialist faith. But during a few years of ministerial life in his native Belgium he found that certain proposals which he favoured met with opposition and obstruction in parliament from persons or groups whose interests seemed to him to prevail sometimes over a rather abstract 'general good'. This, together with a military defeat of his nation, was enough; he solemnly abjured his liberal principles and offered homage to authoritarian and arbitrary governments as alone able to afford the people the comforts of passive prosperity and 'social justice'.[1] Did he then suppose that everything which any individual among us thinks good and useful must meet with no opposition, but be at once accepted and put into practice by other men? Or that there shall be no more intrigue and sinister influence and other trickery? There always has been in the world, and always will be, without bringing the healthy activity and progress of human society to a standstill, as the whole course of history attests. Or did he think that 'la rugueuse réalité' (a phrase it pleases me to adopt from Rimbaud, who used it in his only serious moment of internal conflict) will ever under a new government become smooth by stroking? I fear that, only too likely, he honestly held these strange beliefs, for *semel abbas, semper abbas*; a man who is not gifted with the historical sense and a

[1] Henri de Man, *Après Coup*, Mémoires (Bruxelles, édit. de la Toison d'Or, 1941.)

72

sense for the tragic drama of human life either never really acquires them or could only do so by the blood and sweat which watered the soil in the garden of Gethsemane.

Returning to the history of communism and our initial denial of its possibility: what we intended to deny was not the occurrence of the particular positive facts which are more or less appropriately incorporated in such a 'history', and must certainly be described by general history in their individual character for the sake of their consequences; it was rather that communism has any positive, self-governing principle. In primitive times, in classical antiquity, in the middle ages, in the early centuries of the modern age, manifestations of communism had little importance; they were the rare accompaniment of religious crises or occasional savage explosions or *jacqueries* of oppressed peasants. In the course of the nineteenth century, when genuine socialist parties with appropriate policies were formed, the alliance of socialist with other historical forces contributed at least indirectly to so-called social legislation and made itself felt in other activities of the legislature and administration, and it still proposes and carries ambitious measures of reform. But besides this, communism contributed to a libellous falsification of liberalism, insinuating doubts even into many liberal minds, by describing it with bitter satire as nothing but a set of lies and fictions, conscious or, more often, unconscious, in defence of bourgeois capitalists. Thus liberalism began to lose the vigour of its prime and was shaken in its self-confidence of its high moral character. Moreover it was the aim and purpose of the socialist parties to detach those social classes which they claimed to represent from unity with their state or nation, condemning patriotism and every other moral idea—European federation, the League of Nations and so on—as capitalist and bourgeois. They spoke in the name of a non-existent international proletariat, torn out of the concrete context of historically conditioned interests. Their own acknowledged method was revolution, the very method which liberal policy had tried to replace by that of continual struggle and gradual constitutional progress, leaving to revolution only the rôle of a short remedy for rare cases. When the hope of revolution became a common and usual state of mind, it was in some countries the beginning of an end which was not the establishment of proletarian communism but the ruin of constitutions and the substitution of authoritarian for liberal governments. So the true subject of this history of socialist parties is not after all communism but the *Christus Patiens*, tried and travailing humanity, which is put to the proof but does not yield.

It may be thought that in our description of communism as merely negative and in our refusal to it on that account of the right to a history of its own, exception must be made of the particular communist or socialist theory which takes its name from Marx. This theory, according to its author, has made the advance from Utopia to Science and thereby grafted itself into the course of history, and has moreover opened up a new field of historical facts with a correspondingly new and independent science of history within the field of thought. But, in fact, Marx performed nothing that was promised in this formula, though he and his friend Engels gave themselves no little credit for it. Their boasted grafting of communism on history did not really give communism a positive content, which it continued to lack as it had always done. It was simply one of those ingenious dialectical constructions which the Hegelian school, and especially its left wing, was in the habit of inventing. In this theoretical fabrication the course of history was represented as starting from an imaginary primitive communism and reaching its goal in a developed and self-conscious communism after traversing the three intermediate economic stages of ancient slavery, medieval serfdom and modern capitalism, and as finally girding itself for the leap from this last to a so-called 'reign of liberty'.

The liquidation of the capitalist economy, according to Marx, was the factual criticism of the waste of wealth which that economy brought about by its periodic crises; though at the same time he could not help admiring the magnificent work accomplished in a few score years by bourgeois industry, compared with which the economic losses in the crises of adjustment were almost negligible. Marx exaggerated their extent, importance and regularity. But what the 'reign of liberty' might be, on which he was so eloquent, he was not in a position to say, and never said. He did indeed say that capitalism

74

produced and educated its own 'gravediggers' in the working classes; but it is obvious that gravediggers do not produce any new life, nor are destructive forces, as such, constructive, and it remains a question what new and positive form of life communism bestowed upon the world. George Sorel, who had more warmth of feeling and poetic impulse than Marx, dreamed of a working class which should have developed a more pure and vigorous morality and given fresh life-blood to human society, as had done the Christianity which he delighted to compare with his idol of socialist syndicalism. But this dream soon faded, and he could never define the character nor prove the existence of this new morality which was coming to birth and of which he certainly was neither the Jesus nor the Paul. Marx contented himself with pointing out a promised land afar off, in which classes would have been abolished and there would be no more need of state machinery or coercion, since all would be in the enjoyment of liberty by free association. When he was now and again asked for something less vague he avoided the question by the quip that 'he was not writing menus for the kitchens of the future'. Only one plain word escaped his lips: 'dictatorship', to which indeed he added the possessive 'of the proletariat', but a dictatorship it was to be, in whatever name it was exercised, and one from which men could forsee no release; for dictatorship as a legal expedient depends upon an established constitution, temporarily suspending itself, to which one hopes to return when the emergency is over. But without such dependence (as in the case where a socialist revolution had not only overturned the state economy but destroyed the very idea of a State) dictatorship is not temporary but permanent and takes on a more ugly name. And so, in Marx, communism has no content except the absence of all content, which is signified by the absurd cessation of conflicts and the historical void which is produced by cessation of the conflict of life.

As to the alleged 'realisation' of communism in Russia today, I have already protested against the methodological error of claiming to settle a question of principles by adducing facts which cannot be assumed to be historical facts, that is to say, conceived, understood and defined, except by means of the very principles which are in question, a vicious circle that can only be the result of very inadequate reflection.[1] The nature and self-contradiction and weakness of communism are one story, and what has happened or is happening in Russia is another. Only one who has followed and inwardly digested the history of the Russian people and society and of their thoughts, feelings and customs, and of all that this revolution destroyed and constructed or is constructing, can judge the nature of their revolution. It follows that since, for my part, I do not feel possessed of these indispensable qualifications, I shall not, like so many others, throw out any impromptu criticism on the history of that society; nor shall I accept the verdicts of others, however well-informed they may seem, since, before accepting the judgment of others, one must be able to confirm it critically, that is to say, from experience and knowledge of one's own. In books, mostly English and American, which I have come across, I have read accounts which seemed to shew that of all the items in the programme authorised by Marx, in whose name these revolutionaries began their work, only one is extant, the dictatorship, and a dictatorship, not of the proletariat but of a technical and political bureaucracy. This is a new class, better paid than its subordinates, which educates its successors, sending its children to the universities and preparing them to succeed it in the public leadership and administration; whereas peasants and workmen are not allowed to move from one place to another but are like serfs attached to the soil. Of the 'reign of liberty' prophesied by Marx the very memory has disappeared, and the 'withering away of the state', is, by tacit agreement, no longer mentioned. In its place there has been an increase of state activity, centralising and regulating to its own taste every occupation and every thought, and turning even art and poetry into political propaganda. And what is one to infer from this? That communism, or the society of equals, has not been attained in Russia? But that such a society never could be attained, because of its essential nature, had already been proved in our criticism of its guiding principles, and to that proof nothing is added by the failure to attain it in Russia. It cannot even be said that we have here an empirical confirmation by facts; for a fact which has not happened

[1] See *Russia e comunismo* in *Conversazioni critiche*, series V, pp. 348-50.

now or here might happen in another day or place, if only it were not self-contradictory and therefore impossible, and so we are sent back once more to our logical analysis. So our problem is not the hopeless one of how to accept a fact we do not understand in place of a demonstration of the principle necessary for its understanding, but the concrete historical problem of what advance Soviet Russia has made over Czarist Russia, and of the nature of the new autocracy compared with the old. It is remarked that though the old Russia gave the rest of Europe no illuminating thought, she at least gave it splendid poetry, the tortured and pessimistic poetry of souls darkly seeking their path, which Tolstoy and Dostoievsky taught us to admire and love; whereas from the new Russia we hear only the repetition of Marxist formulas, well known and criticised and out-grown half a century ago by the philosophy and economics of Europe, and a poetry generally inferior because tendentious and, as has been said, polemical. But this negative argument, just because it is negative, is not historically conclusive, for the spirit of art blows where it lists in any social atmosphere.

The materialist philosophy now taught in Russia, which is certainly incompetent to withstand instructed criticism, may nevertheless be a relative progress, or beginning of progress and of elementary scientific training, for a people among whom such things hardly existed, and whose finest natures were nourished on fantastical reasoning and paradoxes. In spite of the well-known absence in contemporary Russia of originality and of philosophical or historic penetration and of wide culture, there is certainly progress in the elementary education generously supplied to the people, which has put an end to the traditional illiteracy of the past. It is also to be noticed that in spite of the official anti-patriotic doctrines, framed on the Marxist teaching which considered patriotism a sentiment or fiction of the bourgeois class, and in spite of the cosmopolitan gospel which resounded so loudly in the Communist Manifesto : 'Workers of the world, unite !', Russia still feels herself a nation among nations. She has political relations and enters alliances as a state with other states, not as one proletariat with others against the capitalist régime; she still fights for Mother Russia. But surprise at all this is the result of a false assumption that the history of contemporary Russia is the history of communism, whereas it is the history of Russian life, which develops like those of other peoples, and like them necessarily moves, in fact if not in theory, even in its times of trouble, towards an ever greater or more congenial liberty, or at least one less uncongenial. We must admit that the revolution did not cut Russia off from a freedom she had previously enjoyed, nor was the new régime less free than the old. After long fermentation of thought and spasmodic attempts at revolution, she made the only revolution possible for a nation like herself, who was neither England in the seventeenth century, nor France in the eighteenth, nor Italy in the nineteenth. It was the revolution which those who knew the real conditions best, saw being prepared by the play of forces in Russia. How the Russian people will develop in the future, clearly only the future can tell. It would be a waste of time to guess here, since our guess would be of no importance, and, in any case, is implied by our whole conception of human life and its history and ideals.[1]

[1]See, however, the conclusion of my *Storia d'Europa nel secolo decimonono* (1932).

8

THE IDEA OF CLASSES AS
REAL ENTITIES

FOR THE LAST CENTURY, but especially in the last fifty years, the world seems to have been invaded, harassed, haunted, terrified, by a nightmare of furies, something like a medieval troop of *hellequins* or harlequins, or a ride of devils, called the 'social classes'. The author who chiefly inspired them was Karl Marx, on whom the final conclusion of accurate criticism must be that, while he was a Jeremiah of revolution and a driving force of social movements, he lacked any great philosophic or scientific talent, which is the talent for truth. He put into circulation a series of queer conceptions, both in philosophy and economics, ranging from historical materialism with its 'ideologies' in the former, to the theory of surplus value in the latter. No doubt the word 'classes' was in use before his day, though only in an empirical context, and no doubt it was used both as a battle cry and a term of abuse, with accompanying hopes and illusions. As the villeins were satirised in the Middle Ages, so in modern times were first the aristocracy and then the bourgeoisie. But Marx petrified the 'classes' into clear-cut logical and even metaphysical categories of 'dialectic'. If this fallacy, of which he is the author and the patron, has any value, if it is to have any influence on the history of thought, it will be by way of reaction in having stimulated a revival and renaissance in the true theory of human history and of pure economic science. Everyone knows what became of feudal aristocracy, bourgeoisie, proletariat, capitalism, in the hands of Marx, to mention only his main conceptions. We all know how these conceptions have to be corrected and melted down so that his myths may give place to the realities which he had distorted by bitter prejudice and question-begging definitions. To this revision and recasting I myself devoted an essay[1] in which I examined the various historical uses of the word 'bourgeois', sometimes as a term of contempt for 'middle-class' minds and spirits, sometimes with the serious political and moral import of a middle-class mediating between two extremes, and lastly with the ideal suggestion of the educated and civilised classes. Only through the fiction of a mythical metaphysic has it come about that the class-names, naturally given to the component parts of society, have given rise to a belief in the reality of classes, distinguishable as sheep and goats, base and noble, healthy and diseased; and so to these 'classes' are applied the verdicts usually passed in social and moral conflicts only on the behaviour of individuals in various temporary situations. I have drawn attention to the uses of the word 'bourgeois', which I have treated elsewhere, but it is also worth pausing to notice that the words 'peasant', 'worker' and 'proletariat' in general have also been used in abusive senses similar to that ascribed to bourgeois. I will not give a list of the types and characters presented by sociologists and by realistic or 'veristic' novelists like Balzac and Zola. The latter ended by rousing the indignation and retaliation of marxist writers, for example those of the *Neue Zeit*, who accused him of libelling the proletariat and of being a lackey of the bourgeoisie. No charge could have been more unjust, since the author's good faith and his aim of scientific impartiality were unquestionable. If in *L'Assommoir* and *La Terre* he had painted the vices of the workers and the grinding avarice of the peasants, in *Le Ventre de Paris* he had done no less for the greasy bourgeoisie, and in *L'Argent* for the business world; while in *Germinal* he had tried to portray the moral motives of the workers' struggles, and in his later novels revealed himself still more as an undisguised humanitarian idealist. It is also worth recalling the verdicts of Maxim Gorky, the Bolshevik revolutionary, who in his later years painted in grim colours the peasant class which, by the Russian revolution, obtained the victory over its masters and land-lords. He set in relief their anarchical, unsocial, unco-operative and

[1] See *Etica e politica* (2nd edition, Bari, 1943), pp. 321-328.

refractory character; their preoccupation with the purely animal egoism of eating as much and working as little as possible; their deep-seated hatred for the city-workers and the civilisation they represent; their lack of any knowledge or traditions of their own past; their minds crammed with superstitions but empty of ideas; the refined and cold-blooded cruelties of which in the revolution they were guilty, even in spite of their political and intellectual leaders; their total indifference to religion. In fact, Gorky saw no future for them except as a sort of drudges in their own business, that is to say in their own interests. For Gorky, the picture of the honest peasant, with a natural sense of truth and justice and humanity, was invented in the writings of 'the friends of the people', which at last aroused protests from authors like Tchekov and Bunin (*Lenin et le Paysan Russe*, French translation, Paris, 1924, *passim*). Verdicts of this kind do not depend on the real character of the human beings to whom they refer but on the simple fact that they are descriptions of 'classes'. All judgments of classes tend to be severe, because in classifications the human reality is mechanically and arbitrarily parcelled into samples, each absolutely determined by a single motive, which of course can only be the desire to defend its own class way of life, to pursue and increase its own prosperity without regard to any other consideration or loyalty. The same result follows from descriptions of all classes within the bourgeoisie, as it is called, as well as of the aristocracy—workers, soldiers, priests and the rest. Truth, justice, kindness, generosity, piety, charm, are to be found in all classes, *nec cubant in ulla*; their foundation lies deeper, not in classification but in humanity. These are what make human history and the traditions of the race with its glory and its strength; not abstract distinctions which, in the last resort, find the determining historical factor in that intractable brute obstacle which always materially conditions spiritual activity, and constantly subdues it to the stuff it works in. That is the logical fallacy of the class theory of human history and life. For the true, rich reality, it substitutes a monstrous history without historical evidence, where all the actors are personifications each obsessed by its own goods and gains and shut off from all its fellows and from communion with its kind. A very different spectacle unrolls itself

F

before the unclouded eyes of the historian. He sees humanity unwearied in self-realisation and in development; ever increasing and restoring what is called civilisation by its intellectual activity, its religious enthusiasm, its poetic inspirations, its deeds of sacrifice and heroism, its laborious discoveries in technical science. He sees that the authors and supporters of these activities are not classes but individuals, who, it may very well be said, emerge from all classes, and not least from those reputed the humblest and most downtrodden. We have no need to be reminded of the peasant boys, to mention no others, who have become philosophers, poets, painters, musicians, inventors, generals and statesmen eminent in the highest offices of the social life. Modern historians after an interlude of dull, monotonous and stupidly materialist class-theory, have instinctively returned to the natural and traditional path, no doubt greatly enriched and fortified in the consciousness that it is the right one. The future is certain, for it depends on the critical spirit, the intelligence and good feeling of humanity, which reveres its noble and industrious past. Antonio Labriola, in one of our Socratic arguments, at the time when historical materialism was the rage, once opened his mind to me: 'Marx', he said, 'has practically proved that for thousands of years human life has been a life of wretches, only worthy of pity, governed in all their actions and in all their quarrels, in all their illusory beliefs and virtues, by nothing but avarice and hunger. A truly human history, without the antitheses of classes has still to begin'. To such blindness could historical materialism and the theory of class-warfare bring even men of distinguished intellect.

But the results of this fallacy in the fields of history and philosophy are less serious, because less directly dangerous, than in moral and political action. There the habit survives of conceiving problems not in terms of men and their actions, and not in terms of the abiding purposes of humanity, but by the formula of classes or, as they are sometimes called, masses, and of conceiving them from the mechanical point of view which this implies. So, instead of bending their hearts and minds to the discovery and promotion of what will from time to time elevate and humanise mankind, men ask what the masses want or what is the will of the people, and plan the mechanism which will produce this or that effect. Apparently, they never suspect that classes and masses are abstractions, incapable of thought or action, and even less capable of thinking or acting rightly, which can only be done by a concrete human individual. By a strange transference, men project into the classes and masses the thoughts and actions of any demagogue who claims to speak or act in their name; though the demagogues have this better qualification, that they are at least men of flesh and blood, real actors, whether their part be great or small, heroic or villainous, on the stage of history. Nor would I deny them the part, such as it is, which they in fact play. They too have an end to serve and a service to perform. Only I would advise those who are not demagogues and who think and act more advisedly and more disinterestedly, never to speak or act in 'the name of classes or the masses', but in their own; let them speak and do, as their own minds guide them and their own hearts move them, for the common good of men, scrupulous always for the fate of every single individual. The man has a real life to live; the life of classes is a fiction.

⚜ 9 ⚜

ARISTOCRACY AND
THE MASSES

IT WOULD BE NO PARADOX to say that the great men of thought
or action are few, and that consequently the fate of human societies
is bound up with that of their aristocracies. Nor is it paradoxical to
add that we must not here think of the old closed hereditary aristocracies of blood, but rather of open aristocracies, continually renewing themselves, whose members, when their work is done, die, or
if they survive their office retire into private life. To contrast the
masses with this aristocracy, as if they were a herd, a many-headed
monster to be repressed and bound and deluded, is the pose of
aesthetes and minor poets, as it was the unlucky habit of the decadent
absolute monarchies. But if the aristocracy of which we speak is an
open one, if it is recruited from the so-called masses, it clearly cannot
treat them as enemies or foreigners nor as worthless matter to be
trampled under foot and haughtily over-ridden. In fact, these are all
platitudes, but still it is true that it is the duty of an aristocracy to
educate the masses.

They must be educated but, what is more, they must be given the
freedom and capacity to educate themselves. Elementary education
is necessary, but in it the part played by the teacher is much greater
than the part which the pupil must take at his own risk and his own
initiative. It goes without saying that the education given must be in
the fullest sense liberal and humane, not partisan or sectarian, for
sects and parties are only a healthy growth when grafted on the stock
of the common humanities. Anything else would not be education

84

worthy of the name but a conditioning for alien purposes and a degradation. At any rate, once the school-time proper is outgrown, men cannot be kept under tutelage with the belief or pretext that their education is being continued, since in this way they will evidently never get education at all. And, as we avoid futile over-discipline by letting boys learn from the experience of their own mistakes, so must we behave also to the men whom we want to train up as citizens to play a part in the political life of their country. Trade unions, trade councils, workers' associations, demands for legal safeguards, strikes, leagues of resistance are ways of carrying on adult education. There is no need as a rule to fear intemperate action or excesses from these members of the masses; action, opposition, argument, facing danger, deciding upon warfare and endurance of its defeats as well as its victories, these are the best pedagogical devices. They give an understanding of one's own rights and of other people's, of what we can and cannot ask or expect, of the distinction between the desirable and the possible, of the limitations imposed by nature and by the historical situation; they teach the virtues of moderation and patience to all in whom these qualities have not yet matured. It is in free conflict that sympathy and toleration are developed. Slaves and men degraded by being kept in leading-strings become bestial and cruel on opportunity. These two stages of education, by the teacher and by life, serve not only to provide constantly new recruits for the aristocratic ruling class; they also provide the environment in which new ideas, bold designs, skilful measures and wise provisions, born and matured in the minds and hearts of a few, may be received with less misunderstanding and opposition, and may find many minds ready to support them and to co-operate in their realisation. When an aristocracy of lofty and acute intellects rules a rude and hostile mob, with no common ground between them, the former is impotent because it has no sufficient power at its disposal, the latter because it has no brains. From such double impotence no historical advance, no increase of civilisation can arise; but the fact that such changes occur in all ages shows that these two opposed classes are not distinct realities but figments of imagination.

The aristocracy and the masses then are not two separate or even separable entities, each a world in itself which cannot influence the other except externally; by their intercourse they compose the single human society and by their mutual interpenetration keep it in a constant ferment of reformation. The intellectual, or aristocrat of whatever title, who presumes that he is set apart from and above the masses by the gift of nature or the grace of God, may chasten his pride by remembering that he too, outside his peculiar office and vocation, is a member of the vulgar herd in all those spheres when he does not employ his talents but follows, more or less passively, common ideas and popular tastes prescribed by fashion or caprice. It is impossible to help smiling when people eagerly and confidently solicit advice on political measures from poets or philosophers, men of contemplation or research who are often more puzzled or helpless than the questioner, without even his merit of being interested. It is equally amusing when, with similar confidence, people try to get guidance from politicians, financiers or soldiers on questions of religion, philosophy, and poetry, piously recording their answers. Both kinds of men are thus tempted to go beyond their proper field, and if they do not know their limitations and feel the dignity of silence, but try to pose as worthy of the rash trust put in them, they talk with extravagant nonsense or platitudes; that is to say they allow the common vulgar part of their mind to air itself, which was previously dormant, or at least carefully confined in some dark corner.

All this, as I said, is no paradox but simple commonsense and right feeling; it only seems paradox in a time when feeling is bad and sense perverted. If it is silly and self-contradictory to call all men superior, and equally silly to draw a sharp line between the superior and inferior, when both only enter this relation within the organic social unity and the course of history, what name does the mystical idea of 'the masses' deserve, which grew up in the nineteenth century and seems now to be in its prime? It is an idea which has had two stages and has taken two forms, of which the second, though developed from the first, is in a sense opposed to it. 'En France' we read in a letter of 1885 from Lanfrey to Maxime de Camp,[2] *'il n'y a plus d'hommes. On a systématiquement tué l'homme au profit du peuple, des masses,*

[1] M. Du Camp, *Souvenirs Littéraires* (Paris, Hachette, 1883), I, p. 275.

86

comme disent nos législateurs écervellés'. As a matter of fact, the fictitious entity called *'le peuple'*, the people, at first signified all that is purest, most noble and most essentially rational in man, the most direct voice of God; then this rather idyllic picture gave place to another, of irresistible, mysterious and irrational power, 'the masses', whose will, often obscure and complicated, has to be interpreted and carried out. The idyllic version gave rise to ill-fated illusions: *'Et puis'*, our letter goes on, *'un beau jour on's'est aperçu que ce peuple n'avait jamais existé qu'en projet et que ces masses étaient un troupeau mipartie de moutons et de tigres. C'est une triste histoire. Nous avons à relever l'âme humaine contre l'aveugle et brutale tyrannie des multitudes'.* But the irrational idea of masses, the second version, falls in only too well with the ruling irrationality of today, so that they will stand and fall together.

🦋 10 🦋

POLITICAL TRUTH AND
POPULAR MYTHS

A RECENT AMERICAN BOOK called *The Machiavellian Defenders of Freedom,*[1] by James Burnham, author of *The Managerial Revolution,*[1] has aroused attention as illustrating an important development of contemporary society and economics. The writer maintains that a realistic political theory, if properly understood, is the necessary presupposition and foundation of any attempt to preach or to defend liberty, and that this pure political theory, discovered once and for all by Machiavelli, is to be found repeated by many who, consciously or not, have recently followed his tradition. Burnham does not know, or has overlooked the great and laborious development of Machiavellian thought from the second half of the sixteenth century, through the many acute writers of the baroque period, ending with Vico and Galiani in Italy and Fichte and Hegel in Germany. Not to speak of my own historical researches and theoretical conclusions, we might be surprised that he is ignorant of Meinecke's *History of Politics,* though it is only one more proof of the disorganization, weakening or complete breakdown of international cultural relations since the 1914 war. At any rate, Burnham's book is chiefly or almost wholly devoted to Italy; besides Dante and Machiavelli, the four Machiavellians whose ideas he expounds and approves are the modern Italians, Gaetano Mosca and Vilfredo Pareto, the half-Italian Robert Michels, and Sorel who had studied and assimilated Italian political literature.

Burnham comes to the definite conclusion that all historical

[1]New York, the John Day Company, 1943 and 1944.

experience proves democracy, in the sense of self-government by the people, to be a fiction, impossible of realisation because contrary to the constant tendencies of society and especially to the necessary technical conditions of social order. And since all social foresight rests on the evidence of the past, and we have no reason to suppose that the tendencies and conditions which have prevented the realisation of democracy in all periods of human history will disappear in the future, we must, as scientific thinkers, expect that future to have as little democracy as the past (p. 326). Politics have always been managed by the minorities capable of it, by *élites*, whatever their origin and character; and their primary object is to maintain themselves in power. But it is just these minorities which make liberty and the common good possible and certain, because they are not united, for they always contain in their own ranks an 'opposition' which turns out to be an opponent. Consequently both parties, the Government and the opposition which criticises it and prepares to succeed it, are driven to enlist support by observing and consulting the essential requirements of the various forces in the society. And if they are not sufficiently united to turn themselves into a dictatorship, this always opens the door to discussions, representations, voting, that is to say, to actual liberty. In this way and in no other, out of the facts as conceived by Machiavelli and his followers there emerges liberty and with it, one might say, the only democracy possible in the world, the only democracy revealed by history in the realm of fact.

This in brief is Burnham's theory, which on the whole I find plausible. I will barely touch on a criticism, though doubtless philosophically important, which I could defend, as to his logical deduction of liberty. By confining himself too narrowly to the purely political forces he makes liberty a purely political product. He thus degrades man to a *homo politicus*, by not recognizing and emphasising another element, active and indeed superior, which may be called either his moral or his religious nature. This was already suggested as against Machiavelli by Tommaso Campanella in his *Atheismus Triumphatus*, and was fully thought out by Vico, who made it the fundamental principle of humanity and its history in his *Scienza Nuova*. Morality is stronger than either the *élite* or the masses themselves, *volentes*

ducit, nolentes trahit; it turns the forms and methods of political power
to its own purposes.

It is, however, incumbent on me to emphasise another difficulty,
which I have noticed and discussed elsewhere, and which Burnham
laboriously and almost painfully expounds. The harsh doctrine of the
Machiavellians has been shown to be the only scientific theory of
politics; in the political world it is the truth. But it is opposed by the
masses, who can never be induced to think scientifically and critically,
to see realistically or to argue logically at the sacrifice of passions
sometimes fickle and sometimes obstinate, but always violent.
Popular education, which the liberal nineteenth century enthusiastically inaugurated, has not fulfilled the hope of making the masses
politically intelligent. They have become more the prey of emotional
propaganda, drawing its strength from passion and imagination; and
woe to them if the propagandist slogan had been true that 'the fate of
the people is in their own hands'. What the people wants is not truth
but some myth which flatters their feelings, and the first and un-
welcome truth they need to be taught is to distrust the demagogues
who excite and intoxicate them. By what means and to what depths
the last and latest of their demagogues has degraded the Italian people,
we all know. The only course then is to put our trust in that part of
the ruling *élite* which is scientifically educated, which can look facts
boldly in the face and be guided by them in its relations with the other
parties. We must trust the class called the 'intellectuals', as Hegel
acknowledged by calling them the 'universal class' or 'the unclassed'.[1]
Their function is to leaven the other parties, their proper policy is
opportunism, not in the vulgar sense of following the current in any
direction and at any speed, but in the sense of suiting the action to the
perceived needs and conditions of the time with a watchful eye to the
future. Certainly such a class will not ruin the selfish interests of the
élite, but it will make the most of their other interests which conform
to the general good and will prevent dictatorships and tyrannies; as
an aristo-democracy it will manage, by opening its ranks, to renew
and rejuvenate itself constantly. Thus it will be able, instead of
crushing revolutions, which would be a crime against history, to keep

[1] *Classe non classe.*

pace with them, and by avoiding ruinous catastrophes, to bring the masses a net profit, an indubitable progress, though one which, like every real progress, is comparative and not absolute. Naturally such a solution, the only one that can be thought of, will not solve all social problems, for these do not depend on the human will; they arise from the unceasing, ever-changing historical process. No solution will secure perpetual peace or perpetual prosperity.

Here, says our author, we are faced with a terrible dilemma. The political life of the masses and the need for social cohesion demand the acceptance of myths which the critical mind uncompromisingly rejects. It seems as if we must deceive the public but not ourselves. But this is more than difficult, it is impossible; one cannot persuade others of what one does not believe, and there is at least the risk that we may become our own dupes and end by believing the myths which we had begun by exploding.

This difficulty Burnham does not overcome, though he observes that it has been practically overcome in certain periods of history, such as those of the Roman Empire, the Catholic supremacy, the Venetian republic and the British Empire. He adds that the failure of all such attempts in the last half century has had and is still having alarming consequences; yet amidst the terrible wars and revolutions of our time, a purge in the ranks of the governing classes has begun on a grand scale which we may hope will continue till it changes the course of history. 'And then', his book concludes, 'though this change will never lead to the perfect society of our own dreams, we may hope that it will allow to mortals that minimum of moral dignity which alone can justify the strange accident of man's existence'. (p. 270.)

This conclusion, with its noble appeal to the moral dignity of man, gives me the chance to repeat that the author should have given more consideration to the moral forces which permeate human history, and which theologians used to call Providence. And I may add that the tragic dilemma he propounds with such misgivings might seem less tragic and less threatening if he would modify his conception of myth. Myth is not falsehood but imperfect truth, one-sided, vague, dubious, mixed with feeling and disguised in images. We can constantly correct it by purifying it, and thus take occasion to fortify the truth and even to enrich it with elements previously neglected. To mythologise in cold blood is tasteless, dishonest and vain, for myths are born, not made, and they are born even of what we call truths and treat as truths in our reasoning. Myths have been born from the idea of freedom, and none are more beautiful than those born from the truth of Christianity, which the vulgar may have taken grossly and materially, but in which purer spirits and finer minds could feel and recognise the deep truth and the high ideals which they embodied. The intellectual class not only opens its arms to recruits from the masses of the people but also to their myths, which it is bound to ponder, to analyse, to reshape, and to absorb in the truth of science and of morality.

✥ II ✥

LIBERALISM AND DEMOCRACY[1]

THE VERY INSTRUCTIVE translations of De Tocqueville's work recently published in Italy bring up once more for consideration the controversy in which, as a young man, I took part between right and left, moderate conservative and progressive policies, between liberalism and democracy. Is such a controversy one between absolutely irreconcilable opposites? And is it well defined by the two terms conservatives and progressives? As for De Tocqueville, he certainly had a vein of conservatism, but it was conservatism *secundum quid*, with the noble motive of love for such traditions, institutions and arrangements as he thought necessary for that liberty to which he had dedicated his soul. But the criticism passed upon his ideas by those who have recently treated of them in Italy has made it clear that his great love of liberty, his fearful anxiety lest it should be lost, had somewhat clouded his theoretical recognition of its inherently creative power, with the result that he sought props for it outside itself. Such props are weak and untrustworthy. The devices by which it was thus supported were bound to suffer change, and, either by their slow decay or sudden collapse, to bring it down in ruins. Even if they proved more or less durable, they would in no way guarantee the vitality which liberty has in itself alone, which, from its own resources, increases in strength, extent and stature, or sometimes weakens and wanders, but only to recover itself anew. Liberty, like poetry and thought and morality, is not tied to any particular environment of institutions or traditions or economic conditions or anything else; all these it can use for its own purposes as the situation

[1]Contributed under the title *On de Tocqueville* to *Critica* of 20th January, 1943.

and the historical process may suggest. Liberty does not conserve anything except itself, which is no 'thing' but a fundamental activity of spirit. The word 'conservative' often has a suspicious and unattractive sound; but surely nobody would complain of those who try to conserve intellectual vigour, artistic sensibility, moral insight or love of liberty; for, in these cases, 'conservatism' means hoarding our resources and equipping ourselves to fulfil our functions and to advance in the struggle of life.

But if liberalism is careful for nothing but liberty as the supreme principle of morality, what is its relation to democracy? It is an elusive relation to grasp; according to the point of view it looks like identity or opposition. Democracy accuses liberalism of conservative tendencies, and liberalism retorts that democracy runs a perilous and headstrong career, which, by the help of a demagogue and a mystical faith in 'the people' or 'the masses', leads to tyranny and the rule of the sword.

The difficulty of understanding the relation arises precisely because liberalism and democracy are at once coincident and divergent, identical in one respect but different in another. They are identical in so far as both will know no rule from above, whether autocracy or theocracy. As their enemies say, both plunge into the same tumultuous anarchy of uncontrolled individualism and wallow together in the same abyss. Their difference is this: democracy has an abstract, naturalistic and intellectualist idea of liberty, liberalism one that is concrete and historical; the former is derived from the thought of the eighteenth century, the latter from the nineteenth. From these two mental attitudes arise all their differences, which, *brevitatis causa*, I will not now illustrate in detail. Nor is it necessary to argue, what is obvious, that the historical thought of liberalism is superior to the abstractness of the democrats, as the nineteenth century mind was richer and more mature than the eighteenth.

In theory then, the conflict between liberalism and democracy can only be ended by the victory of the more adequate and critical thought, which subordinates the latter to the former, much, one might say, as the physics of Aristotle had to give way to that of Galileo. But a very different question arises in the field of practical politics. Here the words 'liberalism' and 'democracy' do not represent merely antithetical ideas but parties or groups. Neither the individuals who form such groups, nor the principles of their grouping, can be simply schematised as a more elementary and a more mature development; for the former differ in their past histories, in their various mental and moral educations; in their temperaments, ways of life and individual strength and weakness.

In this context then liberalism and democracy must be treated not as superior and inferior conceptions but as different and opposed principles, each necessary as the complement of the other and both to that whole which is social or political life. Liberalism has its great quality in its caution, whose defect is to become timidity; democracy, on the other hand, in its radicalism and downrightness, which tend however to substitute quantity for quality and the formal shows of liberty for the reality; when pushed to extremes, contrary to its intention, it actually provokes and facilitates the authoritarian reactions which it abhors.

It seems hardly necessary to elaborate the psychological analysis of these two opposite and complementary political types, both necessarily present alike in good fortune and in bad. In my *History of Italy from 1871 to 1915*, speaking of the conflicts between the right and left parties and of the pessimistic views they occasioned, I remarked that during this period of my life I had been connected with men of the right who were disinterested and most sincere supporters of liberty, absolutely devoid of selfish conservative motives. As the result of reflection on these youthful experiences I discovered and described the weakness in their liberal philosophy as similar to that which is now noticed in De Tocqueville. This led them to overlook the active nature of liberty and to condemn as a lamentable and irremediable heresy the 'revisionist'[1] policy, which after all only repeated, in a modern form, the 'united front'[2] movement started twenty years earlier by Cavour. Italy, and Europe as a whole, prospered under this *concordia discors* of liberalism with democracy. The opposite result, when circumstances destroyed this union, was evident in the

[1] *transformismo.*
[2] *connubio.*

95

European revolution of the last century and a half, beginning with the year 1789. The universal spectacle was one of liberalism becoming sceptical, weak, inactive and even selfish, and of democracy shaking off the bridle whose check and guidance, in the hands of a friendly enemy, its proud neck had just begun to feel and to obey. Then began the headlong career which led successively to the First and Second Empires and other such governments elsewhere. If these sobering lessons from history, which is philosophy translated into action, do not exercise their proper warning and discipline, it will be because our troubled hearts and our distracted minds are in no mood to hear or to take notice, not from lack of evidence for the indubitable truth.

January, 1943[1]

---

[1]Under the Fascist *régime*. (Translator's note.)

❧ 12 ❧

JUSTICE AND LIBERTY

I DO NOT LIKE the popular contemporary coupling of 'Justice and
Liberty', nor yet, with the terms reversed, of 'Liberty and Justice'.
It is the logical implications of the juxtaposition which I dislike, not
the noble moral and political sentiment that inspires it in the verses
of the Italian Carducci.[1] I cannot accept these two ideas thus custo-
marily presented and recommended to us together, as if they were
two fruits set one beside the other on the table. Ideas are not related
numerically like fruits as just two or three; they stand in the living
system of thought. Thought destroys by analysis ideas created by the
imagination and dismisses as alien those of empirical origin and
meaning; to all genuine ideas or conceptions it assigns their proper
place as a necessary moment in the unity which together they
compose, each with its appropriate antecedent and consequent. When
they are torn out of this context they become unrelated and lose their
force and meaning. What then is the really intelligible significance of
of the words 'liberty' and 'justice', and what is the relation between
them? Can one co-exist with the other, or are they mutually exclusive and repugnant? Are they of equal status or can either be derived
from and reduced to the other?

The intelligible significance of the word 'liberty' is simply the
spiritual nature of man; it is identical with activity, which is the
essence of humanity. To deny that man is free and to conceive of

---

[1]"The last survivors among the Gods, Justice and Liberty' in *Avanti ! Avanti !* and
in the ode *A Victor Hugo:* 'He sings of Justice and Liberty to the waiting world'. Less
poetical but more precise in thought are the verses of Henri Becque: *'Sur ce sol que
l'on rensemence, Debout il n'est plus rien resté, Rien que l'arbre de la Science, et l'arbre de la
Liberté'*.

him as a thing whose behaviour is set in motion or deflected and determined by other things, is to take for granted the assumption of a naturalistic metaphysic that such goings-on occur at all in the universe. It is to talk nonsense ; for if we apply the denial to ourselves we shall conclude that in this very denial we are not thinking or reasoning but allowing ourselves to become a prey to momentary feelings of disillusion and abasement, in order to justify to ourselves and others the mediocre standard of our lives. Since then liberty is of man's essence, something he possesses as a man, we cannot accept literally the statement that 'we ought to give it to him'. So far from being able to give it him we cannot even take it away from him. No tyrant has ever been able to do more than kill certain men, prevent, more or less, certain kinds of action, enforce the telling of some lies and the withholding of some truths. No one has ever been able to deprive humanity of the liberty which is the texture of its life. It is indeed well known that all the forces of violence, instead of destroying liberty, give it a new strength and revive it in times of weakness. The only correct meaning of 'giving liberty' is that it is our duty to support and enlarge liberty, that is to say the life of man. On its negative side the maxim prohibits every action that narrows man's life ; on the positive side it commands us continually to widen and amplify it. And since, as we have said, liberty is simply the activity of man, how can we increase it except by increasing human creativity in every field by new conceptions of truth, new scientific and technical discoveries, new creations of art, new achievements of spiritual elevation ? The stupid question is sometimes asked what men should do with the liberty they have or have regained or rather have recreated ; as if it were an idle capacity awaiting some one to employ it, give it orders and keep it to its work. But idle capacities are abstract fictions ; a capacity or power is only real when it is active, that is, creative. Liberty does not go in search of employment or beg it of something other than itself, for it employs itself ; if it were an empty form without matter it would be an abstraction. Its matter, its creativity, its purpose is always moral improvement by means of æsthetic, philosophical, scientific and economic discoveries ; for morality is not something over and above these various orders of creation but is intrinsic to them all, arouses and guides them all, and by them attains its purpose of more and fuller life.

The result of this conclusion is that, since liberty is absolutely identical with the moral consciousness and comprises in itself every moral duty, there is no task which it is not competent to fulfil, none which remains outside its kingdom, looking for some other power to adopt it and actualise it. What indeed could this other power be, if liberty embraces all and is all? That is why I cannot tolerate (logically speaking, not emotionally) the companionship, so often forced upon Liberty, of another idea called Justice, as her friend or superior or rival, to correct or complete her, with whom she may sometimes quarrel and, for better or worse, bargain and compromise. No! liberty has no need of that; whatever morally ought to be done she does and must do of herself, bringing it forth herself, relying on no power but her own.

It will be opportune, then, to examine a little more closely than is often done this Goddess Justice, whose majestic figure combines so many different features of majesty as to provoke criticism and arouse suspicion. It may have been this very superabundance of attributes or aspects that made her fortune in Greek philosophy, so that she actually drew from the prosaic Aristotle a poetical image to express his ravishment ('More marvellous than the morning or the evening star'). Nor did she lose her vogue with the schoolmen, and even today arouses the rivalry of political parties. An examination of this personification will mean the discovery and distinction of the various meanings attached to the term in the past and present, or, to return to metaphor, the resolution of the personality into a welter of different personalities clumsily united or confused.

The first of these meanings needs only be noticed to be put aside, since it reduces itself to the vague use of the word 'Justice' as co-extensive with moral duty. In this comprehensive sense justice has been defined as perfect virtue or the perfection of virtue, and the good man, who resists passion and frees himself from its bondage, is called 'just'. But this is philosophically uncritical; it is only an impoverished form of what in its depth and richness reveals and proclaims itself as liberty. Therefore to couple the two terms together is to unite a precise conception with one that is fundamentally identical but vague, with the consequent confusion of double vision.

There is a second and quite different meaning of the word 'justice', when it is understood in the purely legal sense, and then it is rightly acclaimed as the foundation of all human societies and of every state. Here the idea signified is certainly precise, but for that very reason it cannot be one of the pair we are examining. Law, order, state, rights, justice; these words denote the first basis of practical life, they are the conditions of the moral life or liberty. And since they are conditions, logically prior to it, since liberty pre-supposes and absorbs them, they cannot logically be conjoined with it as an accompaniment or a check. In the Greek thinkers, justice, regarded as obedience to law, took first place and seemed to be all-embracing, just because they did not look beyond the city-state. They never gave to the moral consciousness that emphasis and that pre-eminence which it gained from Christianity. With this pre-eminence, free morality in virtue of the return of spirit upon itself, reacts from time to time upon the conditions whence it sprang, criticises, condemns and reforms them, subverts them or converts them with other institutions of like nature but more apt to its own ends. That is what we see in the history of human progress.

A third sense of the word 'justice', to be met with alike in collo-quial talk and in philosophical books, makes it one of the species of virtue along with a list of others—justice, equity, benevolence, friendship, generosity, courage, prudence, temperance and so on. In this sense it cannot aspire to the rank of a philosophical principle, since it is obviously the word for an empirical generalisation or class-name. From this character of the word 'virtue' several results follow: first, people are led to multiply the virtues indefinitely, with ever-increasing distinctions and gradations, in the vain attempt to enumerate the innumerable riches of moral activity; second, they combine one virtue with another, justice, for instance, with its neighbour equity; finally, they conclude that 'no one virtue can exist alone' which means that, however classified, each is interwoven with all the rest. And this conclusion implies an unconsciously ironical criticism of the whole empirical theory of virtue.

There remains, as the residuum of our analysis, a fourth and last meaning of the word 'justice', which is the most significant of all in the consequences it involves, though it is also the most misleading, being without even the genuine excuses which can be found for the others. In this sense justice is understood as the right of all men to equality, not the equality that is a recognition of the spiritual value of every human being, which is identical with his inviolable liberty, but rather a fantastic utilitarian equality of material goods. This so contradicts the facts of life that it cannot be considered a moral doctrine but, at best 'super-moral', in the ironical sense that, by making it an overriding principle of morality, outside practical life, we banish it to the void. In fact this general demand is specified into two more definite: the one that equal conditions of economic life should be provided for all members of a society, giving each the equal chance of happiness; the other that the social hierarchy should be abolished and all men treated as equal in social capacity and work. As to the first, though the words come glibly, it is not easy to understand what can be meant by 'equal conditions', and still less by 'equal happiness'. Even though, recognising that every part of society is necessary to the others, we must rationally reject the distinction of men into higher and lower orders, or even into worse and better classes, it is still incontestable that individuals find themselves in various conditions and vary among themselves in their needs and feelings. Consequently, however the means of satisfaction might be equalised, it is impossible to confer on them an equal happiness. As to the abolition of hierarchy, the diversity of gifts and ability, as well as of needs and feelings, necessitates social subordination, though, of course, not the subordination of one person to another in all respects. The hierarchical relation cuts across that between individuals, so that he who is superior in one relation is subordinate in others; orders are given and taken reciprocally, and the most eminent statesmen will delegate (to put it mildly) the regiment of the domestic hearth, or at least of the kitchen and the laundry, to his better half. This criticism of justice as the equal happiness of all and the equal capacity of all for everything is an obvious one simply because justice, as the right to equality, is the absurd application of a mathematical abstraction to

the reality which is invincibly concrete, to life, which is unmathe-
matical. Yet this absurdity, with the illusions it creates, incites and
inflames bad feelings of envy for every kind of superiority, not only
of fortune but even of skill, of genius and blameless virtue; whereas
the good man, with a proper pride in his proper calling is dignified in
his modesty and envies not at all. But when a man is once entangled
in this error and tormented by grovelling envy, if he tries to realise
this fantastic and unrealisable equality, he falls into all the inevitably
consequent illusions. He sees on every side, no longer the natural
varieties of feeling and capacity, but the vicious conflict of privilege
and terrorism trampling on each other in barren and gloomy strife.[1]

Plainly in the historical movements marching under the standard
of equality, like the French Revolution, which made *égalité* one of
the three guiding stars for a reborn world, there was more than this
merely absurd misapplication of arithmetic. They cannot be blotted
from the page of history by a simple logical refutation of the theoretical fallacy implied in a word inscribed on their banners. We all
know that there was much more than that in the French Revolution,
which was a turning point in the history of civilisation. There was the
uprooting of old social and economic conditions and of old artificial
hierarchies, which had had their reasons and done good service in
past centuries, but had become, under changed historical conditions,
dead weights, fetters, parasites, iniquity. The privileges of the nobility,
of the clergy, of the art and craft guilds, serfdom and feudal dues, all
these concrete and particular abuses were abolished with good
results. What could not be abolished were the natural economic
inequalities and the system of hierarchy as such, both of which were
reformed and restored for more profitable uses. The radical and
utopian abolition of these economic inequalities and of political

[1] There is an ancient epigram: "Fiat justitia et pereat mundus" which Hegel, by a
clever correction of the consequence, amended in the second clause to: "Ne pereat
mundus", meaning here a justice and order which the moral development of the world
from time to time demands and realises. But from the false idea of justice as equality
with consequent peace and happiness, arises another common saying, or rather sigh of
despair, that "justice is not of this world." Shall we find it then in another? It is
by such sayings, and the pessimism which they sanction, that men arrive, as Kant did,
at the main argument for a future life, in which will be redressed and compensated all
the injustice of this; of this, which is the only life we live and know, in which indeed
are all our sorrows but also all our loves, all the wretchedness but all the sublimity of
man.

hierarchy was a dream founded on the logical fallacy already criticised. Any attempt to realise it in practice, was bound, as we have
said, to end in failure or the exact opposite of the intended result.
The attempt was made by Jacobinism, and more particularly
by Babeuf with his 'Conspiracy of Equals', which originated the
grandiloquent but incomprehensible slogans of 'real liberty', to be
achieved after 'formal liberty', and of 'social equality' to be substituted
for 'equality before the law'.

This Jacobin equalitarianism was the extreme result of abstract
mathematical rationalism in the eighteenth century. Its failure and
experiences gave to the philosophy of the nineteenth century the
opportunity to establish itself and to develop. This philosophy
profited by a new recognition of the relativity of institutions to
conditions and to degrees of spiritual development, and also by a
sympathetic understanding of past history, even of those stages, such
as feudalism and absolute monarchy, rendered more hateful by the
recent struggles. Such sympathy was extended further back to the
middle ages, and even to more primitive times with their religious
fanaticisms, now no longer regarded as engendered by priestcraft.
This new philosophy gave shape to the theory and practice of liberalism, which had its origin in England in the seventeenth century with
the decline of the wars of religion. At that time it was aided by the
idea of liberty in the non-conformist churches, but it was only in the
first half of the nineteenth century that it found its necessary social
conditions, its theoretical justification and its burning practical enthusiasm. At that time, throughout Europe, philosophy, history and
literature came into their own, uniting and leading the forces of the
nations to victory over all autocracies and absolute governments.
But who can always escape the intoxications of hope and triumph?
This victory was accompanied by an extravagant impetuosity, by the
assurance of having at last entered on a career of perpetual and
peaceful progress, 'The Kingdom of Heaven'. Men should have been
put on their guard against this illusion by philosophical and historical
reflection, instructing or reminding them that Satan and wickedness
and slavery breed eternally in men's hearts, disguised under every
historical form of social life. The idea of progress cannot replace that

of cycles, of ebb and flow, of alternations of civilisation and decadence or barbarism, from which man constantly progresses to higher levels. All this must be welcomed, put in its proper place and made use of. How could liberty disown this law of oscillation, if its own essence demands that life must be a conflict, that the conflict must be perpetual, and that the annihilation of good is as impossible as the annihilation of evil? The ethic of liberty, essentially stoical in its perpetual militancy, is constantly confronted by other ideals, more or less eudæmonist, which find the end of life in pleasure, in calm of mind, in happiness, in natural or supernatural blessings. All these are to be possessed or earned in this world, either by subjecting the human herd to a single shepherd, under the names of theocracy and absolute government, or through a peaceful fellowship in satisfied desires brought about by the general will of all the like-minded individuals, under the names of absolute democracy, socialism and communism. No less eudæmonist, at the other extreme, are the ethics of pessimism which despise the vain efforts of liberty. They too harp upon happiness, and despairing of it, or, what comes to the same, despairing of escape from misery, they try to attain their ideal of anæsthesia and stupefaction by asceticism, renunciation, the denial of action, will and desire, and (in all seriousness!) by universal suicide of the race. This last suggestion was put forward by a philosopher of some repute, but it cannot be called very practical, since such suicide would certainly not extinguish universal life, which would manage to produce new beings of human kind with stronger brains and stouter hearts than those educated by the German Hegesias of the unconscious. Against, and above all these theories, the ethical ideal of liberty looks beyond eudæmonism, and beyond the optimism and pessimism which arise from it. It places the end in no self-contra-dictory ideal of happiness, calm and beatitude or escape from pain, but in the clear, coherent, unequivocal ideal of a creation to be achieved, in whose life alone we live. It sees in man, with his passion-ate activity, a poet creating new and complex forms of beauty, and by such self-realisation gaining satisfaction and victory over death.

These inferior eudæmonist ideals, as we have called them, do not hesitate to resort to equalisation[1] as the means of ending strife and bringing peace and ease, with all their accompanying blessings, to be epitomised in man finally released from bondage to the historical process and so, as Leonardo would have said, reduced to a mere food-canal. It is not surprising that, from such a point of view, the idea of liberty had to be opposed and even superseded by that of justice which was here used as synonymous with the desired equality and the equilibrium that had to be established. This idea of equality, an idea which already existed not only in democracy but in the oldest socialism derived from Babeuf, was inherited also by Marx, who, however, saw that it must be conceived more historically, and wrote his *Communist Manifesto* and *Capital* with this expressed intention. But Marx in his dialectic and his philosophy of history was only an inferior follower of Hegel. Hegel had perverted the historical dialectic of liberty into a theological or metaphysical theory which led up to a perfect state, and had failed to see that, though liberty cannot die, it must always struggle to live; and consequently he had opposed and despised the liberal movements which were being initiated in Europe at his day. Similarly, Marx fabricated a mythology of historical development as essentially economic, leading up to the reign of equality, which for some reason, perhaps in conformity to the spirit of his age, he called liberty; though under such a reign there was no room for liberty any more than for a state, as he proclaimed, or for political life or history.

However that may be, the ideal of moral liberty, especially where there are opposite parties with rival programmes, has to confront and contest that of 'justice and equality'. This is in the nature of things and gives us the duty to maintain and diffuse a spirit of criticism, science and culture; for there will always be unreflective persons with simple and childish minds who will stand in need of improvement and development. But the coupling of 'Liberty and Justice' from which I started in this exposition, offends me for one particular reason. It is an attempt to smooth away a sharp and bitter problem of moral theory; it is an eclectic compromise, as distasteful to philo-

[1]Even the pessimist Giacomo Leopardi, in his last poem *La Ginestra*, imagined a confederation of all mankind united in peace and equality by their common conflict with nature.

sophic minds as it is attractive to the lovers of a quiet life and a vacant head, who do not want to overstring the bow of their mind nor to give too great offence to either party. But it also offends me from the political point of view, as a bit of sharp practice towards both parties, the liberal and the socialist or communist or equalitarian; it plays fast and loose with both, and ends in confounding itself by a *corrumpere et corrumpi*. And finally it offends me by the obvious cowardice of failing to maintain in logical integrity the difficult conception of liberty and of compromising it with an essentially contradictory one. This is a trick sure of applause from the majority, or, as it is now called, 'the younger generation' who, to speak frankly, stand rather in need of admonishment, instruction and discipline, both for their own sake and that of the future which is in their hands, than of being ruined by flattery of their youthful simplicity, ignorance and self-confidence. The liberal mind knows very well that it does not bring peace but a sword, not ease but troubles, not idleness but hard work, and it does not mean to flatter or to mock its audience; it prefers a more slow and difficult victory, and is content with fewer if fitter converts, whose practical efficiency is far greater than that of a mob which does not know what it wants, or whose wants are fatuous. The liberal mind shuns the profaner sort of vulgar beings who are superficially educated and reason superficially; it is too proud to go down into the market-place where the vulgar elbow one another, stifling its thought and drowning its well-weighed words with their clamour. Its own field is not the market-place but the larger field of history, where it has always won its victories. There even the occasional defeats are the preludes of victories to come and of those advances in human thought and of civilisation which inexplicably accompany one another and continue from generation to generation.

Now that this unequally yoked pair of mutually repugnant concepts has been got rid of, there remains the one principle of liberty, which has the capacity and the function to take up and to solve all new moral problems which constantly arrive in the course of history; it can solve them all except, of course, the one bogus problem of how to make men perfectly happy. This can be left to the wishful thinking of those who prate about perfecting the world by introducing justice into it and reducing it to equality.

Our examination of these two ideas has led us to a criticism of the false principles, and false combinations of principles, so often met with both in theoretical treatises and in political programmes, which it is essential to correct if clear ideas and close reasoning are the foundation of practical discussion and of achievement. But we must repeat our insistence that to refute theoretical errors is not to refute or deny the pressing practical needs which adopt these errors as arguments and use them as symbols and slogans in the struggle to attract attention and to emphasise their own urgency. Real historical facts must be recognised however they are wrapped up with meaningless theories; social needs must be observed and tabulated; they must be disengaged from the fallacies and fancies which envelop them, if we are to have them before us as data for the moral decisions which it is our duty to make. Beneath the passionate rhetorical invocations of a liberty to be fortified by the new name of justice, beneath a dead weight of theoretical constructions insecurely based upon hazardous foundations, lie the hardship, the suffering, the impatience, the revolt, the desire for better conditions, the hopes and the efforts of nations and of the classes which compose them. These are the realities behind the conflicts and the controversies which seek solution in the attainment of new relations in economic production and in social life. But the problems born of all this can only be stated and solved on the moral plane of moral liberty. Vain have been all attempts to deal with them by materialist tinkering with schemes of social organisation, such as those of *laisser-faire* and of communism or any of the intermediates between these extremes. The defect of all such remedies is that they are neither purely economic nor purely moral, but general and abstract, and therefore necessarily arbitrary. Only on the moral plane can these problems of social regulation be successfully solved as they arise, with due regard to the precise facts of the situation as it presents itself thus and not otherwise. The solutions must vary with time and place, which always alter the conditions; the only constant criterion is that of liberty, which implies that in every case we must prefer the solution which is most favourable to liberty itself and to the advance of civilisation.

But if liberty is to perform the task of making this choice, it must be entirely free from economic prejudice; it must have the courage to adopt means of social progress which seem, and perhaps are, the most various and discrepant. Whether these measures be called *laisser-faire* or communist, they are all good in certain cases if they answer the purpose just described. If they do that, they can discard their former labels and vindicate for themselves the title of morally necessary expedients. For this reason I have applied myself during many years to dissolving the unfortunate association between 'liberalism', as a moral or ethical-political principle, and *laisser-faire*, as one among other possible types of economic order.[1] In this connection I have ventured repeatedly to remark that, if this association were a real one, we should be bound hand and foot to historical materialism, and, like it, we should come to deny the independence of morality, which would become a mask for material needs and satisfactions. There is no precaution which liberty cannot and should not on occasion take in meddling with economic matters, governed by laws of their own and not to be overruled *nisi parendo*; but on the other hand there is no risk which in other circumstances cannot and should not be run. A venture is more resolute and more likely to succeed when it is not made in the interest of any class but is inspired by the voice of conscience and by insight into the ways of history.

Here the philosopher knows that he has gone far enough and that he must leave the field to the man of action, the truly practical man, who is at once bold and cautious, conservative and revolutionary.

[1] See my academy paper of 1927, in the volume *Etica e politica* 2 (Bari, 1943), pp. 316-320; and also my note in the *Rivista di storia economica* of Turin, VI (1941), note 1 (reprinted in *Pagine sparse* III, 30-33). I maintained against Röpke that liberalism must also be disassociated from the so-called 'economics of the market'.

❦ 13 ❧

LIBERTY AND REVOLUTION

LIBERTY CANNOT EXIST without law, rights, a constitution. But law is not liberty, rather it is the framework that liberty makes for itself from time to time in which to act; it is the constitution and system of rights which liberty sets up and guarantees by the power of its will. It sets it up and pulls it down, or, as we say, reforms it, by its subsequent actions; it is always pulling down and always rebuilding to suit the new situations which arise in the course of things. Such is the life of liberty.

This being so, liberty, far from excluding revolutions, necessarily contains them, since it is itself a perpetual revolution, constantly altering, in greater or less degree, the framework of rights and constitutional arrangements in force. Social and political stability conceal beneath the superficial calm which meets our eyes a movement to be detected by the mind. When the usual rhythm of the process is intensified or accelerated, the word 'revolution' springs to our lips and we talk of "legal' or 'peaceful' revolutions.

Such phrases suggest an opposite idea of 'illegal' or 'violent' revolutions as they are called; but if we think carefully we can find no logical distinction between the two kinds. Every modification of law or of rights is accomplished by the pressure of a certain number of wills on a certain number of others; whether this pressure is harsh or gentle, whether its methods are kindly or cruel, the graduation from one to the other is continuous. The two extremes of the scale are no doubt distinct and opposite, but the distinction is only one of degree, empirical and useful for practice, not of kind, and therefore it is useless for philosophy.

The true distinction and opposition is between justifiable and unjustifiable revolutions, between legitimate and illegitimate infractions of legality; and if the latter are called revolutions, especially by those who boast of having made them, yet we feel it is a misnomer and we hesitate to use the word. If revolutions are the perpetual progress and development of liberty they are always essentially 'liberal'; what is opposed to such progress and tries to reverse or retard and impede it cannot be revolution. If liberty is morality and if its development is the widening and the enriching of the individual's moral life, all that withstands this must be a defect and an evil; it must be the resistance of private passions and interests to the common interest, and its occasional and temporary victories depend on the collapse of the moral forces which oppose it. So these self-styled revolutions are properly called 'reactionary' or 'anarchical' according to circumstances, or perhaps 'brutal folly and madness'. Such have been seen in all ages and eminently again in our own, even among peoples trained in liberty and who had long prospered under its laws; they are not revolutions for they do not belong to the active life of liberty. They are part of history and have historical effects, just as disease has in the bodily life but yet is distinguishable from health.

We can define liberty by its essentially revolutionary character, very much as a German philosopher defined walking when he called it 'a continuous process of falling' which, because continuous, never quite lets us down. This was in the minds of those who tried to construct a theory of modern liberalism and who understood liberty as a perpetual motion, an increasing growth and progress. But on this truth was grafted a hope not so much deduced from it as derived from a feeling of confidence in science, in culture, in the mutual understanding and respect of nations and classes, and from a corresponding ideal of ever-increasing unity and good-will among men. It was hoped that fierce and violent revolutions, bloody and ruinous, could no longer find the conditions which occasion them, and that, as the saying went, revolution would be replaced by evolution. It is not the fault of those who entertained this generous hope if it has been disappointed, any more than they could have claimed the merit if it had been fulfilled. It is a hope which, if it would sacrifice the utopian ideal of absolute perfection, should be cherished by all men of good-will as the guide and guardian of their conduct.

🙦 14 🙤

THE THEORY OF LIBERTY
ONCE MORE

THERE ARE ONLY two opposing political attitudes, the liberal and
the authoritarian, however the power may be defined in which
authority is placed—in autocracy, theocracy, or communism (at
least in its marxist and undemocratic form). The difference between
the two attitudes is not that one excludes all liberty and the other all
authority, which would be absurd; but simply that each lays a
superior emphasis on a different principle. Neither side can deny the
fact that both principles are necessary for human life; they can only
understand, and therefore estimate, them differently. Liberalism has
been called idealist and authoritarianism materialist, but, even if we
accept this way of speaking, we find that idealism does not deny the
conception of matter nor materialism that of spirit; their difference
resides merely in their interpretation of the two elements of reality.
Materialism sets out to deduce minds, ideas, thoughts and morality
from matter; idealism, on the other hand, to deduce so-called matter
from spirit, as being one of the instruments which the latter fashions,
or one of its internal contradictions.

If this is true, all the so-called central parties between these two,
such as conservatism, democracy, radicalism, social democracy and
democratic socialism and so on, may have historical justification as
formulas and labels for certain particular, passing needs, or for the
means of satisfying them, but cannot claim any peculiar ideal of their
own. Theoretically their supporters tend now to one, now to the
other of the two fundamental attitudes, oscillating like a pendulum

between the two, but finally coming to rest in one or the other. An equilibrium or harmony of the two is impossible; one or the other must take second place.

The philosophical idealist holds it logically demonstrable that his theory can accept, digest, and justify the opposing doctrine of materialism within his own theory, but that materialism can never explain mind or spirit on its premises. Similarly in politics he claims that his liberalism can give authority its due place, whereas the authoritarian can give no place, however subordinate, to liberty and morality, nor justify their subordination to brutal violence and to the elementary needs of physical and economic life. In short, there is no compromise possible between the two attitudes, because liberalism is itself the concrete synthesis of abstract or unlimited freedom and abstract or unlimited authority. Those who are convinced of these truths must, however, be constantly on their guard to safeguard their integrity in one delicate point, which is the following.

If liberty or morality is the ruling principle of life and our essential attribute, it can and must regulate the satisfaction of those physical needs which are called economic or material, and this is its constant occupation. But in the continual stooping to control our economic needs, and by contact with them, it runs the risk of confounding ruled and ruler, of degrading liberty and identifying it with the materials which it controls, or of making it conditional and dependent on these materials. As an antidote to this we must remind ourselves that liberty is a way of life, an eternal *via docendi et agendi*, not a particular possession nor a way of solving economic problems, still less the actual or proposed solution of any particular problem. Its vitality and its eternal spontaneity belong to it in virtue of this character, just as the vitality and spontaneity of thought resides in its own infinite nature and not in any one of the finite problems which it has solved or is trying to solve.

We must make this distinction a strong and permanent logical conviction in all those who think about politics, and in our time there will be plenty in that field who think before they act and while they act; we must insinuate it in the most acceptable way, in the guise of common sense, into the many minds which are little or not at all disposed or trained to speculation. This has been achieved among some nations, and especially among the English, as can be seen from some of their customs and habits that arouse curiosity and surprise in other peoples. In England it is not surprising to hear someone, like Middleton Murry some years ago, defending communism with all the enthusiasm of a new convert, and inserting the proviso: 'Provided of course there be universal freedom of speech, of association, of elections and of parliament'! This popular loyalty to liberalism in England has been slowly developed through centuries of medieval and modern history from *Magna Carta* and the embryo parliament of 1265, through the religious struggles of the seventeenth century, down to the formation of the new parties when all had become harmoniously liberal. It cannot of course be immune from the dangers of forgetfulness and decay. Other countries may perhaps acquire it with the same firmness and durability if they have learnt the lessons of a shocking and terrible experience. They will have learnt what happens to a highly civilised people, in the full tide of social, economic and moral progress facilitated by liberty, when it allows itself to be snared, stunned, overpowered and seduced, and gives away its government to some cried-up superman and to the gang which serves his fortunes or their own. A people which can find in its annals a page of this kind, if it does not forget it and knows how to read it with understanding, has a source of redemption and salvation more effective than the pages which record its positive but ancient greatness.

I remember that some twelve years ago in Paris, at the house of the great and unfortunate Carlo Rosselli, we were discussing political trends and policies; one of those present, a man pretty well known and estimable for his disinterested enthusiasm and the persecutions he had endured, objected to me: 'My friend, unless along with your liberty you give the people something to flavour it, they will not say thank you'. And in emphasising the word 'something', he made a gesture as if he were spreading a slice of cheese or bacon on a bit of bread. I replied, laughing, 'Don't make that gesture! Liberty is not a crust that wants buttering, it is a religious faith which puts strength in men's hearts and light in their minds, and gives them back the courage to defend their just rights'.

No doubt peoples have sold themselves to absolute governments and tyrants for a mess of pottage, because, in their ignorance, they did not notice they were oppressed but seemed rather petted and flattered; yet in so doing they have always fastened on themselves the fetters of slavery and wretchedness. Certainly, as is but natural, liberals must provide for subsistence; but this is not the way to gain or to keep liberty; that is done in another way which is called education, education in all its stages from learning the alphabet to debating in parliament, the education effected by the liberals of 1860 in Italy. Let us not forget that in that year, at Naples, Garibaldi abolished the lottery, the weekly fountain of dream-fulfilment for the poorer classes. Among the first cares of the government which after little more than sixty years followed him in Italy, was the creation, even before reforming its corrupt and corrupting Italian Academy, of an Italian Monte Carlo, an official gambling hell, in one of the most delightful little towns of our country, as if once and for all to symbolise aptly the striking contrast between two political attitudes and two historical movements.

August, 1943

❧ 15 ❧

JUSTICE AS A LEGAL
CONCEPTION

IN WRITING OF PHILOSOPHY I have not always respected some
highly esteemed virtues, such as gravity and fastidiousness. I departed
from gravity because, if laughter is, according to Rabelais, the
differentia of man, distinguishing him from other animals, I do not
see why the philosopher, who after all is a man, should abstain from
it when occasion calls. I was not fastidious because very instructive
remarks sometimes fall from the lips of people, the very thought of
whom is so repulsive and disgusting that we are apt to be shy of
pronouncing their names. So for my part, when I was expounding
the theory of state law and distinguishing it from morality, I did not
hesitate to cite among other witnesses to the philosophic truth,
instead of some professor of jurisprudence, the famous robber and
murderer Lacenaire. He was guillotined in Paris, about 1830 if my
memory is correct. Between his crimes he not only composed verses
but also reflected on human life and was fond of theoretical discussions. Under examination, giving an account of his way of life,
he frankly confessed : *'Ma tête était mon enjeu. Je n' ai pas compté
sur l'impunité ; il y a une chose, en effet, à laquelle on est forcé de croire :
c'est la justice, parce que la société se fonde sur l'ordre'*. To which the
judge objected : *'Mais ce sentiment de la justice c'est la conscience'*. To
which the accused, sharper than the judge, promptly replied :
'Moins le remords'. (Abbé Georges Moreau, *Le Monde des Prisons*,
Paris, 1887, p. 36.) Here we have defined exactly the sphere of
law, which rests on a principle neither moral nor immoral but

amoral; a principle of practical convenience, to which the moral conscience and remorse are quite foreign. Justice is dear even to ruffians, as Sancho Panza said when he saw how Roque Guinart ruled his men. And when a ruffian is caught and condemned, it sometimes happens that, if he has a quick mind and a stout heart, he resigns himself to his fate and tells himself and those who will listen to him that he has to pay because he has played and lost.

❧ 16 ❧

PEACE AND WAR

THE DISTINCTION BETWEEN the two human activities, the utilitarian or vital and the moral, throws light on the ideas of war and peace. It might seem that, if reality is at every moment an indiscerptible rhythm of peace and war, it is impossible theoretically to distinguish the two states, since they are mutually indispensable. They are so, but in virtue of our fundamental distinction they can be distinguished empirically, since in a state of war the utilitarian or egoistic principle is dominant and in peace that of morality. From this it follows that in itself the nature of war is not immoral but amoral, and hence the vanity of expecting to judge or define or mitigate its methods on moral principles. Even when a ban is laid on certain weapons, and is actually respected in warfare, neither is done out of respect for the moral law, as many would like to persuade us and we might like to believe. The motive is still that of domination, which hesitates at certain actions, since, though they may bring some momentary advantage, they would excite reprisals or perhaps moral indignation. And morality is a spiritual force always to be reckoned with, though it does not touch the hard hearts of those whose only aim is to annihilate the enemy. But the courts, trials, convictions, punishments which are often threatened for enemies accused of moral or legal crimes have the essential defect that they impute responsibility in a sphere where morality has no place and legal ordinance is either suspended or completely wanting, so that a necessary condition of responsibility is absent. In fact such threats are seldom carried out; and when they seem to have some fulfilment it is not a manifestation of legal or moral justice but of passion, uncontrollable anger and revenge. The conqueror has, no doubt, the right and the duty to adopt all the technical means necessary for securing his victory and founding the new order firmly, but only so far as that is done from considerations of prudence and as the means to a higher standard of morality. If he departs from this rule, as has been often seen, he only sows the seeds of new wars, which will soon bear fruit. The complementary truth is that in peace the principle of force, which in war is dominant, has no place. Here its only function is to defend the recognised moral order ; and this is the condemnation of all so-called coercive governments, which provide no real peace since, as the saying goes, you can do everything with bayonets except sit on them. Even the absolute governments which we have to recognise in history relied on some moral prestige—such as the sacred or priestly character of a king, the cult of the divine emperor, reverence for ancient custom, or worship of a man of genius—rather than on sheer force of arms, and only so could they win consent. When such moral forces, whether beliefs, worship or confidence, failed, such governments failed too. It is hardly necessary to remark that our fundamental distinction between peace and war, as two elements inherent in reality, each giving birth to the other, excludes the idea of 'perpetual peace'[1] which is self-contradictory as are all ideas that similarly attempt to break or alter the rhythm of life. Man's nature, and indeed that of the universe, necessitates both together, as was already seen in antiquity by Heraclitus. It is more useful here to recognise that, beneath all the illogical formulas and the ill-fated efforts of propaganda and international associations for peace, there breathes, mixed with sentimentality and rhetoric, a generous aspiration worthy of more systematic formulation and more promising political methods. In times of peace, warlike passion, which is always chafing in men's bosoms, is curbed and mastered, though not stifled or suppressed, by the moral or ethico-political forces and by vigorous minds. Such minds have learnt from experience that the surest course to avoid the shipwreck of civil war is the course of liberty. They let these latent conflicts fight it out under the ægis of the constitution, and so permit the attainment of all the needs or ideals which can be

[1]The title of an Essay by Kant. (Translator's note).

satisfied or realised, more or less readily, in changing historical situations. The same course is followed by a wise ruler in his foreign policy; in his desire for peace he of course tries to satisfy the needs of his own people but is careful not to shut the door to those of others. He is a supporter of peace in so far as he must study how to make his foreign policy more moral, more consistent in its operation, more effective and far-sighted than in the past, embodying it in institutions, varying from time to time, but more solid than before. In such an enterprise, for which our times now call on Europe and the whole world, the cold calculation of interest will certainly not suffice, though that is a secondary motive; we must have the *abundantia cordis* of a human and a Christian heart. Such a heart will feel the baseness and deceitfulness of the pharisaical attitude to other states which was at one time assumed to be proper. Every state then vindicated the enjoyment of liberty and prosperity for itself and left its neighbours free to be enslaved or ground down by poverty; its monstrous hypocrisy was to behave morally to its own people and egoistically towards others, at once civilised and tolerating or abetting barbarism, utterly careless of any sufferings but its own. Such obstinate egoism endangered even its own boasted position of privilege, which could not maintain itself when enclosed, jeopardised and stifled by the surrounding misery and rebellion and barbarism. Even the individual man cannot be moral if he tries to live for himself alone, cultivating either a cloistered virtue, which is nothing but pride, or a narrowly restricted benevolence. Morality is only real when it is a relation to all men, collaborating and striving with them for common humanity. Only by this daily increasing civilisation can peace be long maintained and continually restored on ever firmer foundations. It will not be a perpetual peace indeed, but at least it will not be an empty dream; it will be practicable and real peace, the only kind which the world-spirit allows and ordains, a peace which tames war but cannot absolutely prevent it from erupting now and again in fits of its native savagery if such is God's will.

THE IDEALISATION OF WAR

PERHAPS THE FIRST expression of anti-militarism in the development of historical writing, and an important one though only tacit and casual, is to be found in the eighteenth century. It was an expression of boredom and impatience at books stuffed with the accounts of wars and of the negotiations which prepared and ended them, and was accompanied by the demand for another kind of history to give something really satisfying to the deeper interests of the human heart and mind : histories of religion, of philosophy, of science, of art, of manners and of morality, in a word the history of civilisation. On these lines modern history continued to advance. It not only reduced the excessive space once given to military narratives but inspired even these with a spirit previously lacking. It related them to all forms of spiritual life, which reduces war to a mere means and its results to the material for renewed spiritual labours. Even technical military history, as one of the various techniques of human action, has its place in such a spiritual history, and, more precisely, in that of the various branches of science. But war merely as war does not lend itself to any historical understanding, since it falls under no distinct category or ideal. War, in fact, is a fever which periodically inflames men's blood, so that, while it rages, nations and individuals, however noble their natures, wrestle for mutual suppression and destruction. The cool spectator, following the chances of this struggle from a distance, or reading of them in books, is stirred by imaginative participation as keen or keener than that of the audience in the circus, the palestra or the cinema; but at bottom there is nothing but a restless alternation of beating and being beaten, in which luck plays a great part, and which cannot be put into historical form because the historical connection and the logical significance are to be found elsewhere.

Thus, with the growth of higher intellectual interests and the development of the chronicle into history, the narrative of wars has been outgrown and almost discarded in the way already described. Similarly, as nations emerged from savagery and barbarism and from the renewed barbarism of the middle ages in which fighting was an everyday affair, as other kinds of facts and action attracted their attention and they came to breathe an ampler air, war seemed to fade away on the horizon. Sometimes it came to be thought of as an outgrown stage of human life, a return to which was as repugnant to all civilised and educated men, devoted to quiet work, as an attack of criminal lunacy. Yet, none the less, armaments were maintained with zealous rivalry, since men's inner consciousness whispered the warning that war could not cease in the world, and that they must be prepared for emergency, as doctors, drugs and surgical instruments are provided for some illness which may always reappear. In the years of the glorious Italian revolution, in the midst of the inevitable fighting, men looked at what was to come after, and the Italy which took shape in their dreams was, as Tommaseo said in a poem : 'severe and humble, a lover and in arms'. This state of mind lasted even after 1870 and was only overclouded in Italy, as more darkly in other parts of Europe, at the end of the century. At this time in England universal applause greeted a very wise book, *The Great Illusion*, directed against the idea of war, which was threatening and being welcomed by some who had never felt its wounds. And though, in spite of all, a few years later the plague burst out in that new war which was called 'the European conflagration', yet, so soon as it was mastered and extinguished, the former repugnance to war reappeared in some of the greatest nations of the old and new worlds. They still feared war as a disease, they had not yet made it an ideal. How is it then that in spite of this advanced stage of civilisation, in spite of this general good sense, war has in some intellectual movements been tricked out as an ideal, a sublime, dazzling, intoxicating ideal? Why has the idea of war as a disease been replaced by the identification of a super-war with health? The metaphorical description of life as an unending warfare, means that it is a war against war, a 'negation of the negation' in philosophical jargon, a continued renewal on higher and higher levels, of internal unity and harmony and social co-operation against opposing and impeding forces. Why has this been perverted to mean the exact opposite? How is it that, abandoning the image of an honest man who takes up arms at the call of duty though no lover of battle, and who from his duty derives strength and courage and the spirit of sacrifice, men's fancy has gone astray after strange idols of a very different nature, with beastly shape and cries and bearing, obsessed with the lust of blood and ravin? Unquestionably this darkening of the mind and the imagination must be ascribed to that degraded romanticism, marked by sensualism and materialism, called 'decadence', which ignored or trampled on many tender feelings and subtly corrupted many pure passions, infecting them with lust and sadism. It corrupted, too, the manly sense of duty which determined men to fight in the wars necessitated from time to time by the course of events, and degraded it to the criminal folly of glorifying, provoking and instigating war, thus spreading the very disease that had to be cured. And lastly it corrupted the noble and humane patriotism of tradition into a fierce monster which took from its birth the name of 'nationalism'.

Nevertheless, this ideal or anti-ideal would probably have worn itself out in the inflated rhetoric of literary circles, but for the support given it by a nation of central Europe which made it the guiding principle of its political and social life. The German people lost sight of the more or less universal and cosmopolitan view which had been illuminated by its great age of philosophy and poetry, and turned a deaf ear to the essential teachings of Kant and Goethe. It would be an inadequate and indeed inexact explanation to ascribe this to the fact that Germany was late in achieving unity, and consequently strength, and so found itself impelled by an irresistible necessity of conquest and expansion against other powers who already had wide empires. Such needs might have been satisfied by political means or, even if armaments and war had been inevitable, without poisoning the very sources of the moral life.

The true cause was the reinforcement of decadent romanticism, not so much by political interests as by the traditional ideals of the people. It must be remembered that the starting point of German history, and of its entry into the history of Europe, was not the civilisation of Greece and Rome, nor that of Christianity, but the fierce and devastating outburst of the barbarian invasions. Its early heroes were only petty chieftains, and its epic presents no human figures like those of Greece and Rome or even of France: not Achilles, Hector and Aeneas, not Orlando and Oliver, not Andromache nor Lucretia, but the figures of grim murderers and bloody she-devils. In subsequent and modern history this German spirit found its best expression in Prussianism, from the Teutonic knights to Frederick II of Hohenzollern and Bismarck, the founder of the union, who left as his mark on the new Germany all his own brutality, shiftiness and cynicism, a mark which his successors stamped yet more firmly on her features. From the union of these and similar historical traditions with the decadent romanticism already mentioned sprang race-idolatry, a new biological form of the myth of a chosen people 'which is not defiled with the Gentiles'. It might be said that the war of extermination waged by Germanism against Jewry was only a piece of jealous emulation, since it is well known that the idea of a chosen race was strictly hebraic and was preached and practiced in the fourth century before Christ by Esdras, who indeed had good reasons for adopting it. The cynically or bestially obscene sayings which made men's flesh creep during the present war all came from the mouth of a people which boasts itself by birthright a nation of warriors and despises its enemies as traders. Such sayings are the brutal language proper to war when it is exalted as an ideal, an ideal logically bound to adopt the usual sentiments, attitudes, and accent of the criminal world; they are not the language of the despised trading peoples, whose way of life is sociable and retains, even in moments of passion, the poise and deportment of good education and nice morality. It is probable and quite natural that, when this long and terribly destructive war is over, the world will once more see conferences and plans for the establishment of 'perpetual peace'; and it would be no little gain if even a long peace could be established in which all nations might for a time find some degree of prosperity. Perpetual peace is a perpetual utopia, for its aim is nothing but to break the springs of human action which are to be found in pain and danger. But what we certainly ought to do, and can do, helped by the lessons of experience, is to clear our minds and root out every last vestige of 'war as an ideal'. In its place, we must cultivate the bourgeois idea of the trader, here too learning from experience that traders, when need compels, can hold their own against professional soldiers and defeat them, as has been seen in this war and as was taught to the warriors of Barbarossa by our Italian ancestors of the Lombard league. No nation was ever more cruelly and shockingly entangled in the web of circumstance than were we Italians, whose ancient and modern traditions were exactly opposite to those of Germany and Prussia, but who were forced to carry out a policy derived from these sources by a faction which had seized power and bent to its purpose a King who owed his title to the voices of the liberals and the nation. Then we had to listen to solemn exhortations to make ourselves 'militaristic', a word we had always hated. We had to hear lessons dictated to us in the inspired accents of an elementary school-teacher who has just got them by heart, with-out criticism, like copybook headings, and who is eager to publish what he takes for profound and original scientific truths but which are in fact both platitudes and absurdities: 'Not only do we not believe in perpetual peace; we hold it to be degrading and a negation of all man's primary virtues which are only brought to light by the horrors of war'. As if there was no fear of pain or tragedy in private or public life, no occasion for the exercise of human virtue! Here I will stop; for I feel that I have strayed from my purposed elucidation of some historical and ethical principles to the problems and casuistry of our own day, to whose appeals the intention of keeping strictly to scientific argument cannot always close our minds. But this excursion at least attests the importance of the eighteenth century revolt against merely military history and shows the fruitfulness of the new impetus then given to historians.

✠ 18 ✠

PATRIOTISM: A DISUSED WORD

NO WORD TODAY echoes in our ears so loudly as Liberty, but a term which used to accompany it is no longer heard : 'our country' or 'patriotism', which for us Italians means the love of Italy. Why is this?

It is because this patriotism was corrupted or rather supplanted by so-called nationalism, a name which implied that its opponents were not unpatriotic but 'anti-nationalist'. At the same time there was a certain confusion between the two ideas or feelings, so that the growing condemnation of nationalism carried with it a certain reluctance or shyness in speaking of 'patriotism'. But we must go on talking of patriotism with reverence just because we are opposed to the cynicism and stupidity of nationalism, since the two, so far from being connected are contraries. It might be said that there is a difference between patriotism and nationalism like that between the kindliness of human love and beastly lust or morbid lechery or selfish promiscuity.

Patriotism is a moral idea. Under its standard our severest duties take a definite form which comes near to our hearts and yet represents mankind as a whole and helps us to be active in its cause. Different nationalisms gnash their teeth at one another, but different countries can collaborate, and even if they cannot avoid war their aims are not mutual annihilation but mutual reform and improvement. And since patriotism is a moral idea it is closely allied with liberty. Today we

[1]Written at the request of the editors of *Italia libera* but, for reasons of which I am ignorant, never published. Articles which by implication criticised such deplorable distinctions (*precisazioni*') which, and when they were sent me by acquaintances, I approved without alteration or reserve, were not published either.

are suffering not only from the humiliation, as men and citizens, of losing our liberty, but also from the loss and the shame which have wounded and are still wounding Italy. Italy was once the object of all our thoughts, of our cares and anxieties, our love and sorrow; our hope and our pride; to her we gave the best part of ourselves, labouring to make her more perfect, more worthy of our admiration and respect. Now she is trodden under foot and put in jeopardy by crazy gamblers who stake her wealth and blood in their desperate hazard of tyranny and spoliation.

It may be that this thought and love for our country, this patriotism, will rise again in our hearts more pure and lively. Then the political parties which are beginning to outline themselves will have taken clearer shape and may more easily agree to differ, fighting, as they must, but honourably and without disguise. For as they will all have a common faith in liberty, so they will always have before their eyes Italy and a common love for her; in the welfare of Italy they will from time to time find the limit beyond which they must not push their quarrels, and at any threat to her they will feel their common basis of agreement.

This is the lesson we have learnt from our forefathers of the Revolution, and this is the passionate patriotism sung by the last great poet of Italy, Carducci.

8th June, 1943

☙ 19 ☙

DENATIONALISATION
OF HISTORY

THIS IS ANOTHER instance where a necessity, which has constantly confronted and influenced the writers and methodologists of history, has joined hands with a moral and political necessity of our time.

The nationalisation of history had its origin in the epic character which survived during its early stages and in the tendentious oratory dedicated to the political interests of states and peoples. Later there grew up a bad philosophy which invented the idea of an *esprit des peuples* or 'national spirit', and, later still, the idea of the 'mission' of each nationality. This was a temptation to follow out the history of each of these isolated monads as if it developed independently through the ages, or rather always preserved its original character.

The fact is that what really evolves is not an individual or a group of associated individuals, but the universal spirit which by its spontaneous function, raises up and destroys individuals and nations for its own purpose. So the sole subject of history is the exercise of this human or divinely human function, not any imaginary entities and general names mistaken for substantial realities.

Actually, the history of thought and philosophy kept itself almost entirely free from national prejudices, and valued writers by their contribution to human thought and not by national sentiment or passion. The history of poetry was more exposed to the danger of a national treatment owing to the misleading differences of language which are commonly identified with differences of nationality. Yet it generally, at least in Italy, escaped this bondage and tended to exalt poetry and the other arts to a super-national and ideal sphere. The division of such histories according to different peoples and countries will henceforth be taken for what it is; a convenient division of labour, and a method of classification facilitating reference.

Among histories of practical activity that of the various scientific techniques has no need of denationalisation, since it is almost entirely free from any temptation to prejudice its verdicts by political or moral sentiments or tendencies. On the contrary, by the same line of argument, this need is felt most of all in the history of morals and politics which, as it was the first to appear entangled in these tendencies, will be the last to emancipate itself. Not that even in the past there have been lacking treatises which pointed to the right path and looked beyond states and nations. Such have been the various histories of the religious life and of civilisation, in which writers of different nations collaborated, and which were judged by the joint product and not by the separate contributions. But alongside and opposed to these treatises, which were devoted to humanity as such, there persisted others inspired by the idea of a humanity divided into species, each of whose components was a closed circle; and these were not really human histories but figments due to scientific analogies or metaphysic. We all know the lengths of perversion to which this deification of the national spirit has carried the modern world, which once was the christian world and later claimed to be the world of humanity, liberty and fraternity. In the healing of this poisoned and tormented world, we historians must play our own proper part by pressing on with the denationalisation of history. This obviously does not mean that we should ignore what happens in Italy or Germany or England or Russia or Japan, but that we should try to see it and understand it and judge it in the light of its universal human interest.

PROBLEMS OF ETHICS
AND AESTHETICS

THE INTELLECTUAL LIFE:
MORALS AND AESTHETICS

THE GUIDING THREAD OF modern æsthetic theory in the eighteenth and nineteenth centuries, the thread in which its consistent
character and its strength were most marked, was its criticism of all
doctrines which understood art as the servant of philosophy and
morality, as an attractive form of instruction or a lofty oratory.
Against all such doctrines, in whatever various, fanciful and complicated forms they were disguised, the independence of the æsthetic
activity was now proclaimed. Plausibility had been lent to these
doctrines by some aspects of contemporary works of art, not only
the more or less academic but also the greatest and most inspired,
which, by certain claims that they put forward and in certain parts of
their compositions, seemed to pay homage to the maxims of *docere*
and *prodesse*. Moreover, though these venerable traditions, going
back to classical antiquity, failed to define the essential nature of art,
they were at least inspired by the desire to elevate it by allying it with
all that is noble in the human mind, with the search for truth and
with the love of good. They rescued it from the degradation of mere
entertainment and amusement, to which other theories banished it,
and gave it an honourable function in the moral sphere.

There is no longer any need for this critical polemic; even its
history is almost forgotten; it only survives in learned books, as
happens when a controversy is over and the conclusion is taken for
granted as something to be no more called in question. Supporters of
the respectable ancient doctrine are to be found today only here and
there in academic circles, and do not count. But, in retribution, the

æsthetic doctrine of art for art's sake is now assailed by new heresies, among which the most successful is that of so-called 'pure art', according to which the poetic word or artistic unit is a mere sound, colour, tone or the like. The living artistic output is no longer over-weighted with academic works but with those of a very different appearance, frigid and empty in quite a different way, whose only advantage over the older fashion is that they have a different kind of ugliness, which is indeed a new kind, but still ugly, unpleasant and dull.

This theory of pure art is eager to pose as a consistent and uncompromising philosophy which, as its fundamental principle, strictly defines the nature of poetry and all art as purely æsthetic, since art as such is not, of course, logic nor conduct but wholly sensuous and formal. But it is only a pose; in reality to desire pure art without the necessary conditions of this purity is the gross blunder of desiring the flower without the plant whose roots are deep in earth. This blunder could be expected from the complete ignorance and stupidity of those who so loudly advertise the theory. For the most part, they do not venture beyond mysterious aphorisms and maxims, but when they attempt systematic argument the result is pitiable, in spite of the oracular grandiloquence of their esoteric style. A new theory, or a new elaboration of the theory, of art has always been and must always be the result of real talent and philosophic discipline. And if the test I have just indicated can be trusted, it would follow that the poetry also which these writers encourage with their approval is a true symptom of their character, showing that behind such theories lies a real impoverishment and degradation of mind and heart. An old doctor in South Italy, a man of sound and acute judgment, once wrote to me that when he read verse of this sort he could not help thinking that their authors bore a close analogy, and in fact were the logical complement, to dictators; both are accepted through lassitude; such heroes get the poets they deserve. Indeed such poets have no regret for that liberty which is the wealth of the inner life; they are not even aware of its loss. Irreligious, especially when they ape religiosity or toy with the formulas or ceremonies of catholicism, they are always professing a passion for some debased mysticism which is irradiated by no spark of truth, imbued with no impulse of sacrifice, but is only the sensuous indulgence of wallowing in the dark warmth of blind feeling.

In order to oppose and confute such doctrines however there is no need to reinstate and marshal against them the old arguments which subordinated art to philosophy, morality and religion as their hand-maiden. That theory, as we have said, is dead and buried and cannot be exhumed to serve other purposes than those which, in its day, it performed for the development of æsthetic science. It would be offering an easy triumph, an undeserved justification, to the new heresy, if, in opposing it, we were tempted to relapse into the opposite error as is done by some catholic critics. We must rather hold firmly to the doctrine of art for art's sake, yet at the same time emphasise a vital condition, not always made sufficiently clear, but often over-looked because it was implied as a presupposition. This oversight has never been remedied because the keen intellectual climate in which the truth was first recognised, mentally vigorous and morally earnest, made it seem something so obvious and so natural that there was no need to insist upon it or to elaborate it in formal arguments and defend it on philosophical and critical grounds. The vital condition of art's autonomy is simply the essential unity of the human spirit which, in its various activities, is never disintegrated so as to let each drift in isolation, but is itself always present as the pilot at the helm. A man would not be moral without the capacities for reason and imagination, for intellectual and artistic experience; he could not philosophise unless he had a strain of poetry and a strong and delicate conscience; each several activity draws its specific energy from the spiritual unity, morality, purely moral, rejecting the inroads of sophistic logic, the other, purely speculative, uncontaminated by misplaced edification. So, too, it is impossible to be a poet or an artist without being in the first place a man nourished by thought and by experience of moral ideals and conflicts. Though art is neither the slave nor the handmaid of morality or philosophy, it is always busied with both, for its business is that of the spiritual unity which in it comes to its own as a necessary and unique manifestation. This is the reason why we find in all genuine poets, in all ages and all nations,

133

that breath of sublimity, that *spirare tragicum*, which lifts us on its strong wing to the universal and eternal, an elevation and expansion lacking in the sensual impressionistic art which leaves the spectator on the earth depressed and disillusioned, vainly seeking for something that constantly eludes him. When shall we ever more hear the native accent of true poetry? Or do we ever hear it in some few poets of our own day? When shall we meet again, or do we ever meet the whole man with his search, which is already a finding, for purity and goodness? Only when we again turn our eyes to the heavens and love again the things that are lovely and know how to work and suffer and sacrifice for their sake. Until we do that we may have the desire but not the realisation or the joy of beauty. According to contemporaries who preach and describe what they call the new art and poetry, it is the first that ever has appeared in the world. All that has hitherto usurped the name being mere 'literature'. The inanity of their theory and practice is exhibited by the currency in their jargon of the term 'abstract art', for art is nothing if not concrete and never excludes or abstracts from the expression of feelings, since poetry is simply giving to these feelings the poetic tone which endows them with ideal rhythm. They have also a fondness for the word 'hermetic'; but art is lucidity not obscurity, it does not even play at obscurity, for it is serious. They have a weakness for decadence as being an aristocratic disease; but art is health, not disease, and is not decadent, for it is a cause of life and of greater humanity. Small hearts, small brains, small souls, who have been great poets, are not to be found in history, and will not make their way there by violence like some invader, not only foreign but barbarous, who has no link of common humanity with the past. Mere words, mere images, mere colours, mere sounds are chimeras, not to be found, so far as we know, even in the race of animals. De Sanctis, in refuting certain romantic anticipations of our modern pure art, wrote that the bird sings for song's sake but in singing expresses all its life, all its being, every instinct and every need, its whole nature. So a man, if he is to sing, must be a man as well as an artist.

But since I have touched above on the impressionist and sensual character of much, even of the less empty, of modern art, it is opportune to clear up an old difficulty to be met with in works of æsthetic in the form of a question which persistently returns to the mind. It is well known that many attempts have been made at a scientific graduation of poems and works of art by classing them as great and minor poetry with fine shades between the two extremes. For my part, I have always rejected all such distinctions in principle; for poetry, speaking literally, is neither great nor small, and in a more spiritual sense it is always either great or not poetry. A single line may be a poem complete in itself; the representation of the humblest scene may be great poetry if it is *consule digna*, worthy of the human soul. It is nonsense, a nonsense common enough in æsthetic writers, to classify works of art by the external criterion of their subject. This would be to ignore the question at issue, which is an æsthetic one; indeed the subject-matter is mere matter just so far as it still lacks form and distinctness; it only emerges from vagueness when it is given form which is a quality conferred on it by one of the activities of spirit. Yet, as I have said, this question recurs insistently in all comparative judgments upon the various works which claim to be art or poetry; and for this persistence there must be some ground, which, consistently with our premises, can only be found in differences of the form. Yet we have absolutely excluded such differences by our assertion of the identical character in all poetry and art, the uniqueness of the form which is realised in innumerable individual works but never varies in the fundamental nature of its being. All we can do then is to account for the motive which impels men to this quest for a principle of classification. We must enquire what are the differences they have in mind and which they take to be differences of degree or of precedence, but which are in fact differences of kind. They are differences not between different æsthetic activities, since there is only one, but between other spiritual activities which superficially and colloquially are described as if they were æsthetic, though at the same time, since it is felt they cannot be put alongside art and poetry as such, there is a temptation to treat them as stages or degrees thereof. Great poetry and little poetry, major and minor, turn out to be metaphorical quantitative expressions for things qualitatively different, namely poetry and not-poetry. But what is not poetry need not be bad poetry or ugly, which is the opposite of poetry; it is simply something other than poetry naturally belonging to some other activity of spirit. The kind of works I have in mind—exclamatory, merely symptomatic, prosaic and oratorical expressions, I have specifically distinguished in my book *La Poesia*. There I showed that they may all occur in literature and, indeed, as *belles lettres*, but that they are not poetry since their kernel remains obviously unpoetical, however they may be wrapped up in poetical imagery and sound. I described the various types of this literature as the emotional or lyricism, and the practical or oratory; and I gave as sub-divisions the oratory of persuasion and the oratory of entertainment, didactics or philosophy, history and science, 'pure art' and so on; all of which I further elaborated in another book, *Poesia e non Poesia*. I there called attention, among these forms which are essentially literary but not poetic, to the kind which is neat, idyllic, epigrammatic, or in various ways agreeable. This fills a large space in anthologies and literary histories, and is one of the most likely to be mistaken for poetry by critics insufficiently aware of the severe nature of true poetry, who allow themselves to be seduced by what is merely pleasing.[1] But another type no less worthy of notice and precaution, and more common in our own times, is that of the sensual or impressionistic poetry to which I have alluded. This is distinguished from true poetry by moving only in the sphere of scattered sensations and feelings not integrated or unified in the individual mind; consequently, even when, as sometimes happens, it is in its own line subtly elaborated, it contents itself with *pathos*, and does not aspire to *ethos*. Put it beside a verse from Homer or Virgil or Dante or Shakespeare or Goethe, or even Foscolo or Leopardi or Carducci, and you will feel the difference. You may, if you please, call it poetry or minor poetry, but with the reservation that it is in fact neither major nor minor but, from the greatest to the smallest, quite another thing.

[1] See my remarks on Ronsard in *Poesia antica e moderna*.

ART AS THE FORM OF
PURE KNOWLEDGE

ARTISTS AND POETS, and all poetic and artistic minds, are inclined
to hold that art is the highest and purest, and indeed the only form
of true and intimate knowledge of reality. This idea also found its
way into some philosophic systems of the romantic age, especially
that of Schelling in his first period, and is suggested by thinkers who,
like Bergson, were more or less under his influence. I will not here
repeat the easy refutation of this as a theory; I prefer to take it in its
more spontaneous form, as it occurs in practitioners and amateurs of
art, that is to say, as a way of thinking whose conclusion is erroneous
but which must have some good grounds to justify its origin and its
continual recurrence. What these grounds are we must now enquire.

The explanation is this. Thought indeed solves our practical difficulties and moral problems, but one by one, and by its true understanding of each it engages us in the next. Poetry alone gives us a
glorious liberation[1] from these struggles and difficulties in their
totality, from the whole universe of practical passions. Poetry then
may be called knowledge in the sense of intuition or contemplation,
not theological, not conceptual, not critical. Many philosophers,
unable to understand such a form of contemplative knowledge[2],
reject it. Either they deny it altogether by analysing it as an imperfect
and confused act of thought requiring clarification and correction, or
they find a peculiar character for poetry, sometimes in a dark region
which they call feeling,[3] sometimes in a special kind of pleasure

[1] *catarsi e superamento.*   [2] *teoresi.*   [3] *sentimento.*

which is not sensuous, sometimes in a revelation from on high, and sometimes by other eccentric expedients.

As to this suggested victorious liberation from the whole world of practical action and suffering, it is only in the radiant beauty of art that we can enjoy such serene forgetfulness. Beauty is not the satisfaction in a truth or in any particular good, but in a vision of the universe which inspires joy of a celestial nature. Beauty has often been judged indefinable and mysterious, but on the contrary, it can be and is understood as having the origin which we have ascribed to it; and this origin demands that we should attribute to beauty the cognitive element of pure intuition. This, to many people, is a strange idea, which they cannot grasp; and even those who accept it and glibly repeat the name intuition often have but a superficial understanding of it, or at best catch occasional glimpses of its meaning, as if between the clouds.

It is true that in pure contemplation and under the enchantment of beauty this consoling peace is attained, but only to be lost again immediately. This must be so; not because the cognitive process, which arose with this moment of glorious 'dawn', is annihilated, but because dawn is followed by day, the day in which man must work. In the day, the cognitive process is carried on with a very different spirit, no longer in a calm above the world of passions, but among passions rekindled and under the renewed stimulus to action. What action requires is the mastery by thought of this or that detail in the struggles and tasks which it must undertake and understand. It must master them in all their individual reality, so that understanding may call forth a new action, since life is made up of thought and action, and thought is for the sake of action. So we pass from the poetry to the prose of life, which poetry by its pure contemplation has made possible; we pass to discrimination and criticism, and, in a light that is no longer aesthetic but intellectual, our survey of the universe becomes a more clear and detailed insight into the world of events, a development of our naïve consciousness and a prerequisite of action.

If thought and philosophy were what certain traditions of the schools make them, a mere contemplation of universal reality, a frozen spectacle of the Idea or the Form, they would be a faded and useless repetition of the æsthetic activity. Against such an attempted explanation, which they feel to be false and empty, artists and poets are right in maintaining that thought and philosophy will never attain what they themselves already possess, that living reality of the world which only reveals itself to intuition. But the partial truth thus maintained is driven into self-contradiction and self-correction. It has to be subsumed under the new and true conception of thought and philosophy as historical knowledge if artists are to avoid the extravagant paradoxes to which they are apt, and bring themselves to think clearly. In this, they may be helped by the obvious reflection that they, too, poets and artists though they be, are also men who have to act in the world and cannot avoid thinking about the reality of the world in which they must work and live. But artists are not always content with the recognition that art is an original and essential spiritual activity, and forget that even the greatest human achievement should be modest enough to know its limitations. When they exaggerate art's sphere, as if it were the whole of life, or when, more often, they take up the cudgels for it against every other interest, they run the risk of the disease called æstheticism, in which, not only thought and action, but art and poetry themselves are miserably extinguished. But in purely artistic temperaments, this does not happen. Their obstinate refusal to see further has in it something touching, as anyone knows who has been intimate with them and heard their ingenuous talk. Philosopher though he may be, he will have felt rising to his lips the exclamation of John Huss at the stake when he saw an old woman bringing a faggot for the fire: *Sancta simplicitas !*

And, if I may notice one small trait in the psychology of artists, the unpractical nature of art, as I have defined it, is the root of their frequently remarkable ineptitude and lack of realism in practical life. This is sometimes carried to the pitch of pride and is made a boast of: sometimes it humbles itself to a sense of inferiority and is expressed in lamentations like the moan of the gentle romantic Wackenroder: 'Art is a forbidden but tempting fruit. Those who have once tasted its hidden sweetness are lost forever to the living world of action'.

❧ 22 ❧

THE TWO PROFANE SCIENCES:
AESTHETICS AND ECONOMICS

I

Spirit and Sense

A FEATURE WHICH plainly distinguishes modern from medieval times is the renewal in the former of a vigorous political and economic life and of all forms of art. This is not to say that there was no political and economic or artistic life in the Middle Ages; indeed, by speaking of a more vigorous renewal we imply the opposite. As no man can entirely lack both these mental capacities, neither can any period, even those most barbaric and primitive, when, in fact, there were eminent achievements in poetry and art. All that is intended is to draw attention to the fact that in the complex medieval society the emphasis was not on these activities. Anyone who desires a *prima facie* preliminary proof of this need only glance at the books or architectural remains of this society which survive, particularly from its flourishing time. Let him compare its churches, monasteries and castles with the features of the modern landscape dotted with factories, stores, banks, exchanges, parliament-houses, government offices, and also with museums, picture galleries, exhibitions, theatres, schools and the like. The same conclusion might be similarly drawn from a bird's-eye view of the general character of medieval poetry, literature and art. In the main they were didactic, and propagandist, or narrative and allegorical, very seldom personal or lyric. As to the politics of the times, when not governed by the elementary necessities of life and self-defence, they were directed to unworldly ends, as were the crusades for the recovery of the holy sepulchre and the disputes between the Church and the Holy Roman Empire. The economic life was mainly on a 'subsistence' basis, with little industrialism or commerce. The change began when the Italian cities and great Norman and Suabian monarchies tried to exercise a national or state policy consciously aimed at prosperity and civilisation, under which arts and commerce flourished. This ambition closely followed and sometimes obscured their less worldly plans and sympathies. Finally, with the Renaissance and Reformation began the distinctively modern age; for these two movements, apparently opposed, were in reality complementary, since the Renaissance, seeking Greco-Roman antiquity, discovered the truths of nature, while the Reformation, seeking evangelical Christianity, discovered freedom of thought and criticism. It is because of these differences of emphasis and rhythm that the distinction and contrast between medieval and modern times keeps its place in history, where it serves the purpose of accentuating them. But, as always in history, these distinctions must not be made with a knife; rather must they be thought of as both posited and negated, both sharpened and blurred, in that continuous course of history which exhibits the moving drama of humanity in its passages, at once gradual and revolutionary, from the Middle Ages to the modern world. If these differences of character were denied or underestimated, or if the values we set on the two characters were interchanged, either the word 'medieval' would disappear from our histories or it would be our own days that would be called 'medieval' in the depreciatory sense of 'the dark ages', which is pretty nearly the verdict of reactionary historians and of ascetically religious temperaments.

The growing intensity of political and economic activity, as well as of all forms of art, during the first centuries of the modern era, shewed itself in the appearance of two new lines of thought and study: Economics or Politics (which we may here consider as essentially and philosophically one) and Aesthetics or the Philosophy of Art. Both these sciences were practically unknown throughout medieval philosophy, which in the practical sphere recognised only Ethics and, when it could not avoid political and economic problems, offered moral solutions. In the sphere of theory it recognised only Logic and reduced art and poetry to symbols for popularising divine truth. But suddenly with the Renaissance there sprang up vigorously for the first time the theory of the state and of politics, quickly followed by the technique of statesmanship, and more slowly by economics. The last built for itself laws and principles during the eighteenth century, though it had not yet attained full philosophical self-consciousness. Now law began to be distinguished from morality, and human passions were studied, with the problems to which they give rise.[1] Meanwhile, with the Renaissance, enquiry was again turned to the theories of poetry, the figurative arts, architecture and music. Men began to seek a common basis for all the arts and to define the faculty which gives birth to them; and these enquiries, too, reached a first conclusion in the eighteenth century, when the originality of the new principle was recognised and an independent science came into being with the new name of Aesthetics.

Here, as in all branches of knowledge, we, of course, cannot speak of dogmatic systems fixed once and for all, but of lines on which work has begun and is still continued, because they were felt and are still felt to be inevitable and to lead to profitable results. The essentially unascetic, untranscendent, worldly and profane character of these two sciences was not noticed either by the modern minds which inaugurated and cultivated them or by the older school which should have contested and rejected them, but which either let them pass or actually collaborated in deference to the need and demands of the time. Indeed, the only science which met with reaction, stiff opposition and actual persecution was that of Politics, as the science of 'reasons of state', and this opposition was not directed against the whole science but only rejected the harsh and naked form in which it was presented by Machiavelli and the so-called Machiavellians. Moreover, the opponents of the doctrine were themselves more or less political theorists who tried to embrace both old and new in an eclectic harmony, a kind of conciliation in which it is never the new that is watered down but the old which is eaten away and destroyed.

[1]Notes on these various developments, which superficially seem disconnected but are intimately connected, can be found scattered through my *Practical Philosophy*.

And further, the anti-Machiavellian Jesuits, defending the Catholic Church by modern methods, so effectually made Machiavellianism their own as to apply it, where its author would least have expected, in the sphere of pure morality. The Jesuits likewise contributed to the development of modern æsthetics in their schools of humanistic rhetoric by the theories which they propounded or adopted of fancy, imagination, talent or genius, judgments of sense and good taste. Savonarola as a burner of vanities had no successors in a worldly-wise Catholic Church. Nor did Economics, in its primitive unphilosophical form of 'political arithmetic', occasion scandal or suspicion. Only later and incidentally, when extreme individualist theories of competition broke out, was there talk of 'moralising economics', and, once more, of the *iustum pretium* so familiar in the scholastic philosophy of Aquinas.

Indeed, if either party had at the time been conscious of the nature of these two sciences there would have been no need to expound it now, and this discussion would be superfluous. It is not superfluous since it is entirely due to that growth in self-consciousness which a movement only attains when it has a rich past enabling it to be seen in all its complexity and in relation to its opponents or to the movement from which it issued and which it attacked. Even today this self-consciousness is seldom complete. For my own part, when I have come across scholarly priests or candid monks or other religious persons who had incautiously accepted and employed the principles of modern æsthetics, I have given them the honest warning : 'Take care! You are playing with the devil!' I say 'devil', because I remember that Frederic Schelling, reflecting on the birth of languages and the irrepressible vigour of their individuality, qualified it, in so many words, as 'diabolical' or 'satanic', an idea which the philologist D'Ovidio felt bound to describe as extravagant, and which in fact was hardly the idea of a mere philologist.

What then, in the last analysis, are these two sciences doing? To put it shortly, they are trying by definition and systematization to give theoretical justification, as a creative spiritual activity, to what used to be called 'the senses', something distrusted and feared or even rejected and exorcised by the Middle Ages, but reinstated by the practical activities of the modern world. The term 'senses' however had two connected but distinguishable meanings; on the one hand it referred to those cognitive activities which are not logical or ratiocinative but sensuous or intuitive, on the other to that part of practical life which is not in itself moral or dictated by duty but simply guided by the affections and the desire for what is pleasant or useful. Consequently, the theoretical justification of the senses produced on the one hand, by its science of æsthetic or pure intuitive apprehension, a 'logic of feeling', or 'poetic logic', and on the other a hedonistic logic of utility, economics in the widest sense. And this was in fact a 'resurrection of the body', as the phrase goes, a justification of mere life as such, of human affections in every shape. No doubt this justification of 'the senses' could not be achieved without at the same time spiritualising them. From something external and hostile to spirit, fearful enemies, bestial and full of guile, to be resisted implacably to the death, they were transformed into something within the realm of spirit, into a kind of spirituality with a character, function and worth of its own and necessary, therefore, to a complete and wholesome spiritual life. But if sense was spiritualised by this adoption and elevation, spirit was sensualised, or rather recovered its harmonious integrity, and no longer suffered the former mutilation of organs essential to its life and activity. Logic and ethics came down from heaven to earth; scholastic formal logic was replaced by observation, experiment and induction; morality, instead of an external legislation, became the 'moral sense' or conscience, no longer the enemy of the passions and of happiness, but their indulgent though critical friend. No longer were the passions to be expelled from man's heart, but were to be elevated and purified so as to contribute energy to his life and action.

All the guiding principles of modern philosophy are closely linked with these two new sciences. Without them the old intellectualist logic of the abstract universal could never have been replaced by the speculative dialectic of the concrete universal, for whose formation art or poetry, by analogy, was the pattern, as it was sometimes even thought to be the chief and only adequate vehicle of truth. Without them history could never have been rescued from its humble status, as a mere chronicle or collection of heterogeneous facts or an *opus oratorium* designed to edify by examples, to the highest pinnacle of human thought, to be identified with a concrete and living philosophy. Without these two sciences the immanent metaphysic of reality could never have been rounded off.

Those who know the history of philosophy can supply innumerable details to fill in this sketch of one of its developments in modern times. It would be particularly interesting to record the reactions which were again and again stimulated by every persistence or revival of the medieval opposition to these two sciences, and by every reappearance of a hostility between the flesh and the spirit, even when its motives or its forms were those of modern thought. Among these reactions were the polemic of Vico on behalf of the historical consciousness as against Cartesian rationalism, that of Galileo against Aristotelianism, the protest of Schiller against rigoristic and ascetic vestiges in the Kantian ethics, the rebellion of romantic æsthetics against a frigid classicism, the criticism by expressionists of the æsthetics of the universal conception, even when it was subtilised as the 'Idea'; and so on. The constant motive of philosophies born again from life, experience and poetry was reaction against the lifeless, academic philosophy of the schools, which is usually confined to a world devoid of passion and imagination and tends to abstract logic and pedantic ethics.

Here we must confine ourselves to these mere hints, not forgetting, what has already been said, that the advance of thought is never the victory of a truth or system once for all established, but rather an indication of the road we have to travel, conscious of old difficulties overcome but ready to face and overcome new ones, which cannot be wanting in the present or the future.

K

II

Spirit and Nature

OUR MORE PROFITABLE TASK will be to consider how these two modern and profane sciences have, by their acceptance, completed the boundaries of a philosophy which excludes all transcendence. For this purpose we must pause a moment over the most serious of the distinctions which hindered and impeded this completion—the dualism of spirit and nature.

This is, in fact, a whole knot of dualisms which must be disentangled one from another. The first of these derives its origin, its nourishment and its continual reinforcement from the vulgar assumption of two different orders of reality and in fact two different worlds. These may be distinguished as the world of man and the world of nature, which would include all other beings from animals to stones; or as the worlds of consciousness and of the unconscious, or of life and of mechanism, or in whatever other way two worlds may be more particularly defined as constituted. Though not founded on critical thought but on pictorial imagery, this dualism is most deeply rooted, so much so that thought, which by its very nature must reject all dualism, instead of criticising and refuting it directly, has tried in the first place to save it by a spiritual interpretation of the unspiritual term in the contrast. But such a self-contradictory attempt ended in the surrender of thought to imagination. The most naïve attempt at such a reconciliation was the Renaissance philosophy of nature, which introduced a Pythagorean mythology of personification or animism. The same tendency was more overt in philosophies of idealist and romantic brand which from their first appearance were denounced in principle, as by Fichte, who called them 'visionary' (*Schwärmerei*). They were founded on the idea of something radically 'other' than spirit, an unconscious, absolute somewhat (as if an unconscious absolute were conceivable!), and thus affirmed a primary and fundamental dualism. But they then claimed to have overcome this dualism by considering this 'other', this 'unconscious' as a 'self-alienation' of reason, as 'petrified thought', and accordingly engaged in the task of understanding and reconstructing the unconscious process or 'dialectic' of its alienation. It matters little whether the alleged dialectic was after the manner of Schelling or of Hegel, whether by stages or by thesis, antithesis and synthesis, in which cases the machinery was substantially identical, or whether nature was constructed out of all the activities of spirit or only from those of reason[1]; the procedure was always arbitrary, working with metaphors and imaginary analogies. Indeed these philosophers have been undone less by the criticism of their arbitrary logic than by the ridicule incurred by aphorisms actually preserved in their writings or ingeniously coined by way of parody, as, for instance : 'The diamond is a flint which has become self-conscious' or 'The hurricane is nature's delirium', and so on. As in the natural philosophy of the Renaissance, with which these writers had intellectual affinities and indeed historical relations, there recurs in them the idea of a magic art to be rediscovered and perhaps practised.

The basis of all theories so constructed is destroyed and a new direction given to the philosophy of nature by the epistemological argument through which it has gradually come to be thought that there are not, in fact, two kinds of reality or two worlds, one spiritual and the other material, one governed by final and the other by efficient causes, one living and the other mechanical, but that the one identical, indiscerptible reality can be interpreted, as occasion demands, in terms of spirit, life, purpose, or in those of matter, cause and mechanism. The twofold order of reality, the duality of worlds, then reveals itself as an imaginative externalisation of a twofold activity in the human spirit. So little true reality has it, that not only animals, vegetables and minerals, but man himself with all his feelings, thoughts, actions, and all that he creates, including his history, can be alike schematised, mechanised, materialised and treated as naturalistically determined. And this is exactly what is done by the many natural sciences which deal with the life of the spirit, by that branch of zoology which is called empirical psychology and that branch of physics which is called the linguistic science of phonetic

[1] *Logo.*

laws. When this doctrine of the two ways of studying reality is understood as implying only a duality in the procedures of thought itself, one in relation to the end achieved and the other in relation to the laws of necessary causation, the conception of a natural world wholly determined in the latter way is abolished.

But the conception of a free spirit also seems to be threatened, since, if the one reality can equally well be thought of in two mutually inconsistent ways, it would be to some extent falsified by either, and its true nature would remain impenetrably unknowable. The only way to escape from this dilemma is to recognise one of these methods only as genuine thinking and the vehicle of ultimate truth, and to assign to the other a function merely practical and instrumental or, as it has been called, 'economic'. This is precisely what is done by the modern critical philosophy of science. It may linger in untenable compromises, like that of intuitionism and phenomenonalism, but, whether it likes it or not, it is forced by logical necessity to reassert the exclusive truth of philosophic thought and the absolutely spiritual conception of all reality as history. It is bound to shew that whatever knowledge of truth is afforded by the natural sciences is historical knowledge. In our own times we observe more and more the emphasis laid on the concrete, individual, historically determined facts, in the investigation of so-called 'nature'.[1]

But the dualism of spirit and nature can be understood in another sense, to which the epistemological reduction or destruction of the concept of nature is not wholly applicable. When 'nature' as a separate world or realm of reality has been denied, it reappears within spirit itself as the 'somewhat' with which spirit finds itself confronted; and so within spirit we get the dualism of subject and object. But what could this object, this object in itself, other than the knowing subject, be? It could only be the resurrection of the fictitious matter, unconscious and unspiritual, in fact of nature. It has not been perfectly

[1]See the notes in *La Critica* on contemporary philosophy by De Ruggiero, *passim*. An English physicist, Eddington (*The Nature of the Physical World*, Cambridge, 1927), has humorously illustrated the difference between a living observation of reality and lifeless abstractions: 'A pig may be most familiar to us in the form of rashers, but the unstratified pig is a simpler object to the biologist who wishes to understand how the animal functions.'

dissolved by criticism, or only for the moment, and is quickly recreated by our obstinate imagination to reappear in a new guise. And since such is its character all our efforts to assimilate it to spirit are as vain as those of the old philosophies of nature and result in mere tautologies or quibbles. For instance, the problem is not solved but simply restated by insisting that the duality of the subject–object relation is also a unity. No better are the conjuring tricks by which a profound metaphysic tries to *escamoter* the object by making it vanish only to reappear as the product, as opposed to the act, of thought, that is to say, as nature opposed to spirit, or as the past as opposed to the present, which are merely new temporal metaphors for nature and spirit over again. At the same time while our destructive criticism of mechanical nature as a reality drives us to conclude that the object cannot be this nature, which no longer can be held to exist, we are no wiser as to what the proper object of thought may be; and this lacuna is apt to be filled in by the resurgence of a fictitious nature. Our argument implies that the object cannot be anything but spirit, but it is not spirit in the form of thought, whose activity is always that of subject as opposed to object What then is it?

The answer is provided by the two philosophical sciences which we have described as eminently modern, of which one deals with the life of action, so far as its motives are the passions, and the other with creations of the imagination. These sciences reveal the object of thought as nothing but those passions, motives, impulses, those pleasures and pains, those infinitely various emotions which are the direct objects of intuition and imagination, and indirectly therefore of reflection and thought.[1] On this principle truth must no longer be defined, as in scholastic philosophy, as *adaequatio rei et intellectus* since the *res* has been eliminated, but rather (so long as we take the idea of 'adequacy' metaphysically) as *adaequatio praxeos et intellectus*, a 'correspondence' between action and thought. That 'nature' should be identified with the operations of desire, appetite, lust, alternate

[1] The same conclusion which I reached some five and twenty years ago in my *Filosofia dello spirito* by way of æsthetics and the logic of history, summing up and criticising the traditions of classical idealism, has been reached from a different direction by Dewey. See the article on him by De Ruggiero in *Critica XXIX*, 311-57, especially pp. 345-6.

greed and satiety, was a thought that struck philosophers like Fichte and Schelling, and was the theme of Schopenhauer; but they all, and especially Schopenhauer, hypostasised the Will as something outside spirit, so much so that they thought of it as 'blind' and made it antecedent to any thought or idea.[1] In the same metaphysical manner, Hegel hypostasised the Logos, making it the basis of both nature and spirit, and lesser thinkers similarly treated other spiritual categories. Froschhammer, for instance, gave this dignity to imagination, and Hartmann to the unconscious. On the contrary, we must think of the will (in the sense of nature) as included in spirit, as one of its forms or activities, and the most rudimentary of its practical activities, in which the higher practical activity of morality always has to work and to embody itself. Thought and imagination, too, must embody themselves in it, realising themselves in words or other symbols, and by this self-realisation becoming liable to all the vicissitudes of passion and to the contrasts of pain and pleasure. Even when our thought studies and criticises the thoughts of others and traces their history, it is not strictly thinking about thought but about the practical activity of thinking, for thought is always the subject which thinks and not what is thought about. What, for instance, do we mean by thinking about some thought of Kant's? Simply thinking about Kant at some moment of his life, in some effort of concentration, with all his experiences, ideals, doubts and needs, and with the means by which he tried to satisfy them. We are reflecting upon a practical experience, though one directed to thought. And why ever should we reflect upon it if not to solve some mental problem of our own, whose solution, and not Kant's thought, is the thinking that is active at the time?

But even this last effort to expel nature from the subject-object relation does not exhaust the recurring series of dualisms or finally liberate us from this obsession. Again and again it recurs as an offence and a stumbling block, as a dead weight upon our spiritual life, where it insinuates itself as a disintegrating force driving our wills to evil and our minds to error. *La nature: voilà l'ennemi.* This material, mechanical, necessary nature stands over against spirit, opposing its purposes,

[1] *rappresentazione.*

its ideals and its freedom. The 'will', which was Schopenhauer's name for nature, is the source of pain and wickedness. Whatever he may have tried to maintain, it can never be stayed by any renunciation of the will, which is itself an act of will, or by any ascetic life, which is only a succession of volitions. But if we could never discover a nature outside spirit, no more can we conceive one opposed to spirit; if evil and error are within spirit they cannot be nature.

What then can they be? As we said of the 'object', they cannot be an activity of the spirit, for, if so, they would have a positive and not a negative value, they would be goodness and truth, not evil and error, whereas they present themselves as terribly negative. Nor can they be an illusory appearance, for then the fight against evil and error would be a sham fight and no earnest, whereas it is terribly serious and real. The only remaining alternative is that 'nature' has a double character: it is something positive which takes on a negative appearance in the struggle to pass from one positive stage to a higher, so that the struggle and its pains are serious. It is not the positive stage from which we have emerged that was evil but only the relapsing into it. Such a relapse would be a kind of inconsistency and therefore painful and shameful, for once we have escaped the lower stage we cannot recover it as it was; to return to it with remorse is not to recover what may be called a state of innocence.

Is there then in spiritual life a positive but lower stage as well as a higher? Here we are helped to an answer by the science of what is hedonistically useful, the *quod mihi placet*, the science of those passions, desires and tendencies which are commonly called 'natural', all of which have been classed by this science as the rudimentary basis of action. This is to be distinguished from the higher or ethical form but is not directly opposed to it. It only enters into such opposition when from private utility man rises to morality, and from personal advantage to duty. In the completion of this process arise all the phenomena of evil, which range from the momentary temptation immediately repressed, through all the stages of partial relapse, to what seems total and abysmal; from the inconsistency of a peccadillo to the horrible remorse for a great sin, from firm constancy to wavering and degradation, and from this once more to renunciation, rebirth and redemption. Evil then is the pain of a fall from morality without a return to the innocence of 'nature'. 'Natural' life is in itself good and not evil, though it is a lower good as compared with a higher; it is positive and not negative. It is to be feared that those who obstinately deny any spiritual nature to the natural life and confine it to morality are influenced not by a peculiar strength of their moral consciousness, but by its weakness and indecisiveness. They rob morality of its militant nature or set it to a sham fight with its own shadows. But the idea of the pleasant and useful, as set out by economics, preserves this militancy. It even shows the possibility of victory, which could not be if evil, instead of being a growing-pain in a crisis of development, were a wedge brutally driven into our spirit by the external violence of 'nature' or 'matter'.

So the two eminently modern sciences, aesthetics and economics, tend to reconcile the flesh and the spirit. They free the spirit from the incubus of an external nature, and spiritualise the subject's object; they shew that the conflict of good and evil is in ourselves, and thus complete the philosophy of immanence by rejecting every kind of transcendence. Thus they are the eminently profane sciences. It will not be surprising that one who has long cultivated them and gained great enlightenment from them for his spiritual life, should wish in his old age to offer them this humble tribute.

1931

✣ 23 ✣

THE CONFLICT OF DUTIES

WE ALL KNOW (or at least readers of my past works know it by heart) that spirit is a system of different elements and therefore a unity. If it were not for the differences there would be no unity, since a unity without internal differences is a mathematical abstraction, no concrete or organic reality. And if it were not for the unity, there could be no differences, for there can only be differences within some unity that comprises them; otherwise the word loses significance and becomes mere vocal noise. Since the two terms are thus absolutely identical, it is inadmissable, though it has often been attempted, to think of the unity as the prior term from which the differences emanate, like some mythical God who, in his solitude, makes up his mind to create a world. The true God creates himself and his world together, and creates them with joy and suffering. The same activity which has the specific function of unifying, is itself one of the differences which it unifies, one of the forms of the spirit, and is called the moral activity. It continually overcomes the discord which is the 'negative moment' or subject-matter of every activity, and attains the spiritual harmony in virtue of which spirit advances from victory to victory and life constantly rises above itself.

Discord, the negative moment, is in fact the ever-recurring attempt of some particular form of spirit to maintain and develop itself without taking account of the others. From these it had its birth as a new generation, to grow old in its turn, giving birth to others, and so, with these others, repeating the eternal cycle of spiritual life. Decadent æsthetes, for example, aspire to create poetry, which shall be pure, abstract poetry, from minds empty of human passions and experience, with no effect upon the spirit as a whole, without any

153

consequent mental or moral process. The same may be said of philosophy and action when they strive after absolute self-sufficiency and independence, trying to cut themselves off, the former from action, morality and poetry, the latter from thought, morality and religion. Such error, of course, like every other, is due to a partial truth; each particular form of activity obeys a law of its own and has its own proper 'duty'. The mistake is that a part tries to elevate itself into the whole and thus contradicts its own nature; as a meticulous show of conscientiousness actually results in a violation of duty.

Of all dangers to the moral life this is the most insidious, and one might say the most devilish, if what Dante was taught in the theological schools of Bologna was true, that 'the devil is a liar and the father of lies'. There is no need to go further in search of more examples. During the last few years we have had right under our eyes the spectacle of a nation, which in the past had contributed greatly to European civilisation, stricken with a terrible insanity. It not only elevated the negative into the positive by making its ideal of the good life war, which for centuries had been numbered with plague and famine among the three calamities, an ideal peculiar to a race of warrior-heroes like the German[1]: by a similar exaggeration it made patriotism and the obligation to defend its country into absolute and exclusive duties. Patriotism is justified and morally worthy only when it draws its life and nourishment from the parent tree of humanitarianism, of which it is a compendious imaginative symbol, being also the most obvious, though by no means the sole field for the exercise of that duty. There is a noble sentiment expressed by Montesquieu in one of his notebooks: 'If I knew of an action which would be useful to my country but harmful to Europe, or useful to Europe but harmful to the human race, I should think it a crime'.[2]

'My country right or wrong (über Alles)' is either a merely emphatic expression or a criminal and perverted one. Similarly the military maxim to 'harm the enemy in every possible way' has the logical and moral limitation: 'except in those ways which affect what is as sacred for ourselves as for the enemy'. The destruction of what

[1]See No. 17 above: *The Idealisation of War*

[2]*Cahiers* (1716-55), ed. Grasset (Paris, 1912), pp. 9, 108, 241.

is sacred lessens our own stature as much as the enemy's, and indeed more, for we are responsible and incur the hatred and the shame. This is the moral aspect of the so-called *jus gentium*, natural right or law of nations, which is as much a right as any other. As I write these words[1] I have in mind the deliberate destruction by officers of the German High Command, in brutal reprisal, of the Great Archives at Naples. This impious deed was carried out in spite of warnings that it meant the destruction of treasures belonging not to Naples nor to Italy but to international scholarship. Medieval manuscripts, the register of Frederick II of Swabia, the Angevin registers, the Aragonese Chancellery records, the Farnese papers, documents for Napoleonic history filling gaps in that of Europe and the East; all these inexhaustible sources of valuable information, objects of indefatigable research by Italian and foreign scholars, jealously preserved for centuries, are now no more; they were sprinkled with petrol and perished in the flames. How many youthful hours did I spend studying these volumes and the other files of papers, also reduced to ashes, containing the lives of medieval towns and families! How gladly I returned to them whenever my studies took me that way! I can still see in memory, though my eyes dim with tears, my old teachers, who were the proud and devoted guardians of these treasures in the ancient monastery of San Severino, with Bartolommeo Capasso at their head. This deed, done in the full light of German and international civilisation, is an infinitely greater 'vandalism' than those of poor ignorant barbarians like Alaric and Genseric and such *deustche Recken*, the ogres of German history. It is hard to believe that its perpetrators can have persuaded themselves that they were thereby fulfilling their duty and serving their country. Men who have not utterly cast off humanity know how to subordinate minor obligations to the paramount duty, as Schiller said that he was too religious to accept any of the religions. From the intuition of a sound heart they side with the right, on the same impulse which often springs spontaneously in the minds of criminals, steeped in every kind of vice and wickedness, who have not quenched the last spark of humanity in their souls. Such men have not degraded

[1]October, 1943.

themselves to automata or robots in the same degree as these Germans, whom we have seen devastating all Europe, and who are now systematically and methodically destroying our Italy, not only the lives of her people, not only the fruits of heavy toil which her children inherit, but also that ideal heritage which still makes her the mistress of nations. This extreme degradation of humanity, this conventional obedience to a legalistic 'duty', this monstrous and blind worship of their Moloch, has overtaken them in the guise of patriotic discipline, but has only ringed them round with horror, fear and loathing. 'Inhumanity' is indeed the proper word; I well remember, in contrast, a young Jewess, a student of archæology, who had come to Italy after the beginning of the savage anti-Jewish persecution in Germany, and who still bore in her hollow face and mournful eyes the signs of shocks and privations she had endured; I well remember the accents in which she described, as though it were incredible, the welcome she had found in Italy. 'The Italians are human beings'. We used to love the Germans for their great classics in philosophy, for their music, for Goethe's poetry, for the homeliness of their honourable and industrious way of life; then, too, we came to admire them for their services to pure and technical science, for the wealth and power to which they had advanced their country. It seems impossible that they should have become what they now are, an abomination to every class of person over the whole world, one which presents to the whole world a problem bristling with difficulty for the day when we must after all once more live as neighbours; a problem which certainly cannot be solved by exterminating the German people.

I have never held the belief in the myth of nations or races of unalterable character, nor will I be seduced into it by a spirit of recrimination. I shall abide by the belief, less uncritical and less pessimistic, that such characters are not naturally determining factors, but products of history more or less lasting, varying in strength, which may fade away and give place even to their contraries. How history produced what we now have to face as Germanism or 'Aryanism', I have briefly described elsewhere. But perhaps in the boasted superiority of Germans to all other races, in this bid for

European and even world-wide empire, in their constant preference
for the argument of force and for the hectoring language of their
Brennus, we may discover, what all this at first concealed, a repressed
and tormenting consciousness of inferiority. They have not hitherto
succeeded in rivalling other nations in liveliness and clearness of
intuition, in tact and grace and the arts of behaviour; they do not
move sympathy nor rouse the imagination, they cannot attract
imitators nor set a vogue; they have not the political sense to take
advantage of fortune and to seize the opportunities she offers; they
cannot win respect by respecting. So their boundless ambition and
their cult of the *Kolossal* leaves them no alternative but to impose
themselves by violence. They saw in the whip, the truncheon, and
what more modern and scientific weapons they could add or substitute, a short cut to world-wide dominion. But what such a world
would have profited them, in which all morality had been banished
or rather driven into rebellion, no man has been able to imagine. In
the times when even Germany was warmed by the sun of European
liberty, one of their own poets said: 'Victories spell defeat when their
fruit is weeping and the boundless hatred of the world'.[1]

---

[1]*Triumphe sind wie Niederlagen*
Wenn ihre Frucht besteht in Klagen,
Im grenzenlosen Hass der Welt.

Augustus von Platen, in *Polen-Lieder*, 1831.

24

MANUAL WORK AND
WORK OF THE MIND

NO ONE WHO OBSERVES the conditions of modern society with a critical eye can fail to recognise the diminished honour, not to say indifference and contempt, with which religious, intellectual and artistic activities are regarded as compared with what is called manual labour and the positive and technical sciences which control it. This indifference moreover corresponds to a diminished independence and energy in the spiritual sphere. It is certain that the two spheres are inseparable in the indivisible unity or relationship of the human spirit; but this unity, being organic and 'dialectical', is a unity of differences and even of oppositions, which in history have sometimes been emphasised less and sometimes, as seems to be the case today, more.

The possibility of this difference and opposition arises from the deep distinction between work directed to the preservation and growth of what may be called our physiological, economic or material life and that directed to the corresponding service of the life more eminently spiritual. This is the same distinction as that made in antiquity between the 'banausic' or menial arts and those respected and admired as 'fine' arts, which latter came to monopolise the title of 'art' as identical with beauty. Since the dialectical distinction between the different categories of reality involved a difference of dispositions and aptitudes, education and what is called nature—though nature, too, is a result of education and historical evolution—produced men particularly fitted to one or other of these two kinds of work, manual and spiritual, of which the former class was in the majority.

The difference of numbers may be more or less pronounced, but the indivisible unity of the human spirit necessitates that the smaller class is indispensable to the larger and essentially its ally, not a competitor or enemy which oppresses and exploits it, as exuberant orators have sometimes proclaimed and weak minds believed. Oppression, profiteering, exploitation have occurred and occur in history, and in some times and places have not been felt as such but have been accepted as necessary and legitimate. When this was so they had not really the same character as in those times and places where, owing to changed conditions, they have been felt as tyrannical or insupportable, and, becoming odiously hostile, have earned abusive names. This is 'the tragedy of labour', which Antonio Labriola once outlined to me in a sort of historical epic that he wanted to compose. In this poem there arose in succession different representatives of the labouring generations, with the same miserable fate, from those of ancient Egypt and Babylon to those of modern England, Germany and Italy. It was a tragedy in the sense in which all human history is a tragedy. But the form taken by the development of labour in the three usually recognised stages of slavery, serfdom, industrialism, was not given it by the intellectual minority, but by another, which arose within the majority, among and from the workers themselves, with the same outlook as the workers and the same thoughts, purpose and methods, though differently directed.

The components of this second minority were chiefly those who came to be celebrated as heroes or *patres*, aristocrats and feudal barons, all who founded and still found and govern republics and kingdoms. With them or under them are the leaders of industry and commerce, men of business, to whom is due the advance of society, in production and distribution of wealth, and who are sometimes considered the modern aristocracy that has displaced the old feudal system. Even they did not exist for a purely negative function, which would be a contradiction in terms; though in the days of Rousseau and the enlightenment they were popularly assigned the old rôle of our mythical first parents, who, through eating the forbidden fruit, destroyed the earthly paradise and brought on mankind the curse of working in the sweat of his brow. Even this class of employers fulfilled a necessary function, which they could only fulfil by mastering their fellows, stimulating and constraining them to labour, guiding and disciplining the work. Having thus become the masters, and being flesh and blood, not saints or ascetics, to the work and risks of mastership they added the pleasure of ease and riches. This, under the conditions of the day, represented the reward of initiative and courage and of social service rendered, and came to be looked on as an unearned reward only when such service ceased or ceased to be of value. Any other interpretation of what happened is fiction, not fact; and the pseudo-economic doctrine of Marx is now recognised as fiction, which makes unpaid labour the sole source of profit—a doctrine that only has value as the effective war-cry of an age in which this social relation has proved itself an anachronism in need of replacement or reform.

From this historical movement has arisen the demand expressed in the formula of 'emancipation for the workers', which needs further examination. For man only gets emancipation, if at all, from himself and in himself, in his inalienable liberty and moral worth. Christianity, much more clearly than ancient philosophy, proclaimed and advocated for man this freedom, attributing it to every human being, since all had been redeemed by the blood of Christ. It was in this sense, not in the sphere of actual economic relations (which awaited other and slower methods of decline and decay) that Christianity abolished slavery by abolishing the idea of it and by rescuing from the contempt of the Greeks and Romans the labourer and the artisan. From another point of view any emancipation from the chains which fetter our activity can only be relative and partial. Complete emancipation is not only impossible but undesirable as being devitalising, since the only stimulus to progress and the only material on which activity works are the obstacles that confront them ;—so true is it, that the only people who make this absolute removal of all obstacles their programme are fanatical anarchists or antinomian individualists. Consequently, the so-called emancipation of the worker has only local and temporal importance and meaning within the detailed context of history, in which it must be seen as a historical development. It is then exhibited in the three stages of slavery, serfdom, and industrialism, in the last of which the manual workers are seen governed by the same laws as other men, free and equal before the law, enfranchised citizens and therefore the architects of their own fortunes. Hardly worth refuting is the false and mean contention that ancient slaves were better off than modern wage-earners or proletarians since their masters protected them from desperate daily insecurity by providing them with food, clothing and a roof over their heads, in other words, since they treated them like *res* or domestic animals. But whence has this progressive emancipation of the workers from obstacles to the development of their moral personality derived its enthusiasm, its thought, its language, if not from that minority of spiritual workers which here took the lead, men of religion, philosophers, poets? The men of religion gravely rebuked those in power and worked directly on their conscience; the philosophers, who appeal to the common faculty of thought, are by nature democrats and '*ab optimatibus non injuria sibi existimati periculosi*'; the poets join hands with all men, high or low, in love and suffering, in virtue and in error, in pity and admiration, and have found a humanity worthy of compassion even in the fiery Achilles and the criminal Macbeth, and a generous heart in the mad Don Quixote. All this the workers of the mind have done, not by force or fraud or flattery, but by their sense of justice, truth and beauty, by being disinterested because universally interested. Nor have they adhered to utopias, the barren utopias of fiction outside reality and opposed to it; they expect that events themselves must produce the conditions rendering gradually attainable those eternal aspirations of mankind which they themselves keep alive and active.

In this close correspondence and sympathy between the activities of the larger and the smaller class there is not to be found any hostility or suspicion among the manual workers—peasants, artisans, labourers, the 'people' as they are called—towards the religious teachers, the thinkers or the poets. The humble and oppressed have followed in the steps of the latter with their popular religions, intellectually inferior copies, abounding in fables and superstitions, but retaining

L

the spirit of their originals. We may leave to popular protestant polemic the epithet of 'pagan' which it applies to the religiosity, let us say, of the Spanish or Neapolitan people. The treasures of Christianity here concealed are sufficiently revealed by the cult of the compassionate Madonna. The people have also followed their leaders with a popular literature, not so much created by themselves as selected, imitated and adapted as fitter to their feelings and their intellectual powers. In this they not only poured out their passions of love and sorrow, but also those of daring, heroism and valour; and like their masters, with the same eager enthusiasm, they read or listened to the deeds of heroes in epic or romantic poems. Even proverbs, the so-called popular wisdom, are indebted to the experience and example of a more reflective, thoughtful and learned environment. Among the people a sense of reverence has always surrounded the person of the learned man, the man who knows, who knows more than themselves, though they may not expect to understand ideas which are above their heads.

What then is the real cause of the change? Whence come the indifference, the dislike, the suspicion, shown towards the guiding minority? Only from the interests, whether base or respectable, of those on whose influence this minority has trespassed—from those rulers in the political and economic spheres, who, in certain stages of historical development, appear as oppressors and exploiters of the other workers. There has been not only a tragedy of labour but a 'tragedy of mind', which as we all know, includes countless martyrdoms and constantly renewed persecutions of men of intellect, against whom the lords of the earth, not content with their usual weapons of war and policy, often incite the ignorant and misguided mob. Even the favour which, in other circumstances, great minds have found with the mighty is not to be considered a real sentiment of respect. If the latter, in their times of sure prosperity, in their moments of ease and dreams and pastime, called about them poets and artists, scholars and learned men, their motive was the lustre thus conferred upon their persons and their courts. There was no true sympathy of minds; and rare, even in the splendid courts of the Italian renaissance, were the princes who had a genuine love and understanding of art. In the main the artists, such as Ariosto and Tasso, have left us in no doubt what to think of the princes and courtiers who protected them, and who not only excluded them entirely from their secret councils but used them so far as possible for their own political purposes and to advertise their own praise and glory. Such were the conditions imposed on men of letters by the patronage of princes, which moved the generous indignation of Vittorio Alfieri and dictated his essay *Del principe e delle lettere*, in which he could not pardon even Virgil for having used the golden music of his verse to celebrate Augustus and the imperial family. From the time of Alfieri, Italian men of letters, keeping their eyes fixed on the lofty image of Dante, gradually freed themselves from their bondage to the mighty, rulers and men of affairs, and took up ways of life more suited to their noble calling, jealously independent of every influence but that of truth and beauty. Among the new movements was that towards liberty, with which they united themselves; but there was also the different though related cause of democracy or the preference of quantity before quality; and this, when necessary, they resisted, not even listening to the great moral authority of Giuseppe Mazzini, who in his desire to engage them in the service of his own political ideal, lofty and inspired though this was, would have degraded them from ends to instruments. (I may remark parenthetically that I have heard the sentiment of Mazzini, which taxed Shakespeare with being the poet of the individual isolated from society, re-echoed by a citizen of the Soviet state who, in my presence, condemned a contemporary Russian poet of genius as 'purely psychological' and not expressly representative of the proletariat.)

But the lack of reverence for the work of the mind, its debasement in comparison with material service, and the attempt to enslave it to politics, are found today not so much in the countries which still claim to be democracies but have lost their confident spirit, as in a competitor which has succeeded to this spirit and aims at rivalling and replacing them. This is so-called 'communism', though it preserves no essential feature of communism but is a particular form of national and class government. It is indeed represented in the latest historical development of a great part of Europe, and is capable of great achievements, but it ought by now to be given an unambiguous name of its own and not an equivocal one that is not proper to it.

We must remember the adverse judgment passed by Lenin, at the beginning of the Russian revolution, upon the work of the mind in favour of that of the hands, which alone for him had value. Even if this early attitude has been changed, so that even in that country a fairly wide sphere is allowed to intellectual work, the principle is still that of enslavement. Marx in those youthful metaphysical improvisations, which later took root in his mind with no further effort at self-criticism, had conceived of philosophy, art and religion as mere expressions of class interests and economic relations, especially those of capitalism, which was then predominant and so the chief object of his attack. The ingenuous modern theorists who parrot his teaching have accepted the philosophical argument and the historical interpretation as sacrosant, but have turned them upside down and ordained that religion, poetry and philosophy should be expressions of the proletariat, or of those who practice politics in its name; and they force all three into this mould by violence. This misunderstanding of poetry, art and philosophy, and of moral and religious problems, and this crude way of treating or neglecting them, have now crossed the borders of Russia and penetrated our western countries, where luckily they meet with a different experience, a different tradition and a more sagacious criticism; but, in spite of all, the withering effect of this parching eastern wind is felt. Finally, in Italy there has been planned on paper a cabal of sworn conspirators, 'writers of the left', who call themselves democrats or communists and are ready to prostitute their talent; but it seems that none of them have had the courage to appear upon the scene.

It is curious that all these attempts and all these sentiments pose as 'young movements', though, as I have shown above, they have a history of centuries and have been abandoned as unworthy of the dignity and liberty of letters. But the old, against whom the high spirit of youth is so often invoked and incited, are at least aware of one thing; they see clearly enough that these so-called youthful ideas have very long, grey beards, which yet do not make them very venerable. For my own part I often console myself by repeating an epigram of the elder Dumas which I think is not only witty but sheer truth: that a young man always begins life with an old woman on his arm and an old idea in his brain.   10th April, 1945

PHILOSOPHY OF
HISTORY

25

PROVIDENCE OR THE 'CUNNING OF THE IDEA'[1]

THE GREAT INFLUENCE exercised by the idea of Providence in fostering a just conception of history deserves emphasis, and should never be forgotten. Its earliest form was the theological doctrine of a God who shapes the plans of men to his own ends; Vico subtilised this transcendent, personal God into an 'immanent providence', and Hegel into the 'cunning of reason', or of the 'Idea'. The thought common to all these forms prepared the way for a more 'objective' consideration of actions and events, refusing to regard them merely as they appeared to those who participated in them, as bound up with their personal interests and passions. Men's private motives were degraded, from this new point of view, into mere accidents of the essential and necessary process.

But language is naturally metaphorical, and, in expressing this newer and profound historical conception, it admits, demands and spontaneously reproduces figures of speech derived from the older theological conception. We are told, for instance, that God leads men to his own ends without their will, or against their will, and ignorant of his guidance; from their weakness and vices he fashions avenues and instruments of goodness, and so on.[2] There is no harm in this, rather it lends vivacity and colour to the style; but we must be

[1]In English idiom 'The Hidden Hand' (a phrase, I believe, due to Adam Smith) or 'the divine tactic' (Burke), cf. Hume *Essays* 11, xii. Kant speaks, in this context, both of 'nature' and 'providence'. (Translator's note.)

[2]Kant says 'Thank God for our vices' (*Idea for a Universal History from a Cosmopolitan Point of View*), cf. Psalm LXXVI 10, 'The fierceness of men shall turn to thy praise'. (Translator's note.)

careful not to lose sight of the truth really intended under these forms of speech.

The truth is this : history is the record of the creations of the human spirit in every field, theoretical as well as practical. And these spiritual creations are always born in the hearts or minds of men of genius, artists, thinkers, men of action, moral or religious reformers. Such new births are welcomed and tended in their original purity by the elect who are natural leaders, and by their help are transmitted to the many, and finally to the so-called 'vulgar', who adapt them and bend them to their own personal and private interests of every kind. A little thought shows us that even the poetry of a Dante or a Shakespeare, outside the little circle of those who really feel and understand it as poetry, gets its universal fame from people who either do not know it or at least have never realised it imaginatively. Either they admire it for reasons that have little to do with poetry, or they sing its praises to show their intelligence as superior persons, or they occupy themselves with it for a professional or academic livelihood, or from some such motives. Yet after all, a universal reputation thus gained increases the vital efficacy of these sublime spiritual creations ; even fashion has its uses. Similar is the historical development of philosophical thought, of economic and moral institutions, of religions ; they too impregnate society in the same way, and thus the Republic of Plato, shedding its rays upon the dregs of Romulus, fertilises and prepares the soil for the seeds and the growth of new forms. But it is the duty of historical and philosophical criticism to sense the quality and to understand the place and the relations of these spiritual creations in the historical context. The critic must not be misled by the accidental nature of these methods of popularisation, which are in fact always pretty much the same, that is to say, commonplace, whereas the creations themselves are eminently original. Psychologists, associationists, positivists, naturalists and materialists so far lose themselves when they try to comprehend these methods that they actually end by describing them as the 'causes' of the spiritual creations. They think the creations came about by a set of lucky coincidences and so were themselves accidental. This is the lowest depth of philosophical and historical understanding ; we have seen it in an ingenuous form in the days of the pseudo-scientific method of philosophy or positivism, and we now experience it in a subtler and decadent shape.

I will take a chance example of this relation between the realities of history and the 'accidents' of their development, or, to speak more exactly, between the reality of thought, politics and morals on the one hand and on the other the merely physical reality of appetites, needs, satisfactions and dissatisfactions in the animal life of individuals. I take it from a page of the *Historia de rebus gestis in Partibus Trans-marinis*, that is, a history of the first crusade, by William of Tyre, which I happen to be reading in the old French translation. Having told how the idea of the crusade was propagated by the Pope and by popular preachers alike, and how it spread rapidly through every part of Europe and every rank and class of people, he goes on : 'I do not say that all who adhered to it had any very high motives or very pious intentions towards God (*ne très pure entencion à Dame Dieu*) ; the monks escaped their cloisters without leave from their abbots, many laymen went to keep company with friends, some through vanity and fear of being thought cowards if they stayed at home, some to escape their creditors and postpone payment of debts'. This last motive has, in fact, animated many volunteers in the wars of all ages ; as we read in the memoirs of General Macdonald that in 1789 many flocked to the forces of Condé for this reason. But it is a fact which has not prevented such men from doing honour, by their heroic courage, to the cause which they had joined from selfish motives. The archbishop of Tyre does not fail to distinguish, in his own way, between substance and accident, between the physical reality and the higher reality which he refers to God ; he adds : 'But whatever the hidden motives of the heart, it was plain from the grand adventure which was unrolled before men's eyes, that God therein was operative. And great was the need in those days for so great a pilgrimage, for so great were the sins of the world, which had forfeited the grace of our Lord, that it was most fitting for God to show men a straight path to paradise and to give them a task which might be as a fire of purgatory before their death'. (I Ch. 16.)

Though this explanation by means of a transcendent God and

paradise no longer satisfies us, it agrees with the other explanation, that of the 'cunning of the Idea', in the tricks which the Idea is supposed to play on men. For such metaphors can easily give rise to myths, which are often metaphors taken literally. The true and simple explanation lies in the historical method, which distinguishes the history of essential progress[1] from anecdotal history, from the record of purely personal happenings, physical and transitory. Scientific history elucidates the relation between these happenings and the essential progress, to which, from this point of view, they must take a quite secondary place.[2]

To return to our instance, the Crusade in spite of the low motives of the majority, was a historically important movement, because it was inspired by a purely religious ideal. It was not the first such ideal, since it was preceded not only by the Christian movement but by all those of classical antiquity; nor was it the last, for it was followed by others with different ideas and different forms in medieval and modern times. It was an ideal suited to the conditions of a time which, since it projected true reality and perfection into another world, was bound to feel as a sublime duty the liberation from infidel rule of the place where Christ was buried, and where the drama of redemption from this world by another had been accomplished. Hegel said that the legacy of the Crusade was disillusion because a great enterprise found itself at last before an empty tomb; and the Italian Manzoni, in one of his odes, tells of a voice crying to the Christians who seek the body of Jesus in the tomb: 'He is not here, he is risen'. History confirms that the first Crusade, even in the enthusiasm of its early activity, deviated no little from its original inspiration to the pursuit of political ends, and this tendency was stronger in the Crusades which came later. The appeal for the liberation of the Holy Sepulchre was still heard in Europe for some centuries, but more and more it became a mere figure of speech or a simple-minded delusion; it became a complete farce in the sixteenth century when the Christian

[1] *valori*.

[2] I think Hegel was vainly trying to reach this distinction in his famous 'Note' to 6 of the *Encyclopedia*, where he tried to explain his aphorism that 'all that is real is rational, and all that is rational is real'. But the explanation, far from establishing the dictum, seems to weaken it. See my *Saggio sullo Hegel* (3rd edition, pp. 153-158) and *Ultimi Saggi* (pp. 138-9).

powers, headed by France, made a treaty and alliance with the Turks. Certainly, the ideal expressed by the Crusades belonged to a period when a Christian Europe was becoming a Europe of worldly politics ; it was provisional and transitory like all ideals, for all ideals pass away but none dies ; the old and past lives in the new and living. That is the truth which history teaches.

26

THE HISTORY OF ENDS AND THE HISTORY OF MEANS[1]

IN THE PRECEDING SECTION I paraphrased and analysed the conception of Providence or the Idea or Reason in its relation to human passions. Such an analysis may sadden or shock and antagonise, since it gives a sordid picture of the way in which men's highest ideals, beauty, truth and morality, in spreading themselves through human society, popularise their institutions, establish them, defend them, and thus realise historical progress. The historian must, indeed, concentrate on these ideals and their original character, on their mutual oppositions and reconciliations, and on the spiritual progress they achieve, which is called culture or civilisation. He may omit or take for granted the obstacles to their recognition and success, the accidents, often strange enough, that befall them ; or he may mention all these merely to accentuate the power of the ideals which overcome them. But he must never deny the way in which, as we have said, these ideals realise themselves in the historical process, for what is necessary cannot be denied.

There is an ancient Greek story of how the Muses rebuked a philosopher who dreamt that they appeared to him in a brothel and accused him of having housed them there by proposing to 'popularise' them. The story keeps its worth as an uncompromising warning for the golden hour in which beauty is created, truth grasped or action determined by the voice of conscience, when we live, as it were, alone with our ideal. But it no longer holds good when those

[1] *Valori assoluti e valori strumentali.*

ideals enter into the world of events among human passions; if it did, they would be condemned to an ascetic and egoistic cult, worshipped by their creator only, and must renounce any efficacy in the social life. No less one-sided on the other hand is the hope that all men may one day become 'enlightened', as used to be said, all disinterested, all victorious over the passions which breed error, all obedient to the dictates of reason. Such a hope or conviction is incontrovertibly the fundamental error of sheer democracy. So far from all men, or even all in any society, being perfectible, no single individual, however elevated in feeling and strict in conduct, can ever become an automaton set in motion by abstract reasoning; he is flesh and blood and suffers all the ills that flesh inherits, swept by passions and swayed by them, in little things if not in great, every day and seventy times seven.

But what we have ironically called the ills of the flesh offer an unexpected answer and remedy for the melancholy and pessimistic fancy of an original evil which we can never shuffle off or purge away. Life in the flesh is not a disease but a good; if it were not, no more would truth, goodness or beauty be; if these are good, life is good, if they are things of the spirit, so is our life, which is not material or mechanical as bad philosophers, a prey to naturalistic and mathematical fallacies, pretend. Just because our life in the flesh is good and an end in itself, and spiritual, it has a perfection of its own and the freedom to pursue it; if it had not, it would not be life but death. And though this life must, from time to time, bend itself to the service of other spiritual activities which must be held higher, those which create provision for the eternal needs of the spirit, it cannot do this without first of all providing for its own conservation, its own health and energy and its own contentment. So in one aspect, life in the flesh is a necessary condition of these higher goods, in another it is their rival and their enemy; and this rivalry or opposition is called evil, which, as error, is a necessary condition of living truth, as ugliness, of living beauty, and as 'evil' in the most eminent sense, of living goodness. But evil considered abstractly, as one element in life, apart from its negative relation to other elements, is not evil but good; it is the good of sheer vitality which, however unbridled and excessive, in this way asserts its proper claims.

Is it then surprising that those few in whom the eternal ideals are the guiding principle of all their actions and all their being, who are absorbed in thought, in contemplation, in good works, find themselves faced and outnumbered by the many, in whom the need to maintain and enrich their lives preponderates? Yet the opposition is not absolute; the guiding principle of the first class is tempered by human weakness, the *humanum aliquid*; and on the other side there is no man, however selfish his professions, who has not his slender vein, or his generous moments, of pure idealism. Or is it surprising that the lesser sort should clear the way for the innovations of their betters, sometimes falling under their spell, but more often because in aiding or not resisting them they satisfy those natural interests which appeal to them as personal, utilitarian, economic? If this had not happened in the past, not even liberty, the supreme social ideal of humanity, would have found a footing in the world; if it should not happen in the future, liberty would be extinguished, no doubt an absurd hypothesis but one which it is sometimes useful to entertain in order to emphasise the truth. The essential meaning of liberty and the rigorous logic of its pre-suppositions and consequences is not easy to understand. This can be seen from the facile criticisms brought against it by dilettante rationalists and superficial minds, not without the consenting applause of the vulgar. Yet liberty always wins its campaigns and resumes its power, rising with strength renewed from its very defeats.

Unquestionably, it is one of the ends of civilisation to increase more and more the number of those by whom the higher ideals are valued for their own sake, on their merit, and not for incidental purposes. But however great we may hope and believe this increase will be, there will always be a large residue. Not to mention the knaves and fools, criminally or weak minded, there will always be the easy-going people who see nothing but their own peace and happiness, for which alone they will make efforts and sacrifices, or at the most extending their interest to their families and friends. This majority of mankind is sometimes sneered at by the 'elect' as being the 'belly' of the human race; but, for all that, the belly is part of the organism, which has its function, and by its health contributes to the physical health of the offspring, who often, with an inspiration different from their fathers', raise themselves above them to ideal activities. Moreover, it does not seem probable, at least from a medical point of view, that the 'ethereal' parts, the spiritual, should ever supersede the 'fleshy' parts, the carnal, as the Gospel calls them. Life has need of both.

The vital force is not only necessary but beneficent and gives rise to a philosophy of its own, the theory of the useful or economics. This I have already treated, distinguishing it from the other branches of philosophy[1] and expounding it under the general name of 'History of Technique'—technique in the widest, most comprehensive sense, in all its various forms. This is the history and the philosophy of something which has value, whose useful discoveries, like those of the activities called superior or intrinsically good, only make way in the world with the co-operation and resistance of human passion and self-interest. They have to make terms with the quick intelligence which helps them and with the stupidity or presumptuous ignorance which obstructs and opposes them. All this is familiar from the lives of inventors, among whom also can be found heroes and martyrs.

I now leave these dark phrases of 'Providence', and 'the cunning of the Idea' sufficiently elucidated. There follows from this elucidation not only a justification of the historians' proper method, but a reconciliation of the divine in man with his human life, which is demonic and, in its way, divine.

[1]Logic, Aesthetics, Morals (or Practical Philosophy). (Translator's note.)

27

THE HISTORY OF EVENTS AND
JUDGMENTS OF VALUE

THE WRITING OF HISTORY is simply a logical judgment of the only true kind; it is the bringing of the individual under the universal, the intuition under the category. It therefore excludes the intrusion of 'judgments of values' in the proper Herbartian sense, according to which they are extra-logical appendages (*Zusatz*) turning out on analysis to be nothing but expressions of emotion with practical motives. This is an essential point of philosophy which must never be forgotten.[1] This maxim of historical writing is implied in the common saying that history should be objective, not subjective, though this leaves it undetermined, or at least unexpressed, whether the subjectivity spoken of is that of passion and propaganda or that of the intellect which rules and criticises passion. The best confirmation of the definition of history as the union of universal and individual is by a comparison of history with poetry. Poetry consists not in a logical judgment, but in what used to be called a *judicium sensuum*, that is, a logic of the imagination, or in one word, imagination itself. The poet also, so far as he is conscious of his imaginative act, resists the temptation to the propagandist expression of feelings personal to himself. Even poets of great genius sometimes allow their works to be coloured, or rather adulterated, by such practical aims; but then their works are poetry only in the parts unaffected by such adulteration; and, as critics, while recognising their genius, we accuse them here or there of a lapse in style. Simi-

[1] See my discussion *I giudizi di valore nella filosofia moderna* (in *Saggio su Hegel seguito da altri scritti di storia della filosofia*. (3rd edition, Bari, 1927), pp. 396-410).

larly, those readers who cannot stick to the poetry, but take upon themselves to admire or detest, to praise or blame the things and persons of the poet's imagination, show bad taste, since they either do not feel the poetry or do not mind its adulteration. In historical works also we sometimes find this admixture which has to be mentally rejected, leaving the historical element pure. As I write this, there comes to my mind a life of Benedict Spinoza, written by some contemporary Lutheran parson, in which the symptoms of detestation ('abominable', 'wretched', 'poisonous', 'devilish', etc.) are quite becoming to a pious minister, though the historical narrative is sufficiently objective to give internal evidence of Spinoza's lofty mind, sincere spirit and ascetically saintly life.

It is hardly necessary, but may not be superfluous, to observe that in excluding emotional expressions of praise and blame we are condemning the emotive intention of these expressions and not the actual words which, though commonly used with such intention, may easily find a place in the most severely logical of histories. It would be pedantic to repeat to oneself the maxim of Epictesus in his *Manual*, 'If a man washes perfunctorily, do not say that he is dirty, but that he washes perfunctorily. If he drinks a great deal, do not say he is a drunkard, but that he drinks a great deal'. Heightening or understatement is a matter of style and of context. The exactness which must be observed in strict philosophical discussion is relaxed when it is no longer a question of defining concepts, which may be easily recognised under the metaphors of ordinary speech.

It will be objected that history thus conceived and described as a texture throughout of logical judgment will be a frigid history. But we need not be troubled by this criticism, which is identical with that brought against pure poetry by all those who seek in it stimulus for their loves or hatred, the very things which it is the function of poetry to allay in the tranquillity of recollection. The alleged 'frigidity' of history is in fact the white heat of historical truth.

Moreover, we have not implied that history cannot be repaid in another way, which I have already hinted at, for the abstention thus imposed upon it; namely by 'anecdotal' history, the history of mere events, which, though not true history, has its right to exist and may yield a rich harvest. In one of these gossiping histories, for example, I read the detailed account of the sufferings of the little eight-year-old king Louis the Seventeenth, in the Temple tower, separated from his family, and of how he was persuaded to vilify his mother and to abuse her and his aunt and sisters. '*Ces sacrées salopes*', he was heard to say, '*qui ne sont pas encore guillotinées*'. And with all this they amused him by games and romps and kept him cheerful. 'There is a tragic coincidence of the date with the words: *the young Prince burst into laughter.* It was on the 25th *Vendémiaire*—that is to say, the 16th of October! Perhaps at the moment when Marie Antoinette's darling child was thus enjoying himself with his gaolers, the Queen, at the point of death, was writing the heart-rending farewell which was interrupted by the executioner; perhaps the tumbril of Samson was already dragging her across Paris. His gaolers knew it; they could not have helped thinking of it; yet they could excite his childish laughter; they could mock his candid gaze . . . what men and what days!'[1] The final exclamation finds an echo in the reader's feelings, and might have been left to his imagination as pretty obviously implied by the style in which the story is told. But we must remember that this is not properly history. The *raison d'être* of a historical account would have lain in our political and moral need to understand how the little King and Robespierre and Chaumette and the men of the Paris Commune came to behave as they did in this and similar cases. We should have been told all that went on in their minds—the ideals, intentions, ideas, reasonings and hopes, so that the facts might appear to us as necessary elements of a movement in which a social and moral transformation precisely like the French Revolution was being realised. But if my quotation was not history, what was it? It was a narrative of fanaticism, violence, perversion, which has the interest common to any human spectacle, as the aphorism reminds us: *humani nil a me alienum puto*; it was a 'human document' which, we must remember, is commonly and properly distinguished from a 'historical document'. By such an insight into humanity it enriches our experience with data from the past and,

[1]Lenôtre, *Le Roi Louis XVII et l'Enigme du Temple*, Paris, 1921, p. 183: cf. the same author's *Vieilles Maisons, Vieux Papiers*, Paris,, 1914, II, 20.

moreover, it suggests moral reflections; as, for example, that brutal and inhumane actions arouse in the persons they were intended to humiliate moral reactions and impulses beyond their ordinary reaches. It suggests political reflections, too; as, for example, that brutality has the unexpected result of surrounding its victims, such as Marie Antoinette, Louis XVI, Madame Elizabeth, with the halo of martyrdom and winning them the pity accorded to all human creatures cruelly sacrificed; it weakens its own cause and strengthens that of its enemies. In other words, such stories provide didactic rhetoric whose effects are by no means negligible.

All this, as is well known, was a prevailing character of ancient histories, one which lasted till the renaissance, and did not disappear then, but was only put out of date by the historical thought of the nineteenth century. But it is out of date only from the point of view of history in the strict sense, and because we have to emphasise the true nature of that history and to develop it consistently. To do this, we must purify our true history from the superfluous elements which distract it from its true path, leaving them to their own place where they fulfil their proper office of moving and didactic rhetoric.

🙐 28 🙐

IN PRAISE OF INDIVIDUALITY[1]

I

IT IS OFTEN POINTED OUT, not without regrets and protests, in academic treatises and reviews that I have denied 'universal history'.[2] But this contention is very incorrect; those who make it have either not read or have misunderstood my express attempt to show that all universal history, if it is really history, at least in those parts of it which are vitally historical, is always particular history; and that all particular history, when and so far as it is real history, is bound to be universal. The former in its particularity embraces the whole, the latter refers the particular to that whole of which it is part. In fact, I identified the two things, since the mental process involved is not two but one.[3]

What I denied is universal history in the vulgar sense, which tries to supply its lack of a genuinely intelligible universality by a material universality, a very large 'thing', a compendium of all the particular facts that have occurred or been recorded in the five continents. Even in this sense a really universal history is impossible; there is no logical justification for separating history from pre-history, nor human from natural history, nor the history of the earth from that of the other planets and of the stars.

Moreover, the claim to enumerate all facts is as desperate as the attempt to distinguish historical from unhistorical facts is vain. What

---

[1] Croce's alternative title is 'Against Universal History and False Universals'. (Translator's note).

[2] But see *Teoria e storia della storiografia*, pp. 41-42.

[3] In this essay, while avoiding repetition, I reconsider and amplify some ideas in my essay *Lo storicismo hegeliano e quello nuovo*, which seem to have no little importance, but rather great urgency, in the moral and intellectual conflicts of our time.

is actually produced by this kind of universal history is a compilation or conglomeration of a certain number of chronicles, or of histories modelled on them and combined, which by the method of their combination set out to compose a great *Chronica Mundi*. The plan and contents of such a chronicle differ at different times; those of our own day, for instance, are no longer those which obtained for centuries, *de quatuor imperiis*, the histories of the four empires. As if to prove the slight intellectual value of such compilations, they have passed more and more out of the hands of writers to those of publishers who contract to have them executed. Nor have these often at their disposal any one individual, I will not say, of sufficiently wide and deep intellect, for that would be little to the purpose, but with broad enough shoulders to carry the immense burden. Consequently, they enlist squads of workers to share out the job, among whom there may happen to be found one with the historian's spirit and habit of thought, whose contribution, whether of a section or a chapter or a volume, leaps to the eye as out of harmony with the rest. But though such a collection always as a whole, and generally in its parts, avoids any historical problem and the thought which that would need, it at all events satisfies the simple ambition of the respectable householder to have stowed away in a row on his bookshelf the complete history of the world. It is seldom opened for any intelligent reading, still less does it minister to any education of the historical sense, which, if it ever attempts such reading, retires distracted and disappointed.

At this point, having shown, as a simple fact which can easily be verified, what the real nature of universal history amounts to, we might say no more about it, but turn our backs on it, as on a crowd of uninteresting strangers. But, though in itself it is too vague to be called either true or false, it has become the starting-point and provides the material for a much more important phase of culture, important, in the first place, as the expression of a need and striving for something better than mere chronological compilations, but still more important as a form of error. This form of error is the 'Philosophy of History', which is a philosophical elaboration of the so-called universal history. Like all forms of error, it necessarily stimulates the mind to react against it and so to appreciate with deeper understanding the nature of history.[1]

The fact is that the human mind cannot feel at home with what is disconnected and unintelligible, and is dissatisfied with this merely mechanical union, this heap of facts which is at bottom a mere chaos, however superficially systematised. This uneasiness is felt by the authors of universal histories themselves; though they persist in their procedure, from the very first they look for some fact to unify their facts, for example the fact that Europe is the centre of the historical world. Or, like Ranke, seeing that this is not good enough, they define universal history as the history of peoples who have developed in relationship, with mutual effects on one another—which is obviously little better.[2] But no set of facts can find its organic unity merely in one fact more. For such unity, it is no use to go above the earth to the sun, whether this be the sun of Copernicus or Galileo or even the 'Sun' of Campanella. We must mount or fly to him who moves the sun, and the other stars, to what is no mere thing or fact, but God, and this is the flight ventured by the philosophers of history, whether the ideal after which they name their god be 'The Idea' or 'Spirit' or 'Matter'. But it is a flight of Icarus which soon crashes to earth, where they fall to blows with one another, for instead of flying they ought to have been thinking. They should have been thinking about reality, and, to begin with, patiently and courageously disentangling the web of abstractions which fill the chronicles and the universal histories; they should be breaking the ice and finding the living water which it conceals. Instead, they religiously maintain these abstractions and classifications and divisions, these *idola theatri* built up by long tradition. They even add to their number, or substitute new ones of the same nature: East and West, Sumerians, Babylonians, Assyrians, Indians, Persians, Egyptians, Romans,

[1] It may not be out of place to say here that my above-mentioned book, *Teoria e storia della storiografia*, had its origin about 1910 in my undertaking with a German publisher to write for an encyclopedia he was producing a volume on the Philosophy of History. I intended to develop it as a criticism of that theory, emphasising some of its merits; but my criticism turned out so thorough and so satirical that I begged the publisher to release me from my undertaking, to which he good-naturedly enough consented, at the same time asking that he might himself publish this other book of mine in German, as he eventually did.

[2] On this point see a note in my *Teoria e storia della storiografia*, pp. 295-96.

primitive times, classical antiquity, the middle ages, modern times and so on. And they claim in the last resort to make a philosophy from this rigmarole of abstractions by elevating it to a higher power and, precisely, to the power of God, whose activity, it would seem, consisted not in creating the concrete, individual acts and thoughts of men but in an elaborate game with the abstractions which men for their own purposes have invented.

The rule of this game is as follows: to discover the 'meaning' of history; to look outside and beyond history for the meaning that, in fact, it has in itself, in its own real truth, for every mind which reflects on it, in every act of life, since life is always accompanied by self-consciousness which is self-history. In this absurd theory, there is on the one hand, an exoteric history, which, it is contemptuously said, the historians write, and on the other, a promised esoteric interpretation, the privileged work of the philosopher, who, consciously or not, adopts the method most ready to his hand, that of allegory. This was the method most common in medieval times, which were the first great age of the Philosophy of History.[1] Allegory, however, which is a sort of hieroglyphic, demands no logical connection between symbol and meaning, but a purely conventional one. Philosophy of History, on the other hand, substitutes for the symbolic relation a supposed real one and makes out of the allegorical 'meaning' a kind of super-history which reveals the motive power in history, a hidden hand which is supposed to guide the visible facts, nobody can tell how. Nobody can tell, because once the fact has been divorced from the reason for the fact, and this reason has been exalted to some transcendent sphere, a dualistic breach has been opened in reality which, at this level of thought, can never be bridged.

But one term of this dualistic relation, namely, the alleged meaning of the allegory, cannot be logically derived from the other, namely, the facts to be interpreted. Consequently, it has to be discovered and brought in ready-made from some other source, from some belief of the philosopher, in fact from a theoretical assumption he has already made. This may be true or false, logically justifiable or a mere product of imagination generated by desire or repugnance or other passions, either a systematic theory or a mere myth. It might, for example, be

[1] See my *Storia come pensiero e come azione*, pp. 139-141.

one of two different axioms, either : 'Spiritual life runs through a cycle, passing from imagination and reason to practical activity, and, owing to the feeling aroused in this action, passing to new imagination and thus completing the circle'. Or it might be : 'The abstract idea of pure Being arouses in opposition its own contradictory, that of not-being or nonentity, and by the negation of this negation, comes back to itself but this time as concrete Being'. Both of these axioms may, for the sake of argument at least, be taken as true. Or there might be others which we should believe or suppose to be untrue, for example : 'Humanity, divided into classes, goes through three stages in its purely economic life, to its final goal of a classless society, a progress which is disguised under the forms of religion, poetry, science, politics, morals'. Or again : 'History consists in a struggle between nations or races, among whom there is one chosen people destined to lead and rule all the others'. Or there might be an institutional dogma, as in the universal histories written by churchmen. Or there might be a pessimistic creed, looking with despair on human life, such as is sketched by the pessimistic dialectician Hartmann, or the irrational creed of those who are pleased to imagine that history is accidental and unintelligible, not seeing that they are revelling in their own wretchedness.

But whether these propositions are true or false, they all become untrue when they are distorted into descriptions of historical developments. Then the abstract categories of thought, instead of being used as predicates for our intuitive perceptions in concrete acts of judgment,[1] are used as substitutes for thinking and judging, and so create veritable chimeras, hybrids, incapable of generating truth and, instead, staging a ballet of ghostly abstractions.[2] This is the inherent vice of all attempts to do the work of thought twice over, to philosophise on the thought of the historian, whatever plausibility, whatever high aims or deep thinking may be involved in the attempt. Attention has been drawn to the importance of the moral value conferred upon history by Christianity in its construction of a philosophy of history.[3] But the true importance of this is in Christianity's wonderful

[1] e.g. 'Descartes was a great philosopher'.
[2] e.g. 'The Dark Ages' 'The Age of Enlightenment'. (Translator's Notes)
[3] For example, by Windelband, *Lehrbuch der Geschichte der Philosophie*, ed. Heimsoeth (Tübingen, 1935). §21, pp.213-25.

deepening and refinement of the moral consciousness and of its religious character, and not in its superstructural philosophy of history. The former laid down a new principle which for centuries has worked and always will work within us as a constantly regenerating force. The latter was the model to succeeding ages for similar fabrications, all now in ruins, whose accumulations it is our business to clear away.

Another damning consequence necessary to the above-mentioned confusion between categories of thought and perceptions is the tendency of all philosophies of history to produce a closed system, either treating past history as a development that has reached its ultimate goal, or, which comes to the same thing, logically deducing the history of the future. In the latter alternative the picture presented is not really of the future but only of a past that is in a sense present, for there is no knowledge of what agents will do but only of what they have done, nor of what will develop but only of what has done so. Moreover, philosophies of history present to us, as something once for all determined and done with, not only the whole trend of history, but every one of its phases or stages. Everything is then self-contained and final, as if it were a summing up, delivered at certain intervals by God or the Idea, or to speak even more vaguely, by historical necessity, which we must respect and obey. But since what is real is always developing, it cannot be conceived as stationary at any point but always as moving through it. No verdict on it may not be contested, there is no victory which is all triumph, and no defeat that has not its victory; no present which is not impregnated by all the past and pregnant with the future. The false idea of historical necessity breathes harshly like an east wind on moral effort; that is plain enough; but still worse, it carries the seeds of a pernicious sophistry, particularly vocal in times of political reaction, particularly acceptable to those 'unfair minds', as an old Italian poet called them, 'who cannot abide reverses'. They cannot abide them because they will not assimilate them, but prefer to bury them in haste, with hypocritical submission to the will of God, which is only a cloak for their own ease and advantage. The so-called 'necessity of history' is in fact only a necessity binding on the historians; it is the rational necessity or obligation to understand the true nature of the past, whether it merit praise or blame, which are here both out of the question. This necessity of facts in no way contradicts the liberty of obedience to the 'moral law'; rather the two are necessarily inter-dependent. We might say that the necessity of historical fact is the theoretical aspect of moral liberty—the condition in which it can rationally act.

The transcendent character of the Philosophy of History, which explains history by a power outside it, is like that of every other theory of transcendence; and is identical with that of the Philosophy of Nature, which flourished and decayed with it. Like every theory of transcendence it takes two forms, one mythical and the other metaphysical. These are not rigorously distinguishable, since all metaphysic has a mythical element in the language by which it is pictured, and every myth has a metaphysical or logical meaning, which makes it a myth and not pure imaginative poetry. Yet they can be to some extent differentiated by a distinction analogous to that between religion, which is myth, and theology, which is metaphysic. Religion and theology, however, are to be distinguished from philosophy of history, and over against both stands critical philo-sophy. It is worth noticing that precisely these three attitudes of mind were adopted by the philosophy of history for its schematization. As those know who remember their Turgot and their Comte, it pictured three historical epochs of humanity, the theological, the metaphysical and the critical or scientific. But these are not historical epochs, but non-temporal ideals. They are present as elements in all our thinking, and from its constantly renewed struggle against myth and metaphysic thought ever rises refreshed and renewed in its critical vigour.

II

I have described the method of the philosophy of history as employing philosophy not integrated in the historical framework, but rather to interpret such history as is found in the compila-tions of universal chronicles. To illustrate this description, it is not necessary to go through all the manifestations of the method, which indeed can be found well set out in various books devoted to

PHILOSOPHY OF HISTORY

the subject. It will be enough to concentrate on the famous and certainly the most weighty work which the method has produced, Hegel's *Philosophy of History*,[1] by a philosopher of genius who also had an acute historical sense.

Hegel started his theory with the conviction that no work, ancient or modern in any branch of history, had conformed to the true method; and this he undertook to establish in the summary which precedes his new work. He divides all previous histories into two main classes, the 'direct' (*ursprüngliche*) and the 'reflective' (*reflek-tierende*). The former he exemplifies by the histories of Herodotus, Thucydides, Xenophon, Polybius and Caesar in antiquity and of Guicciardini, Cardinal de Retz and Frederick II of Prussia in modern times. These are by writers contemporary with the events narrated in which they either took part or were present, and for that reason they cannot view them philosophically.[2]

The latter kind of histories, which do not confine themselves to the writer's own times, is divided into four sub-species. They are (1) 'General Histories', compilations from other people's narratives of events in a nation, country or the whole world, like those of Livy and Diodorus Siculus in antiquity and Johannes Müller in modern times. (2) 'Pragmatic Histories', which accompany the narrative with moral and political reflections, as may be seen in Müller. (3) 'Critical Histories', which examine the truth or credibility of the 'historical tradition' and are in fact histories of histories, like the work of Niebuhr. (4) Finally, 'Special Histories' of the arts, religion, science, law, navigation and so on, which in a sense mark the transition to 'Philosophical Universal History'.

This cannot claim to be a reasoned catalogue of the phenomena of error[3]; rather, it is an arbitrary classification, or mere enumeration of abortive histories. For, according to Hegel, that is all which any historians can produce, who have not achieved a third main species, in his view the only genuine one, that of 'Philosophy of History'.

Unfortunately, this classification omits just the one kind of history which deserves the name, history which is in itself 'philosophical' because it has been thought out, and which is to be found in the

[1]English translation by Sibree. (Translator's note.)   [2]*levarsi di sopra ai fatti.*
[3]*Una dialettica fenomenologia dell' errore.*

properly historical parts of the very books he mentioned and in others he has passed over. Such history, philosophical in its own nature, does not advertise itself by that title; certainly, it is not the so-called 'philosophy of history' or 'philosophical history' in which the epithet 'philosophical' is both redundant and tendentious. The latter is in fact a philosophy that, instead of understanding history, passes it by, or only condescends to offer it a verification to which it is quite indifferent—a 'super-history' as we have called it.

Hegel treated the work completed by historians as a sort of unskilled and inferior labour to be used by him for the purposes of his super-history which pre-supposed it as already done. He designed this super-history on the ground-plan of his *Philosophy of Spirit* as that determined his stages in the development of liberty. In the first of these stages, which may be called that of infancy, one man only is free and all the rest obey him, in the patriarchal manner, as children or servants. In the second stage, that of adolescence, this naïve trust and obedience is laid aside and individual liberty is achieved, but a liberty that is 'unsubstantial', being purely individualist, subjective and capricious. In the third stage, like the prime of life, the individual pursues his own ends, but only by putting himself at the service of the community, the State, whence arises a conflict between his self-satisfaction and communal service.

In the fourth stage, which should correspond to old age (a metaphor that Hegel cannot help using but very quickly drops), the private or subjective spirit reconciles itself with what is objective, namely, the State, and is now perfectly free with a liberty that is 'substantial'.[1] The carrying out of the scheme, the undertaking of the Philosophy of History, consists in showing that this *a priori* scheme is and must be verified by experience, that is to say by the facts recorded indeed in the history books but 'without understanding'.[2]

A 'philosophy of spirit', or idealism, can certainly give an intelligible meaning to this doctrine of stages of liberty, understanding

[1] The implication of this word in Hegel seems to be that the individual, apart from loyal membership of a state, is an abstraction. He is or ought to be an element in (or adjective of ?) a state which is the 'concrete substance'. So he is only 'substantially' free when he uses his personal freedom patriotically. Acts of affection, ambition, covetousness, honour, revenge, are not 'really' free. (Translator's note.)

[2] *Vorlesungen üb. d. Philosophie der Geschichte*, ed. Lasson, pp. 135-37.

them not as a temporal succession, but as aspects or 'dialectical moments' of a single idea. For instance, it can treat as the crudest aspect or 'thesis' the subordination to one individual of all others; as the contrary aspect or 'antithesis' it can take the liberty of all individuals who pool their powers or voluntarily employ them to some common end of their own choice; and it can take as the 'synthesis' or perfect conception of liberty a self-devotion, in the very act, to an ideal.

This perhaps, or something like it, was Hegel's thought as a philosopher. But to abstract these aspects from one another and treat them as historical epochs, and then again to treat these epochs as rigidly distinguishable in thought, is to substitute a mythology for the real historical development. The true conception of such development arose as a reaction against those dualistic creeds which inspired both the making and the writing of history in the eighteenth century and which regarded history as fundamentally irrational. Against these creeds it maintained the rationality of the real and the reality of the rational.[1] Such, it is well known, was the solemn aphorism of Hegel himself, who then unworthily proceeded to weaken it by the limitations of his appended exposition.[2] In the same way, he invalidated and retrenched and falsified the consequential true conception of development. Under the influence of traditional religious formulas, he reduced it to a process towards a given end, the process by which the 'Idea' or reason realises itself in the history of the world, passing from potentiality to actuality[3] and thus achieving its purpose. He said that, without an event to which history moves, development would be reduced to mere change of quantity and not of quality, a mechanical accretion.[4]   The fact is that in historical thought there is no proper application of the idea either of quantity, which belongs to mathematics and physics, or of quality, in the strict sense, which is appropriate to the consideration of the fundamental activities of

[1] I have preserved the ambiguity, which I find both in the Italian and the German, of the word 'rational' which might mean either causally explicable or agreeable to our moral judgments. (Translator's note.)

[2] See my *Saggio sullo Hegel*, pp. 156-58, and *Ultimi Saggi*, pp. 238-39.

[3] Italian *in-sé* and *per-sé*. German *an sich* and *an und für sich*.

[4] *Philosophie der Geschichte* ed. Lasson, pp. 129-38.

spirit[1] and the unceasing cycle of their interaction. What is appropriate to history is the concrete universal of the judgment which comprehends unity in difference.

Through this fault Hegel, instead of allowing both the historical judgments and the history on which they reflect to grow out of the pure categories or elemental activities of spirit, tried to work with mere generalisations.[2] These are taken for granted as already to hand, and are used as a dodge for artificially dividing or classifying facts as if on some philosophical basis. But the 'facts' so dealt with are not the facts of living experience or intuition; what he calls 'experience' is nothing but the bulk of universal history already produced in the traditional schemes, which he scarcely modified. Thus he found it convenient to preserve the divisions between history and pre-history, between the history of civilised peoples and that of savages without development or with one early arrested; yet he rightly rejected the idea of a golden age of high wisdom and pure morals, an earthly paradise, an idea preserved and refurbished by some of his contemporary philosophers of history. At the same time the primitive or prehistoric period was sharply cut off from the historic by the *a priori* argument[3] that since the former did not know the State it could have no history worth remembering or relating.[4] This is as much as to say that there may be intelligent creatures devoid of any historical experience,[5] whereas thinking is always judging and all judgment is historical judgment; it is to suppose that intelligent beings can herd together without the most rudimentary form of state, which is certainly untrue even of those African tribes whom Hegel excludes from history as utterly devoid of any such idea.

He also preserves the other usual distinction between the history of the East and that of the West, in which latter he includes the new Europeanised world of the Americas. But this distinction too he treats as a rigid and logical one instead of merely relative and geographical. He argues that, though the earth is a globe, its history does not return upon itself but has in Asia an essential Orient, where rises not only the physical sun which sets in the Occident but also the inward light of self-consciousness which has a brighter noon.[6]

[1] *Categorie.*   [2] *pseudocategorie.*   [3] *taglio concettuale.*   [4] *Ed. cit.*, pp. 138-146.
[5] *non storicizzino.*   [6] *Ed. cit.*, pp. 232-3.

He preserves, too, the current classification of ancient and modern peoples and indeed gives them historical individuality and personality. No doubt these had been already transfigured during the eighteenth century into *Esprits des peuples* or *Völkergeister*, but he actually rationalises them as the personifications of philosophical categories. He allots one of these categories to each people, whose mission it is fully to exemplify it and then to perish. No people can play more than one part in the historical drama, for if it came upon the stage again, it would have changed its rôle among the categories and so become a different people.[1] He preserves as the boundaries of history the six thousand years given by the ordinary handbooks of universal history, and places at the end of this period the final goal to which the struggles of all preceding centuries had moved—the elevation of the spirit to self-consciousness.[2] Then the dialectic of these allegorical folk develops on the following lines. China represents a stage where man only becomes of any account when he is dead; India represents man as physically and spiritually dead, and by his annihilation absorbed in Brahma; Persia lets light into the spirit, man's personality gets the upper hand, but his physical limitations are absolute; Egypt escapes this entombment in nature and sets up a kind of fermentation. At last, in the West, in Greece, where dawn broke over the western world, the separate elements of the oriental spirit were united in a concrete unity and man's spirit became aware of its true nature.[3] Here the formal Egyptian distinction of subjective personalities is overcome by a more objective realisation of the truth,[4] individuals are reunited by a general principle of patriotism and become essentially capable of moral rights and freedom. In this way Hegel effects the transition from East to West and all his other and minor ones. But the main and fundamental one is that just described, from the East, where a single despot is free, to Greece and Rome, where many are free, and to the Christian-Germanic world where all are free;—and the Philosophy of History lives happily ever afterwards.

The German people here alluded to are alone, in Hegel's view, competent to heal the flagrant breach which Christianity has revealed between our aspirations and the facts of life, between the Church and

[1]*Ed. cit.*, pp. 148-63.   [2]*Ed. cit.*, p. 165.   [3]*Diventa qualcosa per se*
[4]*La particularità e la formalità degli Egizi è superata nell' oggetività.*

the State.[1] And here we notice that the mythological element inevitable in his or in any metaphysic or philosophy of history, has been infected by the partiality of feeling, which is necessarily personal, as arising from national or racial prejudice and not from universal humanitarianism. It was from universal humanity, on the other hand, that Kant could derive his *Idea for a Universal History from a Cosmopolitan Point of View*,[2] which dreamed of a world-federation, the State of States, to guarantee the rights of all men. Even a recent exponent of the Hegelian *Philosophy of History*, who pronounces it to be, in its own sphere, "the supreme and most powerful product of human intellect", is constrained to admit that, in the last analysis, it 'must be judged and prized as the myth of the Christian-Germanic soul, and a myth second to none in profundity'.[3]

This is in marked contrast with Vico, though he too lapsed into the same logical error of treating the categories of his profound philosophy as historical events, when he put forward his theory of historical cycles. Here he made abstract elements[4] into empirical epochs, and so precluded himself from the idea of perpetual progress, the very definition of the spirit which perpetually develops itself. Vico, however, as a point of philosophical honour was severely impartial, and never perverted his vision of history by private, emotional propaganda nor with the 'jingoism' which he despised. He was a humanist, and drew his embodiment of abstract categories not from the void but from the detail of historical reality, within which he sometimes over-emphasised the outlines, but never invented them on abstract principles. Hegel's draught of universal history was an imaginary 'ballet of bloodless categories'; but in Vico the transition from pregnant primitive barbarism to Greek and Roman civilisation, and the collapse of that civilisation in the new barbarism, no less pregnant and 'propitious'[5] (as he called it), of the Middle Ages, and the issue of this barbarism in the new Renaissance civilisation—all these are no product of imagination. It is on Vico's

---

[1] *Ed. cit.*, p. 748.

[2] English translation by Hastie. (Translator's note.)

[3] See K. Leese, *Die Geschichtsphilosophie Hegels, auf Grund der neu erschlossenen Quellen untersucht und dargestellt* (Berlin, 1922), v.p. 312.

[4] *Momenti ideali.*   [5] *Generoso.*

foundations that historians have continued and continue to build, though they may be inclined, in their picture of the 'dark ages', to give a greater and even a predominant part to the influence of Greco-Roman civilisation, transformed by Christianity, and finally, with the energy and prestige of humanism, leading to the crisis and dissolution of the medieval outlook upon life.

Moreover, in Hegel's philosophy we may also notice what we have called the logical tendency of philosophy of history to deny and undervalue the idea and the love of liberty and of morality, though it was his intention to make them his guiding principle. But since this tendency is implicit in the very form of all such doctrines, we must not look for its origin and motive, when we are examining Hegel's work, in his personal character. No doubt, as an obsequious subject and official of the Prussian Government, he neither understood nor liked the liberal movement in Europe of his time, but allied himself with a bureaucratic and administrative monarchy which tolerated some feeble surviving institutions of medieval liberties or privileges. Nor need we emphasise some slurs on morality in such of his sayings as the notorious description of 'historical' or 'super-men' and 'heroes' whom he defined as 'agents of the world-spirit', and who, according to him, cannot be judged by a moral standard since 'world-history moves on a higher plane than that of morality.'[1] In these pages, among the most warmly coloured that he ever wrote, there is really no more than a just indignation against the arrogant stupidity, so common among pedagogues, of abusing and morally condemning historical personages instead of examining what they achieved. At the same time it must be granted that Hegel's theoretical argument on this point is here and there carried away by his vivid imagination. It seems as if he wanted to distinguish great men from little and to allow the former a moral licence denied to the latter. And he attributes achievements too exclusively to leading individuals, who, no doubt, make a greater impression in life and in histories, but whose deeds are also the deeds of all the other minds which aided or opposed them. All, whether they be called great or little, have directly or indirectly made their contribution and left their mark. Hegel's

[1] *Ed. cit.*, pp. 74-84 and 153-154.

treachery to moral ideas is particularly revealed by this deification of the *victrix causa* as against the *victa*, as if the former alone were real and the latter illusion, the former the rising sun and the latter the shades it puts to flight, the one dead and only the other living in this new history. But each of them may be called in a sense alike dead and living, since history has not come to an end, as Hegel and other philosophers of history supposed, and therefore knows nothing of final incorrigible judgments to be now filed in the archives; every event is 'to be continued'. Hegel, like other German historians and his disciples and kindred spirits, was prejudiced[1] against Cato of Utica to whom, though not a Christian, Dante assigns a Christian office and whom Campanella puts besides Socrates and Christ.[2] This is significant for our point, if we remember that Cato still lives in history as actively as Caesar. If Caesar contrived a longer life for Rome in founding the Empire (by a sort of discharge in bankruptcy, as I think Mommsen once called it),[3] Cato has stood face to face with him through the centuries, constantly bringing back liberty to our minds, our actions and our conditions.[4]

III

Though the philosophy of history had its forerunners in the Messianic ideas of the Hebrews and in oriental cosmologies, it was from Christianity, and particularly patristic literature, that it got its

[1]Particularly in *Die Verfassung Deutschlands* (1802) in *Schriften zur Politik und Rechtsphilosophie*, ed. Lasson, pp. 113-14.
[2]Contra sofisti Socrate sagace
Contro tiranni venne Caton giusto
Contro ipocriti Cristo, eterna pace.
[3]Hegel himself gives to the conditions of the Roman Empire a negative character of decadence and despotism, its positive and progressive element consisting in Christianity.
[4]I am glad to mention, at least in a note, a criticism of Hegel's doctrine by Engels (in *Ludwig Feuerbach und der Ausgang der klassichen deutschen Philosophie*, Stuttgart, 1888). He says that Hegel claimed both to justify what has come to pass and, by antithesis, to condemn it; so that if on one side he was conservative, on the other he was a revolutionary, and his authority could equally be invoked by Prussian semi-feudalism and by a proletariat rising towards communism and the abolition of the State. Unfortunately in this context Engels himself was not free from the logical vice necessarily common to Hegel and all philosophers of history. That is the vice of forgetting the influence of human beings and compounding instead ready-made results, which are caricatures of philosophical categories. The outcome of such a method is Engel's dogmatic prediction of the future and of the disappearance of history in a super-historical reign of freedom, founded by the proletariat. He did not see that it was precisely by this method that Hegel too, like other philosophers of history, was bound to foretell a culmination and end of history, though he sometimes shied at this logical conclusion and tried in some degree to loosen the net which he had first so busily woven.

first well-known form, which it substantially preserved under a later and less ecclesiastical guise. We need not here mention all the variations introduced into the picture by such medieval thinkers or mystics as Gioacchino di Fiore. At the Renaissance, under the influence of Greece and Rome, historians began again to write without mythology, and to assimilate by degrees the new ideas of the time, ending with those of rationalism and the 'enlightenment'. Philosophy of history was then confined to ecclesiastical writers, catholic or protestant, and ignored by lay historians, who had no motive for criticising it since they did not feel themselves here opposed by any arrogant opponent or rival who might corrupt the interpretation and narration of history. Vico himself paid no attention to it, indeed in his own rich union of philosophical reflection with sheer historical insight he revived, with profounder meaning, some formulas of pre-Christian antiquity. The eighteenth century, for its part, understood by 'philosophy of history' merely history told in an enlightened and liberal spirit with comments of the like nature.

But in the German universities the medieval tradition in these matters was stronger and more lasting. Here the methods of the old philosophy of Christian history, forgotten elsewhere, were revived by post-Kantian idealists and romanticists and culminated in the work of Hegel. He, as we have seen, despised every other sort of history and claimed as the only authentic revelation of truth a history of which historians, as he thought, had had no idea, having never gained the point of view which could conceive it. When this line of thought became fashionable, the former indifference to a philosophy super-vening upon history suddenly gave place to violent rejection and contemptuous satire. Hegel's own work, as I have said, was enriched by wide historical reading, and abounded in original and sound judgments which are still worth attention today. But there was also too much, both in his imaginary and metaphysical scheme and in the reduction of particular facts to its presupposed categories, that was bound to be a scandal for exact and scrupulous historians. Far worse extravagances were to be found among his companions and followers; either they crudely entangled themselves again in myths derived from biblical sources and from oriental Christianity, or they enthusiastically devised new and contradictory ones, turning out an apocalypse of humanitarianism.

We may enumerate in passing, and rather at random, some of these extravagances. According to Frederic Schlegel, world-history displayed itself as the fall from a primitive state of innocence and lofty wisdom to a state of atheism and impurity owing to the strife between the children of Seth and those of Cain. Similarly it was divided by Görres into stages corresponding to the six days of creation, in which, among other details, Christianity represented morning and Mohammedanism evening. The younger Schelling indicated a transition from a static primitive monotheism to polytheism, a fall into sin, an 'Iliad', followed by an 'Odyssey' or return of humanity to God. The minor philosophers of the school went on in the like strain with imaginative variations and combinations. Somewhat differently but still assuming a primitive state of innocence, in which reason instinctively ruled like a second nature, Fichte followed it by a state of lost innocence and sin, where reason was merely personified in authority; and this was followed by a third and totally depraved period, in which he himself lived, where even authority was no longer respected. Krause put after the germinal stage of innocence governed by nature and God a stage of growth and adolescence. These last two writers both completed their historical maps by deducing the future. Fichte pictured a fourth stage, which was to be that of Science, and a final fifth stage to be that of Art, in which Religion would take the form of Beauty. Krause foretold a glorious perfection of humanity, with complete and harmonious development of all its faculties, in perfect control of nature and of itself, when all states and societies would unite in one vast collective personality; and so spake all the prophets. The characteristics of races and periods were more and more stereotyped and desiccated. We read, for example, that the ancient world is the natural or physical side of history, opposed to the modern world, which is the ideal or spiritual side, as nature is opposed to mind or the finite to the infinite; or, again, that the principle of the ancient world is sense and that of the modern intellect, and that peoples are distinguished by the pre-eminence in them of some particular faculty, the Chinese by reasoning, the Indians by imagination, the Egyptians by penetrative intuition, the Hebrews by strength of will. Of these and many suchlike characterisations nothing can ever be made; it is impossible to overcome one's boredom and impatience, and one is driven to refer the reader to the old book by Flint, which gave a catalogue or anthology of such audacious or fantastic inventions.

Yet the indignant challenge and satire of genuine historians who worked on the texts and documents, who were by no means always mere chroniclers or philologists, but had a grasp of the real problems and a natural if not systematic philosophy, did not suffice to refute the pretentions of the Philosophy of History. They were still met by the specious claim to derive the truth of history from experience by an *a priori* interpretation. But this was not the pure *a priori* method of the formal categories, rather, as we have seen, it was metaphysical and mythological. To refute it adequately, it was necessary to carry the discussion on to the plane of methodology and logic, that is of philosophy in the special or technical sense, which could analyse the error and, by accounting for its origin, provide the dialectical argument which destroyed it. But the next generation of philosophers were positivists who with the philosophy of history threw away philosophy itself, and thus sacrificed the only weapon capable of this critical work. For metaphysical idealism they substituted an equally metaphysical materialism, and, being ignorant of Kant's 'immanent purpose', they enthroned once more mechanical determinism, thus abolishing not the philosophy of history but history itself. They tried to violate and suppress history by substituting for it an impossible natural science, and in so doing overlaid it with an abstract system of classification called 'sociology', which still has adherents who even hope by its means to discover at last a law of historical development that shall enable us safely to prophesy the future.

The Philosophy of History, like the historical determinism which followed it, can only be refuted by a fundamental consideration of the nature of that thinking activity which generates every historical judgment. This is an activity which we all perform every day and which is performed on a grander scale and with more profundity in the pages of the true historians, or at least, in those of their pages which are true. Such a consideration is found in the doctrine that the historical object of our thought is always contemporary with that thought.[1] This doctrine maintains that the act of historical thinking is born of a need, determined by our particular desires,[2] to act or to equip ourselves for action, so as to alter some situation in which we find ourselves. To do this we must first know the situation, our place in the surrounding world, and therefore must know the world and the forces at play in it. Every historical judgment is therefore limited, and only so made possible, by the need which is its motive. From this limitation there is no escape without falling into the void, though that void may be the spangled vault of heaven, which together with its illusion of solidity offers also the deception of unfathomable depths. A historical judgment is always the answer to a question which life sets us in order to generate further life. When we have learned what we wanted to know, cleared up what was obscure, there is no more to ask; when our path is illuminated we must take it. Another demand and another historical response can only come about with the formation of a new situation and a new need. Histories stimulated and guided by no practical problems would be at best virtuosities or fairy-tales, not serious history.

And that is eminently the character of the claim to elaborate, by a philosophy of history, those historical answers which already are philosophy since they imply a consciousness of the essential activities[3] of spirit, activities which can only be found, where alone they exist, in the concrete historical judgment. In this point is summed up the justification of our doctrine that philosophy and history are complementary or rather identical, which can be stated in a convertible proposition : 'the whole of one is the whole of the other'. This truth was glimpsed or guessed by Hegel, but quickly confused or lost sight of when he conceived the design of 'applying' philosophy to history, a philosophy already made to a history already there, each having been completed without the other. Those who today say and believe that the doctrine of the identity of philosophy and history here formulated is only a repetition of Hegel can have considered neither

---

[1] *La dottrina dell' ideale contemporaneità di ogni storia pensata.*

[2] *Praticamente individuato.*   [3] *Categorie.*

his books nor the newer doctrine, or else they must be seriously deficient in the sense of the difference between words which sound alike but take their meaning from historical situations and different backgrounds of culture. So much I must say once and for all, not through any fatuous pride of originality, but that the ideas I am using may be understood.

Yet though a ready-made philosophy is one not made to the measure of historical judgments and interpretations, there is a further work to be performed on these latter which is not the work of thought or philosophy but a sort of memorisation of the innumerable historical judgments we have passed and made our own. This is done by classification, which renders the particular general and the individual collective. It is something we are all always doing and which historians in particular carry to perfection for their own ends. It is an operation never without some more or less profound and clear consciousness of its nature, a consciousness deliberately cultivated by those who specially study the methodology of history. It is the consciousness that the value of these classifications is instrumental and not cognitive, depending upon the capacity to retranslate them, when occasion requires, into their component particular judgments which originally were, and still remain, the only really cognitive ones. Yet this consciousness may be lost by the very man who has fashioned the classifications as his instruments ; he forgets what he is doing and, however quickly he may recollect himself and pause, he may stumble, or at least be tempted to treat his *memoria technica* as a cognition, being caught in the net he had woven for another purpose. More often it is his fate, with anger and disgust, to see his work ill-treated and misunderstood by others. He may know very well the uses and limitations of the delicate instruments he has fashioned, their temper and brittleness.   Those who pick them up as he has left them clutch them in their clumsy fists, and handle them like wood-choppers and brandish them at random, hewing and lacerating and mis-shaping the truth of history. In either case it is such a blunder and absence of mind which is the psychological cause why men string together ideas or words that they have not thought out, and which are the seeds whence again and again springs up the deplorable Philosophy of History.

What, it may be asked, can be more natural than to arrange many
of the historical judgments in our possession according to races,
nations or states, and to write histories of Italy, France, Germany,
ancient Greece and Rome, Persia and Japan? These judgments, since
they are about reality, are not possessions of nations or states but
belong to the kingdom of truth. Yet it is convenient thus to group
them, when addressing them to men of understanding, who under
these titles will always be studying the single drama of humanity.
But, for men without understanding, national characters, abstracted
for definite purposes, become rigid, exclusive and static; from
mental generalisations they are turned into metaphysical entities; and
when they are thus personified we see before us the actors in the
Philosophy of History, whom we have described, who divide between
them the parts in its mythological or metaphysical drama.

Similarly, it is very natural, when we are setting out the growth of
a certain institution, idea or moral tendency, to divide it into periods
or epochs, each of which represents one of its stages. Thus we speak
of Greece as creating eternal patterns of beauty; of Rome as the
home of law; of the Middle Ages as ascetic and transcendentally
minded; of the Renaissance as giving back a value to mortal life; of
the seventeenth century as forging the weapon of a reforming,
revolutionary rationalism. But when we speak thus we always tacitly
bear in mind that these are mere compass-bearings for the problems
which concern us, not realities in the sense in which our mind, that
invents and understands them, is alone real. But even these mere
orientations are turned into the pawns of a metaphysical game, and,
by giving them chronological order or developing one from another
through dialectical opposition, we think we have grasped universal
history when we have in truth only observed a psychological fact of
our thinking. The naïve and childish imagination of untrained minds
actually ends by giving 'objective reality' to the most elementary
classifications. It visualises the Greeks as constantly occupied in the
creation and admiration of perfectly beautiful statues or poems; the
Romans as invariably austere; the Germans as always thirsting for
battle, slaughter and booty; the Italians of the Renaissance as strangers
to melancholy and without sense of sin, wrapped up in the investigation

of nature and the practice of the arts; the French of the seventeenth century as completely logical and consistent. As the witty Princess Matilda once slyly asked the learned Gebhart, who was left dumbfounded and embarrassed: how was it that with the ancient Greeks and Romans it was always holiday and sunshine and blue skies and 'ne pleuvait jamais'?

In the same way, by combining the classifications of peoples and periods with those of the various mental activities, men come to characterise the arts or the philosophy of a people or a period. So we hear of the intellectualism which is the property of the French genius, of English empiricism, of German idealism, of Greek naturalism and modern spirituality; or again of the classical form in art and poetry peculiar to Italy, and the harsh vigorous style peculiar to Germany, of the eloquence characteristic of French poetry, and so on. But when, as so often, we are tempted to mistake these formulas, useful enough in their place, for realities, we must quickly escape by recalling that anything general or collective is neither art nor philosophy nor life but an abstraction. What is real is only this or that thought, this or that poem, this or that moral action. 'History repeats itself' and 'History never repeats itself' make not a contradiction but a single true judgment, that of the individual-universal or unity in difference. This is quite different from *das Allgemeine*, the generalisation, or numerical universal, which would seek a place between true universality and individuality though it has nothing in common with either, but is, as we have said, a practical device.

In other cases these classifications and the reifications resulting from them are not even derived from historical judgments directly, but from sentimental and practical prejudices. We may cite, from the medieval heresies and the great Lutheran reformation, the idea of a primitive church with simple faith, no hierarchy, no wealth, no politics, to which a return was now preached; or, from the passionate and turbid writings of the romantics, the idea of a serene Greece and later of a middle age purely religious and chivalrous. Both of these were projections of their authors' feelings and without historical basis. Such beliefs obscured the facts they were meant to explain and called for a polemical criticism to restore a true picture. To be brief, what on earth is 'modern art', 'modern life', 'the modern ideal', of which we all talk, and must talk, since, after all, we are men and men must chat and make conversation? Is 'modern art' something existing independently of us, or is it rather the art which each of us, humbly but at the same time proudly, creates or admires, and calls new because it is beautiful and therefore necessarily original, different from the old, new-born like a bursting seed—in a word living and 'modern'? The same may be said of philosophy, of life, of our ideal, which we adorn with splendid images and metaphors and similes. In doing so we run the risk of externalising them, of cutting off ourselves or the best part of ourselves to objectify it in a transcendent metaphysical reality. And the enemy whom we have been pursuing in this essay, the Philosopher of History, snatches it and makes it a pawn in his game along with the other pawns he has filched or fashioned. He puts this supposed reality as a starting point or crowning conclusion alongside all his others, as if they and not we had produced it; as if they could prove its necessity, beauty or sublimity. But these qualities are precisely what cannot be either produced or proved, but exist by their own nature, by an impulse that externally renews itself and by its very existence proves its necessity.

IV

We have dissolved some of the commonest working ideas of the historian: the characters of races and periods, classifications of primitive and civilised, history and pre-history, historical and unhistorical countries, eastern and western cultures. All these we have reduced to empirical distinctions and devices of discourse which do not indicate what alone is true or real. We have utterly annihilated the imposing synthesis of world development offered by the symmetrical, complex and dazzling picture of Universal History, which we have irreverently described as a *species sine cerebro*. As a result, we have limited all serious and profitable history to the apprehension and understanding of single individual actions, which, whenever we turn our attention to them, our mind can interpret by entering into them imaginatively and making them its own. But when the beginner in such studies reads all this he is seized with dizziness and

PHILOSOPHY OF HISTORY

dismay, as if he were asked to sacrifice a great treasure and to get in exchange a few scattered and elusive grains of truth. Is that, he asks, our boasted historical science, the highest and only genuine knowledge we can ever have of reality? Is the human spirit confined to such a Platonic cave, where there is only a chequered sunlight, and where in vain it sighs for escape to the open day, in vain yearns to embrace the Absolute which is for ever hopelessly hidden from its eyes?

Such questions may be depressing and even torturing, but it is not hard to bring comfort and reassurance by a simple scholastic method which dissipates the gloomy cloud that had thickened round us. We have only to ask what we are doing and what happens to us when we read poetry. Clearly at any one time we can only read one poem, since if we tried to read two or more at once we should read none, as each would obliterate the other. And we do not complain of this as a loss, but in an ecstasy of love abandon ourselves to the reading, intent on every word and every accent in that poem, surmounting every difficulty we meet by the way, re-reading a passage the better to imprint it on our minds; until we have breathed into our hearts the perfect spirit which inspired and shaped it, and then we rest appeased. And when we go on to a new poem we are in a new world; we are in love again, with a different passion, but one that, like the first, sways our whole being. From Homer we pass to Virgil, from Dante to Shakespeare. And not one of these poems that we may have read and made our own is lost to us, for out of them and all our aesthetic experiences we have made our living, active selves. And in the same way other men will read and make their own some or all of the pages we have read and others which we have not read because we have not come across them or because they will be written or discovered after our time; and their experience, like ours, will be at once perfect and incomplete, perfect in quality but limited in extent which is never perfect. But would anybody exchange the individual poems, few or many, that he has understood and enjoyed, for a visionary whole of poetry in all its infinite developments? Who would try to embrace a cloud? No doubt there are people who yearn and sigh for the possession of an abstraction, for the pure Idea of

203

Beauty, and who despise the menial task of creating or recreating and enjoying a single actual poem. We know what to think of them. And there is also a cultivated set which knows pretty well all there is to know about the universal history of poetry in all times and countries, but knows it from outside, at second hand, from summaries of its content, knows it in the way of erudition and bibliography, but has perhaps never got at the heart of any of it. We laugh at them, as (if I may be pardoned the reminiscence) I once laughed at a friend of my youth, well and honourably learned, to whom I had given a college essay in which I threw some light on a forgotten book by a forgotten writer of the sixteenth century. He told me, with touching complacency, that he prided himself on not having omitted to mention this author in his history of literature. Not that he had studied or read or even seen the book, but he had unearthed the title and incorporated it with other titles in his accurate compilation. Such at bottom are the 'histories'—the universal histories or however named and presented—of all those who undertake to enumerate many or very many or, as they suppose, all the relevant facts, heavily documented and catalogued. They are chapter-headings without chapters, fictions rather than facts, because they have no individual physiognomy, which must depend upon actual birth and history.

Every single historical judgment that we make presupposes and includes within itself all the others which we have already made, builds upon these and relies on them. And in these judgments which we possess there have been and continually are incorporated the judgments of other men, critically sifted, and the process goes on continually and cumulatively in all men. Hence grows what is called the historical culture of a society or an epoch, which is none the less real for being, like every reality, unstable and full of inconsistencies. But this historical culture has its only and perennial source of life in individual judgments made in particular situations. These judgments are mutually related, sometimes supporting one another and sometimes contradicting, and are finally worked into a consistent whole which is no sooner achieved than it suffers a stimulating inconsistency to reappear. To look for a consistent whole of truth outside of this eternal and living process, or to think one has found it in some pontifical authority or in a revelation from on high, even from the high heaven of some ineffable metaphysic, such as the Philosophy of History, is to make a bargain like the man told of by Lichtenberg, who bought a beautiful knife but without blade or handle. This generation of consistent truth, in which we all participate by virtue of the truth that each contributes for himself, is the definition of freedom of thought and the proof of its necessity for the intellectual advancement of mankind.

What has just been said implies the refutation of another error and the dissipation of another fear. We have called attention to the individual situation in which each man stands, and advised him not to let his attention wander from it but to concentrate all his efforts on mastering it and escaping from it by his own thought and action helped by historical knowledge. And this advice may give rise to the suspicion that we are harbouring and preaching a sort of selfishness, or at least egoism, and recommending the prosaic maxim of expediency:—'Everyone for himself and God help all'. But, as I say, the cure for such suspicions has been implied. This attention to one's own need, with the appropriate thought and action, is, just as much as the pursuit of truth, a moral action and, as such, something universal and more than self-regarding. It conspires and collaborates with the moral actions of other men to produce what is called co-operation, society, civilisation. So it comes about that in one sphere or another, in this or that crisis, one man becomes in his turn the ruler of others by their will or consent, as Thucydides says that Pericles was rather the guide than the minister of the free people of Athens, a king in a democracy. Cavour too seems at times to have been himself monarch, parliament and ministry, and was in fact all three, since all three lived and worked through him. That is how great men influence the world by the necessity of nature. What would be more absurd than to rival them by drilling the world and magisterially instructing it how to live in perfect peace and honour? As if the world were an infant in arms or a child whom some stupid teacher did not teach to act for himself but trained like a mount or beast of burden to show its paces or to bear the yoke!

No doubt there is evil as well as good in men's behaviour; yet what is the evil but the instinct of self-preservation, the necessary condition or material of all action? What strength could we put into moral action except the strength we have? And this strength sometimes serves the higher principle and, at others, rebels, and challenges it to summon all its forces in defence of its prerogative. Could there be life without death, beauty without ugliness, truth without error, gain without loss, good without evil, pleasure without pain? Is it likely then that some supercilious edict can wipe evil out of the world and so destroy both physical and moral life by breaking their very main-spring? The selfishness or egoism of which we are accused is then simply the eternal struggle of good and evil, by which individual and social progress is realised; this is the definition of political and moral freedom, as the individual generation of truth was the definition of freedom of thought.

There is no reality outside the passion which we feel, the truth we know, the act we will; all is rounded within this circle of the spirit. Here the universe is concentrated, or rather this is the universe, as lovers tell us in prose or poetry, whatever the object of their love. Progress, which we have mentioned, like other abstract elements of spiritual life is projected by abstract thinkers into an external reality and then looked for where it cannot be found, as if it were something either to be realised once for all or never to be realised at all. But true progress is our own progress, the progress of the world in and through us, which is always going on and so is without end. We all feel this progress in every good or useful action, in every new truth, in every experience of beauty; and in feeling it we rejoice that the world is alive and going forward in spite of trouble, ruin and disasters. Of no other progress can there be any need or desire or idea or reality. Here once more nothing is effective but the efforts of individuals, in which they constantly renew their strength as the mythical giant did by touching the earth. In our intercourse with other persons, in our family, in society, in the state, in our country, there arise quarrels and misunderstandings and painful situations. If we do not then sacrifice our own conscience but play our part even when all are against us, we may comfort ourselves with the sublime sayings of the poets; and so in the truest sense reconcile ourselves with all, family, country, state, humanity. Then we are loyal if unrecognised collaborators with all of them because we rediscover within our own individuality, the universal, the God who inspires, sustains and guides us, and to whose glory we do all. This continual redemption and salvation which the individual effects in himself and for himself corresponds to our definitions of freedom of thought and action. It is the definition of religion.

℥ 29 ℥

PROUST: AN EXAMPLE OF DECADENT HISTORICAL METHOD

THE HISTORICAL CONCEPTION of reality is profoundly religious and moral, the only one which is adequate to the essence of religion and morality. Determinism and fatalism affect it neither directly nor indirectly, for it reveals necessity as nothing but an aspect of freedom. We can never pass beyond the historical course of events to any reality outside and above ourselves, so that, while history of the past takes on the character of intelligible necessity, history in the making is constantly being created by freedom. Omnipotent time, the master of men and gods, the mathematical time which mechanically divides the continuous course of history, is not, as vulgar thought supposes, the framework within which history moves and which confines and determines it. History is its own frame and contains time, which it uses for its own purposes. The life of reality engages the whole activity of spirit in its complex unity, all thought and action, all truth and goodness; it is a perpetual growth and a gain in perpetuity. It triumphs over death, for nothing that we truly love or desire or value can die; what dies is only our own passing joy or suffering, the tumult which is silenced in the eternal. Knowledge, which is always at bottom historical knowledge, unfolds itself in the service of the moral life; since, in the history constructed by our minds, we step by step become aware only of those series of facts which must be known if we are to fulfil some particular obligation as it arises. Apart from a moral motive, there is no historical knowledge of reality, no historical consciousness.

With these and similar principles in mind, with which I had become familiar by repeatedly developing them, it may be imagined with what mixed feelings of surprise I read, more than twenty years ago, the Volumes of Marcel Proust *A la recherche du temps perdu*. These works had stirred up great discussion and argument, occasioned by admiration of the author's originality, by attempts to interpret and define the new philosophy he seemed to offer, by inquiries into his relation with the philosophy of Bergson and with the physics of Einstein. It was confidently asserted that Proust had revolutionised the idea of time, and that the modern novel would have to adopt what was called 'a totally different perspective' in its narrative. I did not let myself be stunned by the shouts of admiration nor fascinated by the hopeful prophecies of a philosophic and æsthetic revolution. I did not think the true significance of Proust's work had been grasped; to do this would have needed a firm hold of the principles above stated; only so would it have been possible to see that Proust's theory oscillated between an intuition of reality as history and a dilution and impoverishment of the truth intuited.

The taste of a bit of biscuit dipped in a cup of tea or the unexpected sound of a doorbell is enough to move us and to call up past events, and *la recherche du temps perdu*. In trying to feel more intimately the sound of this bell which echoed in the mind, '*C'est en moi même*' writes Proust, '*que j'étais obligé de redescendre. C'est donc qui ce tintement y était toujours, et aussi, entre lui et l'instant présent, tout ce passé indéfinement déroulé que je ne savais pas que je portais. Quand il avait tinté j'existais déjà, et depuis, pour que j'entendisse encore ce tintement, il fallait qu'il n'y eût pas eu discontinuité, que je n'eusse pas un instant pris de repos, cessé d'exister, de penser, d'avoir conscience de moi, puisque cet instant ancien tenait encore à moi, que je pouvais encore le retrouver, retourner, jusqu'à lui, rien qu'en descendant plus profondément en moi. C'était cette notion du temps incorporé, des années passées, non separées de nous, que j'avais l'intention de mettre si fort en relief dans mon oeuvre*'.[1] That is how he describes the process from a present impression to the reconstruction of a past one, but his account differs in one point from that which I briefly gave of a truly historical process. In history, the

[1]*Oeuvres Complètes* (Paris, 1929-36), in the part entitled: *Le temps retrouvé*, II, pp. 252-3.

o

starting point is a moral necessity to throw light on the past in order to indicate the action that has to be performed; and this necessity is satisfied by an act of thought which issues in a judgment or series of judgments. For Proust, the starting point is a feeling of mixed pleasure and pain which recalls a chain of similar images which were already attached to it when it first arose in the mind. The difference can be illustrated by the picture of a man who is thinking hard in order to prepare himself for action as compared with that of one who relaxes in ease and idleness and daydreams. The latter has merely the pleasurable satisfaction of a bodily need; which is not an intellectual process just because it is not also a moral process. A proof of this is that Proust uses for the reconstruction of his *temps retrouvé* the vulgar subject of so-called good society, the 'good society' which Goethe loathed and stigmatized as impossible for poetry and whose one unifying principle clearly enough is an over-ruling sexual pre-occupation.

The true human drama, the drama of man toiling in the creation of the spiritual world, is not to be found in Proust's mind or in his pages; if he ever happens to mention it, it is only to misrepresent its motives; if they stare him in the face, he is tempted to explain them as habits acquired in a former life, which is simply to deny that they are real powers and components of the only life we live or know. '*Tout se passe dans notre vie comme si nous y entrions avec le faix d'obligations contractées dans une vie antérieure; il n'y a aucune raison dans nos conditions de vie sur cette terre pour que nous nous croyons obligés à faire le bien, à être délicats, même à être polis, ni pour l'artiste cultivé à ce qu'il se croie obligé à recommencer vingt fois un morceau dont l'admiration qu'il excitera importera peu à son corps mangé par les vers—Toutes ces obligations qui n'ont pas leur sanction dans la vie présente, semblent appartenir à un monde différent fondé sur la bonté, le scrupule, le sacrifice, un monde entièrement différent de celui-ci, et dont nous sortons pour naître à cette terre, avant peut-être d'y retourner revivre sous l'empire de ces lois inconnues*'.[1] This imaginary 'former life' of his would be a purely spiritual world, a category 'empty', as Kant said, because lacking the terrestrial 'matter' which, in its turn, would be 'blind' because lacking

[1] In the part entitled *La Prisonière*, Vol. 1, pp. 247-48.

any spiritual guide for its movement. So we have the idea of a world divorced from the reality of this world, a piece of philosophical nonsense, which the author only fails to formulate in these precise terms because he does not see that he is talking nonsense.

The feeling aroused in Proust by this vision is one of bondage, oppression and debility, exactly the opposite of that excited by genuine historical vision in men of sound heart and head, to whom it gives counsel and comfort, the spirit of emulation, the courage to act. '*J'éprouvais un sentiment de fatigue profonde à sentir que tout ce temps si long non seulement avait sans interruption été vécu, pensé, secrété par moi, qu'il était ma vie, qu'il était moi-même, mais encore que j'avais à toute minute à le maintenir attaché à moi, que j'étais juché a son sommet vertigineux, que je ne pouvais me mouvoir, sans le déplacer avec moi*'.[1] Instead of the strongest self-concentration and an increase of individual energy he feels only the disassociation and disintegration of his personality. '*Mon amour pour elle n'avait pas été simple : à la curiosité de l'inconnu s'etait ajouté un désir sensuel et à un sentiment d'une douceur presque familiale tantôt l'indifference, tantôt une fureur jalouse. Je n'étais pas un seul homme, mais le défilé, heure par heure, d'une armée compacte, où il y avait selon le moment, des passionés, des indifférents, des jaloux—des jaloux dont pas un n'était jaloux de la même femme*'.[2] Nothing is left him, but the pain of memory which can only end in death. '*Et c'est parcequ'ils contiennent ainsi les heures du passé que les corps humains peuvent faire tant de mal à ceux qui les aiment, parcequ'ils contiennent tant de souvenirs, de joies et de désirs déjà effacés pour eux, mais si cruels pour celui qui contemple et prolonge dans l'ordre du temps le corps chéri dont il est jaloux, jaloux jusqu'à en souhaiter la destruction. Car après la mort le Temps se retire du corps et les souvenirs—si indifférents, si pâlis—sont effacés de celle qui n'est plus et le seront bientôt de celui qu'il torturent encore, eux qui finiront par périr quand le désir d'un corps vivant ne les entretienne plus*'.[3]

It has been said that the 'catharsis' or consolation of such a tragedy, the solution of the problem stated by Proust, is to be found in art, where alone life finds calm and tranquillity. And in fact Proust

[1] *Le temps retrouvé*, l.c., p. 253.　　　[3] *Le temps retrouvé*, II, p. 253.
[2] *Albertine disparue*, Vol. I, p. 102.

persuaded himself that his recollection of his past was art and poetry. 'Or la récréation par la mémoire d'impressions qu'il fallait ensuite approfondir, éclairer, transformer, en équivalents, d'intelligence, n'était elle pas une des conditions, presque l'essence même de l'oeuvre d'art telle que je l'avais conçue tout à l'heure'?[1] But this is not the true definition of a work of art, because, as has been noticed, it describes a process which is not contemplative but practical, an unburdening of the nerves by the imagination. In Proust's actual work, with all its acute and subtle observation, with all its accurate description and analysis of sentimental subtleties and complications, I cannot easily discover any poetic inspiration.

An important but little recognised fact is that the philosophy of history and the theory of the historian's art have been little, if at all, developed in French thought and literature. It will be opportune here to refer to an article written more than sixty years ago by Anatole France, Les torts de l'histoire, in which the French anti-historical tradition of Descartes is ingenuously noticed. 'Les philosophes ont, en général, peu de goût pour l'histoire. Ils lui reprochent volontiers de procéder sans methode et sans but. Descartes la tenait en mépris. Malebranche disait n'en pas faire plus de cas que des nouvelles de son quartier. Dans sa vieillesse, il distinguit le jeune D'Aguesseau, et le favorisait même de quelque entretiens sur la métaphysique: mais un jour l'ayant surpris un Thucydide à la main, il lui retira son estime : la frivolité de cette lecture le scandalisait. Avant-hier encore, étant assez heureux pour causer avec un philosophe dont l'entretien m'est toujours profitable, M. Darlu, j'eus grand peine à défendre contre lui l'histoire, qu'il tient la moins honorable des oeuvres d'imagination'. The article went on to praise a book 'tout à fait solide et puissant', which was Bourdeau's wretched L'Histoire et les historiens, where, after denying any truth to any history, the author, in order to escape such a world of frivolity and fable, suggests its replacement by 'factual statistics of the communal life', a positivist corollary to Descartes' contempt of history. To which the only objection of Anatole France was to beg favour for books of historical narrative which appeal to the imagination and are exciting or amusing. When I think of the many who have argued and still argue in

[1] Le temps retrouvé, II, p. 251.

this dogmatic strain (and among contemporaries Valéry, who has also had his say about history) I have no desire to reply. They really seem to me, in things of the mind, to be men *penitus toto divisi orbe*, happy and self-contented in their immeasurably distant abode, free from any gadfly of self-criticism, and so certain of living in the clear light of truth that it is impossible to get into touch with them or to exchange ideas.

The only moment favourable for the growth of a deeper and more serious conception of history in France was the period of the restoration, the golden age of the widening and invigorating of the French mind under the influence of German thinkers and of the Italian Vico. But this good beginning came to nothing in a quarter of a century and was never repeated. Even when some necessary presupposition of historical thought was formulated, as in Bergson's criticism of the popular idea of time falsely imagined in terms of space, the suggestion was never developed into a logical theory of history. For Bergson never got beyond his so-called 'intuition' nor rose to a philosophical and dialectical conception; his culture was and always remained, in origin and at bottom, naturalistic, anti-historical or unhistorical. This intuitionist philosophy, not used as *fermentum cognitionis* but accepted as dogmatically self-contained, was popular with decadent men of letters like Proust who, in sheer ignorance, treated the noble matron history, mother of stern men trained in stern thought, as if she were a shameless hussy to provide exquisite titillations for their jaded nerves.

VARIOUS
THOUGHTS

SEXUALITY AND SPIRITUALITY

THERE IS A TENDENCY in contemporary science and philosophy, parallel with our decadent literature, to widen the scope of the sexual relation so as to make it not only the master but actually the source of what is called spiritual life. But why not reverse the process, even if our decadent literature and the pseudo-poetry that goes with it had to be greatly shaken in their self-confidence and perhaps to disappear —which I should think no great loss? What, in short, is the nature of this spiritual life, what is its activity and its satisfaction? It is the creative activity of thought, of poetry, of morality, of technique; I do not think we either need or can find any further definition. And what, on the other hand, is the physiological relation of the sexes if not the instinct to create or generate new life through the necessary cycle of distinction, opposition and conjunction? Does not that account for its central throne in the organism and its primacy—let us agree—over the nutritive instinct, and also for its repercussions and over-tones, even for its obsessions and perversions? That may be the reason also why there are so many preachers of erotic theory, and so few like Brillat-Savarin, who have hidden their thoughts under a mask of irony. And that may be what has stimulated so many poets or scribblers of love lyrics, who, as has been said, fill the pages of literature, and who now knock on the doors of science and philosophy, while the poetry of gluttony and deglutition is only represented by the parasites of Greco-Roman or Italian sixteenth century comedy and in popular farce. When the place of the sexual instinct in the cycle of life is thus sensibly and fairly explained, it is placed in the realm of the spirit as the most elementary form of practical organic life; it enters the sphere of the useful, pleasurable, profitable, or whatever branch of 'economics' may be assigned to it. Being thus in a degree spiritualised, it is far from sensualising or materialising the higher activities as is maintained in clumsy sexual theories of æsthetics and even of logic. There has actually been recently given to the world, or at least to the German world, a sexual analysis of the categories and dialectics of thought; a pretty extravagance, but certainly not without significance for the tendency I am discussing. If we take the opposite road which I have commended, and grasp the creative and spiritual function of physiological life, we may repeat, without fear of the morbidity that often affects mystics: 'The law of the spirit is love'.

✎ 31 ✎

OUR DEBT TO THOUGHT

EVIL IRREDEEMABLE and really 'desperate' is the 'metaphysical evil', for in all other evils, since they are only partial, there springs up perpetually the hope of change. But this is a universal evil, a sense of hopeless shortcoming, *Weltschmerz*, the misery of the world itself, which strikes at the root, not the leaves or flowers, which disposes and impels to melancholy and to suicide. I am speaking of those who are in earnest with it, certainly not of academic or literary persons who dilate in their arm-chairs on the irrationality of the real, nor of the fashionable folk who talk so lightly of 'this mad world', and fear it so little that they can speak with a smile on their lips. But for a universal evil there is a universal remedy, and metaphysical evil is cured by thought. Thought analyses the unity of the real into its opposing aspects, without losing sight of the unity, and thus it weaves its web and performs its miracle of reproducing the harmony of things in its own harmony; thus it restores a wholesome world to those who in the tumult of passion or in unrequited love had felt it as infected with vileness; thus it restores an ever youthful world to those who in a frightful dream have seen it rushing to destruction. From time to time we call upon this healing minister, which restores us to our life's work calmed and comforted, and there rises from the depths of our hearts a kind of gratitude, a thankful impulse, like that which rises from religious souls to God. Or is it the very same impulse? Thought is in us and is the ruling part of us, and God is only in us and is the source of all our strength. Do we then thank God as men thank one another in the world, in order to repay benefits with praise and to encourage their continuance? That is not a kind of thanks very pleasant either to give or to receive for gentle natures who know that the right return for kindness is intelligent appreciation and rivalry in well-doing. 'Thanks be to God' is a metaphorical expression of the poets that symbolises our recognition of a power above all others which we can only reverence by exercising it ourselves.

Sorrento, 1943

℣ 32 ℣

THE 'ETERNAL PROBLEMS'

MONTESQUIEU (*Cahiers*, p. 139) remarked that at one time '*on était philosophe à bon marché*' by discussing three or four questions : 'What is the chief good ? What is the principle of all things ? Is the soul immortal ? Does providence govern mankind ?' and, he went on, '*celui qui s'était déterminé sur quelques unes de ces questions, était d'abord philosophe, pour peu qu'il eût de la barbe.*'

But as philosophy has come to feel the pressure of worldly life, or secular life as it may be called, with its manifold needs and forms of activity, there have gradually grown and developed particular philosophical branches of study which professional philosophers have always considered subordinate to their main philosophy, though in fact these are the whole substance of philosophy itself. These studies contain in themselves the questions and the answers, even the vague ideas, which the earlier philosophers held to be pre-eminently or uniquely philosophical. Their discussion of these lofty topics was vague and inconclusive for lack of the necessary implementation, which could only be afforded by those other studies which they wholly despised and treated without seriousness if at all. Finally, the crisis has come to a conclusion, or perhaps only to a head, with the daring definition of philosophy as neither more nor less than the scrupulously careful 'methodology of historical thought'.

Naturally enough there are still pretended philosophers, even some '*avec la barbe*' who protest against this. If they did not protest and find some means of keeping alive their endless discussion of 'the eternal problems' and of the 'riddles of the universe', they would have nothing to talk of, for there is nothing else they know. Specialised philosophy needs too much study and too much culture and too much talent for them to be willing to attempt it. What is certain is that nothing else has any value for practical life.

221

☙ 33 ☙

ETERNAL TRUTH

THERE IS A WIDESPREAD recurrence of the longing for eternal
truth, for a truth not to be discussed or corrected or modified, a
constant rule of life for humanity, a sure guide to the haven where
it would be. And since the Church of Rome offers such a rule and
such guidance more generously than any other existing institution,
it is on the need for an eternal truth that it most effectively bases the
appeal to take shelter under its wings. In the eighteenth century too
it was by this argument, which he called 'triumphant', that Gibbon
was made a convert, however temporarily, to Catholicism. 'There
must be', he writes in his autobiography, 'an infallible judge some-
where; and the Church of Rome is the only Christian society which
pretends or can pretend to that title'. Eternal truth, a universal creed,
a perfectly ordered society, perpetual peace, are all mutually inter-
dependent and indeed inseparable. And since all such ideas in the end
deny the whole conception of life as essentially and unalterably
change and movement, it is not hard to see that they are self-
contradictory and void of logical significance. Lacking this significance, in whatever logical forms they may clothe themselves, they
can only be symptoms of passion—cries of distress, sighs of lamentation, ravings. Even the aforesaid 'triumphant argument' is not logical
but 'emotive', or, more properly, oratorical; of power to move
men's minds in favour of an institution, the Church of Rome or
some rival with a numerous and faithful following, such as has
appeared more than once in our time and whose fate has yet to be
decided.

Is then human life a kaleidoscope of change, whirling us from one scene to another, with nothing that abides, no solid ground on which to plant our feet? We are conscious of the opposite. Change is on every side, but within us abides inexhaustible the power to will and to effect changes, that power which the ancients called the *pectus* and the *vis mentis*, the unconquerable mind. There and there only at every moment we discover a sure support in action, a safe refuge and resting place to refresh from time to time our spirits and to renew our life with stronger and with better heart.

What then is the significance of this lonely longing, so noticeable today, for a truth embodied in fixed formulas, alien to us and imposed from without, beyond the reach of our own minds and hearts? Alas! When we are seized by such a longing, it is the sign of bafflement and of enfeebled mental and moral force. When, as today, such longing is widely spread, it is the sign of a lowered spiritual vitality in society. An old man, in the decay of his vital forces begins to ask the help another's arm can give him to guide his tottering steps; the young man, who feels life warm within him, confidently seeks the conflicts which others shun. Happily human societies only grow old metaphorically and temporarily. They grow young again and renew their spring, and in all their labours they see hope on the horizon. The light-heartedness of the Renaissance is to be found again and again in the revivals of all the centuries which preceded and followed it, and will be found again in the future. And in such new springs other loves blossom than the plaintive passion of weak spirits for eternal truth and for the fixed formulas out of which an exhausted vitality weaves its appropriate ideal, an ideal of exhaustion.

❦ 34 ❧

'THE FINAL PHILOSOPHY'

IS THERE A FINAL PHILOSOPHY? In spite of the claims of some systematic doctrines to this monstrous title, and their shameless assumption of it, there is in fact no such thing. There cannot be, because there is no philosophy which is not a step in the historical development of philosophy, and no poem which is not a step in the historical development of poetry—we cannot conceive a 'final poem' which would be a substitute for all the others which have appeared and will appear in the world.

No doubt there is something 'final' or 'perennial' in all philosophies, but it is not strictly their philosophy, rather it is the unchanging subject-matter of all philosophies. This is self-consciousness, which is only active in the perpetual posing and solution of particular problems, an activity it could not perform if it were not essentially one and unchanging in its fundamental and eternal categories. It is impossible to pick out these categories and to establish them above, and in abstraction from, the particular philosophical context with which they are not so much combined as fused. The evidence for this impossibility is to be found in precisely those treatises which might be thought to achieve it, those which claim to be 'pure' philosophy, not a step in a historical development. Every such attempt to demonstrate and define final concepts reveals, on due analysis, the historical context which has contributed to its result and which makes it a determinate philosophical theory *hic et nunc*, sufficient for the day (which is a day in history), but not sufficient for the morrow, when it must be refreshed or reformed. There is no thought except in a historical context; not even thought can rival the famous feat of Baron Munchausen in pulling himself out of the water by his own top-knot.

❧ 35 ❧

'ETERNAL LIFE'

THE LIFE ETERNAL is not only to be vainly hoped for in a 'beyond', but something that we already possess and experience in every action, whenever we know a truth, realise beauty or do a good act. How else would we have come to the thought or name of 'eternal life'? In every one of such acts we feel that we have put off our corruptible, mortal body, and raised ourselves to the incorruptible and eternal by unifying ourselves with God. For that very reason it is absurd to desire or demand or conceive a life eternal for that part of ourselves which is only instrumental to those other parts in whose service it is worn away. Our bodily, 'organic' life is by definition transient and perishable; it is precisely the not-eternal stepping-stone to something higher, constantly abandoned in our advance. The illogical idea or confused picture of an eternal life for our sensuous and emotional nature presents itself with two faces; the one is terrifying and fills us with dismay and horror for a bodily life to go on for ever in a meaningless round of pains and pleasures, a drama without plot and without climax; the other is sweet and comforting by its promise of a pure, unbroken joy, with no shocks of pain in its pleasure, but perpetually self-sustained.

⚜ 36 ⚜

THE IDENTITY OF PHILOSOPHY
AND THE MORAL LIFE

WE MUST MAKE UP OUR MINDS to give up the traditional distinction between plain thinking and philosophical thinking, between empirical and speculative thinking; and consequently we must also give up the idea of philosophy as a study of what is beyond ordinary empirical thought. This is not the place to enquire into the motives which originated and maintained the distinction (such as philosophical pride, the survival of a transcendent theory of revelation and the like) nor into the amount of truth contained in some of its applications (such as the proper demand to be freed from the tyranny of empirical and mathematical logic). It may be enough to remark that this dualistic idea of two kinds of thinking either rendered ordinary thought and experience superfluous or made the boasted philosophy useless, since all thought is ordinary thought and always linked with experience.

We must reformulate our definition of the specific difference of philosophy on quite a different plane and from a different point of view; no longer as a logical difference in the quality of the thought but as a purely psychological difference of interest and attitude. In general terms we may say that the distinguishing feature of philosophy is consistency. Non-philosophers are those who are not troubled by inconsistency or incoherence and do not trouble to escape it, philosophers are those who experience these troubles vividly. But since this distinction is, as we have said, merely psychological, we must at once modify it by adding that no man is either a pure philosopher or quite unphilosophical. The consistency for which the philosopher strives implies the continual resurgence of incoherence in his mind, even though at a constantly higher level; the cessation of the process would be the death of thought.

Starting from this psychological criterion, it is possible to classify men as thinkers according to the emptiness or richness of their thoughts. In one of the lowest classes will be put together those who are usually described as 'incoherent' minds, 'self-contradictory', 'impulsive', 'cloudy', frivolous in their ideas and judgments; in other successively higher classes will be those who succeed in attaining coherence in some sphere of their thought but not in others and not between the different spheres. Among this last class, for example, are to be found so-called specialists who argue well enough in their own subject but like children in others, and even in their own subject stop at a certain point and can give no account of some of their assumptions nor of the relation these bear to the assumptions of other sciences. In fact they are hedged in by incoherence and yet feel no stimulus to escape, and as a rule, do not even notice that they are imprisoned, but contemptuously ridicule as dreamers those who with good advice or with a helping hand would try to liberate them.

The highest class is that of philosophers properly so-called who feel this stimulus constantly. I should be sorry if the word 'philosophers' should call to my readers' minds certain figures and faces which would interrupt their reading for laughter, so I will explain that I do not mean professors or writers of philosophy. A man may be a philosopher without writing philosophy or even knowing the meaning of the word, for he may have practised and be always practising the labour of clarifying his mind and getting clear ideas, as they are called, about the world and human life. He may be open to doubts, which always have the virtue of stimulating thought, and by quite unacademic ways may constantly attain as much philosophy as he needs. It is not without reason that we sometimes admire the 'philosophy' of very unpretending people, working men or peasants such as used to be called 'born philosophers'; because they think and speak wisely and are secure in the possession of the substantial truths.[1]

[1] 'He was a born philosopher, and a man of few words', said Franco Sachetti of a soldier of fortune. And even as early as in Paul the Deacon (Hist. Lang. VI, 58) we read that the Longobard King Liutprand was *litterarum quidem ignarus sed philosophis aequandus*

This is no metaphor but the proper use of the word; it is used metaphorically when it is bestowed on writers of theses and dissertations and on lecturers who are void of the philosophic spirit. When a philosophic mind attains the depth and intensity which can embrace all or most of the typical problems of the time, we have the philosopher in the highest sense or rather a philosophic genius, who seems so far removed from other men and yet is so near akin to them. He gathers up their scattered efforts, summarises precisely their obscure and anxious questioning, and gives answers which, if most men do not at first understand them, yet are gradually reproduced in common convictions and decisions and in time affect the social and historical environment. The philosopher by calling is consumed with the passion for clear thinking. His case is analogous to that of the poet. In the greatest excitement of practical conflict, in his most bitter sorrows, no sooner does there arise in his mind from these experiences some doubt or contradiction or incoherence, giving rise to a problem, than he falls into abstraction, is engrossed in thought, and remains absorbed till he has found or recovered the logical link which was missing. Once this is secured, he recovers his self-possession and with it the strength of mind to hold his own, overcome his sorrows and continue his work.

This sketch of the various types and grades of mental coherence may be paralleled in the practical sphere to shew who are the me 'of character', as the phrase goes, or 'without character', meaning moral character. Here again we must treat the distinction as not logical but psychological, not one of kind, but of degree, and here again our criterion must be that of coherence, which is as difficult to achieve in the moral as in the intellectual sphere.

The different degrees of this coherence may be compared to a long and arduous march in which some drop out or rest after a little way, others after longer or shorter stages, and some, outstripping all the others, seem to have reached their journey's end, though in fact the end is never reached since at every turning the road stretches out anew. Those who gave up at the first stage are called 'men of no character', the majority are men of little or too little, and the few or very few remaining are 'men of character' and therefore objects of our respect. All men would like to be good, there is some spark of goodness even in so-called villains; and since they want to be good they must co-ordinate their actions under some principles of conduct, that is, render them coherent, and character consists of this coherence. But few men carry out this process to the end. You may see them coherent in one sphere and incoherent in another: good husbands and fathers but bad citizens, industrious in their trade or profession, but careless and dissolute outside it, capable of doing their duty in spite of some difficulties, temptations or dangers, but not in greater or different ones; whereas what distinguishes duty from expediency is that it is unconditional and has no exchange value. Those who are called eminently men of character feel the inter-connection of all spheres of action, and that they cannot be truly or sincerely virtuous in one unless in all, since all depend on the one principle of conscience. They feel that he who yields in one point has no security against yielding in others, and that the man who prevaricates with his conscience corrupts and ruins it, unless his faults bring such shame, remorse, and reform as to restore it to greater vigour because it is now more experienced and scrupulous.

Like the philosophical genius, the man of eminent character, a hero or a saint, who seems so far above humanity, is in fact intensely human; not only because, for all his heroism or sanctity he knows he is a sinner and is therefore humble, but also because he works for mankind at large. It is he who in the hour of disaster saves the honour of an army or a nation, gives examples which will bear fruit and creates moral standards or institutions which will help other men in the good life. It would be inhuman to deny the moral nature of other men, the majority, because they are not proof against every duress; the hope of making all men equally constant would be as visionary as the alchemists' dream of transmuting base metal to gold or diamonds. True humanity consists in contriving for others the conditions in which those who cannot escape their limitations can yet do the work they are fitted for, and in which the weak are not called upon beyond their powers but may be inspired and aided to persevere and to reform. Those who think otherwise are like those who would deny the rationality of other men because they have not the wide and deep intellectual consistency of Aristotle or Hegel; as if these great ones were not the providential instruments for communicating to lesser minds the benefit of truth or at least of its indirect consequences.

Can the two kinds of coherence, the philosophical and the moral be mutually unconnected? We should think so if we relied on the common observation that there have been great thinkers whose moral life was weak or culpable, and men of strong moral character weak in power of thought. But clearly that is not the point. We are not concerned with the empirical observation of individuals in the various actions of their life-history. So far as that goes, we may allow at once that a man who will never hear of the 'synthesis *a priori*' may be capable of a miraculous synthesis *a priori* in his moral life, giving up his life for his ideals. And conversely, the man who perfectly understood the cogency of experiment against the scholastic syllogism may have been an unscrupulous administrator of public funds.

The same contrast or distinction is allowed by the often repeated indulgent saying that no philosophical doctrine can be subject to moral blame since it is an act of thought and not of will, not obnoxious to moral judgments. This saying is undeniable, so long as it is strictly used to imply that moral immunity is guaranteed to philosophy only so long as it is an act of truth, or in a word, true. It is just here that the problem arises, rather further back than is commonly supposed. How can a man achieve anything so pure or disinterested as an act of truth, unless his mind is similarly pure, that is to say morally disposed, or rather filled with moral enthusiasm, and therefore sensitively respondent to every moral demand in every sphere of life? If philosophy is knowledge of the life of the spirit and the life of the spirit is morality, how can one know what one does not possess or create or as Vico would have said, '*non si fa*'? What pure truth could a coarse and lustful creature discover or understand? Just so much or so little as corresponds to the small amount of pure disinterestedness that, like every man, he possesses. Anything more that he says will be parrot-talk and not thought, or abstractly not concretely thought, or literature and not poetry, or rhetoric and not philosophy. The falseness of a philosopher's theory, as distinct from its imperfection (for none are perfect), can only be owing to the lack of moral scrupulousness in his thinking and to his lack of experience in human life, including the moral experience. On our moral responsibility for intellectual error I think I need not insist; that, too, is to be understood as a doctrine of indulgence.

We may then assert that, though philosophy is not morality, philosophy is more philosophical, more rich in truth, in proportion as the mind that thinks it is more profoundly moral. It might seem impossible to convert this proposition and to say that the moral life is richer and more purely moral in proportion as the mind that lives it is philosophical. But such impossibility is only apparent and arises from the false idea of philosophy, which we tried to expose before by pointing out that philosophy is nothing but intellectual coherence. This coherence is to be found in men confined to a materially restricted sphere of life, men whom the overweening learned call ignorant, whereas in all that matters it is not they but the learned who are ignorant. Underlying every moral action is a thought, a judgment, a recognition of the true nature of some given situation, a recognition impossible without philosophy. As the sphere of a moral man's knowledge widens, so does the sphere of his moral action, and as it grows more profound and coherent so does the morality of his action.

Strangely enough, people have been tempted to deny the classical distinction between theory and practice, between thought and will in the interests of the unity of the spirit. But this very distinction is the basis for that unity, since each in its way presupposes the other, will having thought as its starting point and thought will. That is why spirit can be defined neither as thought nor as will nor as a mere union of the two, but only as their relationship, which is not static but dynamic or 'dialectical'. Perhaps this same denial was itself directly produced by an inadequate acquaintance with the moral and intellectual life and by a superficial view of the life of the spirit, derived from the reading of philosophical literature and not born of direct experience and knowledge of the human heart. Such thinking is carried on as a skilful systematising and relating of ready-made ideas, with no serious attempt to follow Hamann's advice, and boldly break the ice in which these ideas are frozen and find the living water beneath it. So it is possible, continuing the metaphor, while skating over the ice, to forget the original motive power of the will and actually to believe that we can define the spirit as mere thought. But this thought cannot after all be mere thought, but turns out to be also will. And so clumsy is then the attempted unification that each element in it neutralises the other and the result is something much like blind impulse, brute fact, mere chance, or lust. That is the doctrine which contributes to muddy the more turbid currents of contemporary life.

37

SOLILOQUY OF AN OLD
PHILOSOPHER

ANYONE WHO LIKE MYSELF was born and grew up in the early
years of the unity and liberty of Italy must proclaim in every
company and against all opponents, that he knows what it is to have
lived the greater and best part of his life in a sublime spiritual atmosphere. He 'knows', he does not merely 'feel' it; for these words of
his are no mere effusion of a nostalgic sentiment for the past, or even
an imaginative picture of it, but an affirmation of the very truth. And
as an affirmation, in the strict sense, it claims to be distinguished from
that sort of utopia projected into the past, which leads men to think
that some golden age ever fleeted the time in 'blissful ignorance', a
phrase which is purely nonsensical. At the time of which I speak, as
in every other, men lived a human, not a superhuman or heavenly
life, a life marred by cares and griefs, sorrows, solitude, despair,
sullied by reprehensible deeds. It could not even be called more
moral or less moral than the life of earlier or later generations, for
morality is an inner energy, whose quality cannot be measured, and
whose external manifestations, which alone can be measured, are
mere events, and as such neither moral nor immoral. A sophistical
trick used to discredit the age of liberalism, and invented by the
vulgar for the vulgar, is to air all the dirty linen of this period, the
poverty, the blunders, the pride, the scandals, the crimes, of which it
may have been guilty, in order to shew that it was politically inferior
and contemptible; as if a similar collection of anecdotes could not be
made, and a similar picture as fairly painted of any other stage or
period of history.

233

A historical period cannot be truly described or judged by accumulating scandalous stories, but only by pondering and enquiring whether it had a moral ideal governing and illuminating the minds of those members of human societies who are capable of ideals; capable of loving something above their own happiness or that of others on which it depends, that of sons, wives, friends; capable of something above the 'natural' or 'sensual' love (to use an old phrase of the Churchmen) for the persons or things with which, for all of us, the 'joy of life' and self-preservation is interwoven. There are historical periods in which the power of such moral ideals grows faint, and almost seems to disappear, and these are called ages of barbarism or decadence; while other periods are active and flourishing and signalise advances in civilisation, and the attainment of richer and deeper ideas, with corresponding progress in practical activity.

The period to which my thoughts and memories now recur rejoiced in the calm assurance of a secure, full, and fruitful expansion of energies, and a noble co-operation of man with man. It saw all men as possessed of equal rights, without slavery or despotism, all at liberty to express their thoughts and to further their policies, under the free judgment of public opinion, which, in spite of inevitable oscillations and mistakes, usually in the end supported truth and equity. At this period the development of the human spirit had attained in Italy and Europe a more reflective self-consciousness, coherence, and harmony than had ever before been reached by that dynamic tendency to liberty which gives history its positive progress. It was an exalted ideal of liberty that now shone forth as the rule and guide and ultimate criterion of every effort. Behind this new form could be recognised, illuminated by a new light, the stern ideal of the old Greek and Roman heroes of liberty, but also the more intense and continuous influence of a process, begun or quickened by Christianity, towards a humanity united in love and sorrow and sublime aspirations. The Christian ideal had been brought down from heaven to earth at the Renaissance; it seemed to be denied by the Enlightenment, which celebrated the cult of abstract reason but in fact by this very 'reason' worked towards the same ends, dissipating darkness and promoting liberty, equality, and fraternity. And now, in the time I am speaking of, Christianity reconciled to the long, painful development of which it had been the seed, arose, one might say, refreshed by its contact with philosophy and history. The fact that, nevertheless, the Roman Church grew intolerant of liberation was due to the way in which she came to mould Christian minds into conformity with her political ends; but the close bond between the two was felt, not only by pure liberals, to whose lips religious phrases and metaphors so readily sprang, but also by liberal Catholics, who were the deepest thinkers and most generous spirits of their Church. We still have the proof of this bond today, a proof that liberalism is essentially Christian, when we see that those who hate and abuse it most are either inflamed by the passion for extolling and reviving distant epochs of pre-Christian history, such as paganism, or frankly profess the most crudely materialist, utilitarian, fratricidal conception of human life.

Certainly the ideal of liberty which flourished in the nineteenth century can and must be deepened, defined and widened; and this will be the business of the following periods, whose growth and progress will depend upon new experiences critically sifted and assimilated. But since its essential principle is moral, or rather is the development of morality itself, that principle can never be denied or replaced by any other; nor can we go back on its past history, or abandon the point it has reached; we can only advance further

It is, of course, possible to 'deny' it by vocal articulations, signifying nothing, and to refute it or claim to refute it, and to cry up as the true ideal its opposite, and to triumph over its supposed death. But since this proclaimed opposite is self-contradictory and morally unacceptable, the idea of liberty remains after all invulnerable, and when the storm has blown over it blossoms freshly and renews its youthful prime.

'When the storm is over'? Is there something in the world which can resist and impede and delay and shatter, for however short a time, the practical influence of this high ideal? Most certainly; and we should not be surprised at it, nor be panic-stricken for the fate of the world, as if it were thereby irrevocably compromised or beyond hope ruined. Nor, on the other hand, is it for the enemies of the ideal to argue that therefore it is essentially invalid and inadequate, and that their substitute has a monopoly of power and permanence. The delays and breakdowns in the advance of liberty are in fact evident in past and present history, the history which goes on within us. But the reason and justification of this fact is not far to seek, and though some through thoughtlessness seem not to see it, or to have forgotten it, a little reflection will bring it to their mind.

The obvious reason is that there can be no life or reality without differences and perpetual opposition or composition of forces, without war and peace, war which brings peace and peace which leads again to war. This is the plain truth, accepted by common sense no less than by profound philosophy, but contested and denied by all Utopians, pessimists and sceptics, ever seeking a good unconditioned by evil, a life whose complement is not death ; who, when they are unable to find this good in reality, shudder, or prate about the inscrutable mystery of things. Seen in the dialectical conflicts which are the law of history, man's moral action does not stand alone, an abstraction in a world of abstractions, but, always in relation to that which is at once its material and its instrument, its enemy and its ally, the vital force, whose moving principle is the prime mover. It is this force which continually contributes to the creation not only of the earth with its 'lovely family of beasts and flowers', its volcanoes and earthquakes, but also, by continual conflict, of ever-changing conditions of life. And most directly it operates in that sphere of human life[1] which is called 'the world of affairs', that is the world of business[2] and of practical politics, which is always engendering new patterns of nations and of states.

It is the professed ideal of liberal statesmen, not to extinguish economic and political rivalries, as some airy castle-builders might desire, and thus dry up the very spring of all activity and advance, but so to guide them that they may develop and give room for the necessary changes and re-groupings. Hence the internal policy of liberal states is to maintain with scrupulous firmness a respect for general liberty, and hence also their vigilant precaution that the powers of the government should not exceed its legitimate authority.

[1]*Spirito.*   [2]*Economia.*

Hence too the anxiety of the leaders in such states, of the ruling classes, and of all men of goodwill, however they may differ in other opinions and policies, to preserve international peace and to substitute for physical combat diplomacy, compromise and treaties. But all such action, whether internal or external, is itself a kind of warfare, though as we have said, not fought with weapons, or at least with different weapons, and, like other warfare, it has its turns of victory and defeat.

When these defeats occur, liberal constitutions and the love of peace are overcome and destroyed, and for a longer or shorter time, in greater or lesser degrees, give place to their opponent, the savage vital force. Such are the changes which succeed one another on every page of history; and it is unthinkable that this rhythm of victory and defeat should ever cease. The very idea of its cessation, the idea of a liberty completely and finally achieved, settled and immutable, of a liberty without dangers, or with only those fictitious dangers, which can always be escaped or checked, is as self-contradictory and empty as the idea of an end of the world and of universal life and being. But being cannot be annihilated since not-being is within its realm. Serious thinkers will never take the absurd line of preaching and demanding the abolition of war, and the establishment of perpetual peace and of static material equality. Nor, when they see unleashed the violent wars and revolutions which they have vainly tried to avert by defending peace and liberty to their utmost, will they cherish the equally absurd design of sitting in judgment on these mortal struggles and of arbitrating between parties while passions are still high. Strife knows no law but strife; its only arbiters are the actual results in which it will issue, and what these are to be is no man's secret, for no man knows. It is 'God's secret', as the wise proverb says. And philosophy agrees with common sense in refusing to individuals, each of whom has to fight his own battle in the universal warfare, the right to make himself judge and master in matters too high for him. Each must be content to fulfil his individual duty, in his own situation and state of life, as the voice of conscience bids him. Who, indeed, however sure he felt of rare intellectual and political genius, however sublimely self-confident, would accept at

God's hand the task of deciding human destiny? Who would presume to decide, by such criterion as he might vainly seek in his own mind, what can only be decided by the outcome?

But it is only in souls apt to despair and to lose their way, only in minds apt to confusion, that the necessary rhythm of history, with its recurring horrors of war and its recurrent back-slidings from peace and liberty, can inspire the thought that liberty can ever vanish even from a world which desires to be governed by a different law. Is liberty then a by-product, which dies and is not born again? Is it not the very *activity* of man, which is by definition free, and which nobody has yet ventured to define as determined?[1] It is within the realm of possibilities that the liberal period of the nineteenth century, which men of my generation have seen, and to which some of them are still loyal, splendid in its achievement, proud of the mutual respect of its citizens, will one day be compared with the great periods of philosophy and art, the Athens of Pericles, the Italy of the Renaissance, the France of Descartes, Corneille and Racine, the Germany of idealism and romance. Such periods open rarely and quickly close, leaving admiration and regret behind them. But though such marvellous seasons of blossoming pass, not for that reason will art and philosophy be banished from the world; arts and philosophical genius will arise again in men as great as those of old, and, what is more, the search for truth and the worship of art will never fail to inspire love and longing in the heart of man, and to shine there with all their former splendour. So too liberty has fallen, and will again, on days of opposition, of indifference and of persecution, but none the less it lives in the hearts of its lovers, it lives and operates in the sphere of action, where by right it moves, and which it naturally enlarges. Liberty can settle its account clearly enough with everything that neglects it or opposes it, for whatever 'comes to pass' and comes under its thought and judgment has 'passed' into the conditions of its own activity. The functions of liberty are different in the church triumphant and the church militant, but it can never be condemned to impotence or death, or at least no man has the power to execute the sentence he pronounces.

[1] *Un essere che serve.*

I have now brought back my argument to its main point of moral duty; I have shown that duty alone can be the end of all our efforts and all our practical activity; I have shown that moral duty is not subservient to the traffic of the world, or to its violent deliriums, to its demands or their satisfaction and appeasement. For the world, as Campanella wrote with lyric admiration, is a 'great and perfect animal' which goes its own way and finds its own means from time to time of accomplishing the various stages.

And now I can conclude my argument by pointing out that our duty likewise has its own good and its own means. And one of its first demands is that we should refute the illusion, which these vital forces suffer or create in their activity, when they claim moral worth and the right to fix our standards. No doubt, in political and social struggles, banners are hoisted, slogans are shouted, idols of love and hate are fashioned; and men inspired or maddened by these symbols are ready to fight and die. But all this is quite different from the moral ideals or from the ideal of liberty which comprises them. Factions fight to keep what they have or to gain something for themselves and their own party, where one man's loss is another's gain. But the moral ideal of liberty is a message to universal man as man; it is no incitement to the pursuit of private interests or more or less general goods, it is an educative and redeeming revelation to the heart. Even when, as sometimes happens, the aims of parties are inspired by a moral spirit, that is the moral ideal entering into them and beginning this education, converting them and raising them above themselves. This can be seen in the word 'patriot' which at one time expressed the reverent pride, the loftiest feelings, and the noblest dreams of all who could claim it. Indeed it symbolised their devotion to the cause of humanity, a meaning exactly opposite to that of the word 'nationalist', which came to be substituted for it, as was 'my nation' for 'my country', as though it were a translation, though in fact it was the expression of dominating and predatory natures.

Political ideologies, and slogans bandied against slogans, have no doubt their necessary uses, they call to arms, unite the combatants to attack and defence and intoxicate them with the hope or joy of victory; but they leave empty the heart of man in his simple and essential humanity, which only finds itself at home in union with the universal. It seems as if there were two histories, and two ways of relating history, which run closely parallel but never meet, the political and the moral. But in truth they are two aspects or 'dialectical moments' of the one history, which is the constant creation of life and the perpetual elevation and sublimation of life in its dedication to the universal. A man whose mind is so religiously disposed gladly leaves the care of political history to the politicians and soldiers and economists. He fixes his thoughts on moral history where is unrolled the drama which also goes on in himself, and where throughout the centuries he meets his fathers and brothers, who loved liberty as he does, and like him knew how to work and suffer for her.

January, 1942